BECKETT'S LATER FICTION AND DRAMA

Beckett's Later Fiction and Drama

Texts for Company

Edited by James Acheson and Kateryna Arthur
Foreword by Melvin J. Friedman

MACMILLAN
PRESS

First published 1987

Published by
THE MACMILLAN PRESS LTD
Houndmills, Basingstoke, Hampshire RG21 2XS
and London
Companies and representatives
throughout the world

Typeset by Wessex Typesetters
(Division of The Eastern Press Ltd)
Frome, Somerset

Printed in Hong Kong

British Library Cataloguing in Publication Data
Acheson, James
Beckett's later fiction and drama: texts for company
1. Beckett, Samuel—Criticism and
interpretation
I. Title   II. Arthur, Kateryna
828'.91209   PR6003.E282Z.E282 Z5725 1987
ISBN 0–333–39951–X

Contents

Foreword

Samuel Beckett's work belongs to world literature perhaps more emphatically than that of any contemporary. Not only has he been producing texts insistently in two languages, French and English, during the past forty years, but he has actively been involved in the translation and performance of his fiction and drama in a third language, German. (His collaboration with the translators Elmar and Erika Tophoven and with the performers at the Schiller Theater in Berlin has a passionate and consuming involvement.) Bibliographers have naturally been uncomfortable about where to place his work, although usually it finds its way into assessments of the twentieth-century French scene, such as in volume six, part three of the standard *A Critical Bibliography of French Literature*.

If Beckett's *oeuvre* belongs to more than a single literature, his versatility surely does not stop at that point. He started his career as a critic and poet. His flirtations with these forms eventually gave way to his more realised talents as fiction writer and dramatist. The ease with which he moved from genre to genre is almost unprecedented in the history of literature. In this respect he might appropriately be mentioned in the same breath as Goethe – who, incidentally, often thought of his own work as belonging to world literature as he added the grandiose word *Weltliteratur* to the German language. Some of the experiments of the French Symbolists, especially Mallarmé, may also have some relevance; Mallarmé's generation witnessed the breaking down of all classical distinctions so that poetry and prose were no longer generically different, so that fiction and drama were often to melt into each other and become (in S. E. Gontarski's happy phrase) 'textually androgynous'.

It is clear, then, that Beckett's work stands at the cutting edge of international literary experimentation – as it goes its unique Anglo-Irish/French/Germanic way. It defies many of the premises underlying conventional dramatic and fictional discourse, which depends so crucially on words. In his later texts Beckett has reached the enviably minimalist position that Mallarmé strove for in his final verse. Jacques Moran, in the second part of *Molloy*, came up with what proves a telling formula for Beckett's prose and drama of the past two decades: 'It seemed to me that all language was an excess of language.'

Beckett's Later Fiction and Drama, a genuinely international gathering as befits its subject, offers a series of elegant commentaries on these later works which manage with so few words. The essays themselves engage the matter of Beckett's discomfort with language, in the brief prose texts as well as in the drama. One contribution even looks at the crossing over from one literary form to the other, what Ruby Cohn once called 'jumping genres', with the result that the narrative *Company* was translated from page to stage. Another essay raises the generic question about a group of the late plays: 'Are these works inherently dramatic, or are they essentially works of prose fiction enclosed in a theatrical conceit?' Rarely have works of such startling brevity and skeletal dimensions been given such close examination and scrupulous concern as in *Beckett's Later Fiction and Drama*.

When Paul Verlaine remarked defiantly in his 'Art poétique': 'Prends l'éloquence et tords-lui son cou!', he could almost have been offering Samuel Beckett a poetics – at least for those 'queer little pieces' (as Hugh Kenner once called them) which comprise his work since *How It Is*. The poetics for *Texts for Company* in a sense is offered by Martin Esslin's 'Towards the Zero of Language'. While this seminal essay is mainly concerned with Beckett's dramatic work, many of its insights are also applicable to the late prose texts. Esslin examines the growing distrust of language, the 'steadily increasing interest in drama, as against narrative fiction', with the result that 'the image tends to override the words'. Esslin sees in the group of television plays written between 1975 and 1982, including *Ghost Trio*, . . . *but the clouds* . . . and *Quad*, wordless visual experience, to the point where they can no longer be classified as literature. He especially sees *Quad* as marking a crucial touchstone on the way to 'wordless poetry'.

Robert Wilcher ends his study of the radio plays with the useful reference to 'the silence that engulfs all radio drama'. His own essay is a painstaking examination of the texts for radio, with illuminating readings especially of *All That Fall* and *Embers*. Wilcher is successful in placing these works within what he calls 'the evolution of that lifelong "work in progess" in which individual items can best be appreciated as parts of a greater enterprise'.

S. E. Gontarski and Colin Duckworth are both concerned with the staging of Beckett's work. Gontarski's essay looks at his own adaptation of *Company*, performed in Los Angeles in February 1985, 'the only adaptation of his prose work with which Beckett has directly involved himself'. The theoretical underpinnings of the discussion – the possibility of crossing over from fiction to drama when 'generic androgyny' seems especially pronounced – reveal another way that Beckett's late texts have suggested tampering with traditional notions of literary and dramatic discourse. Gontarski seems to revel in the paradoxical nature of an enterprise which depends crucially on 'a tension created by playing narrative against visual imagery, ear against eye, the story we hear against what we think we see'.

Colin Duckworth takes a more jaundiced view of another staging, the 1984 production of *Waiting for Godot* by the San Quentin Drama Workshop. After examining this 'new' *Godot* with admirable patience, basing his essay in large part on a recorded interview in Melbourne with several of the actors, he remarks with a certain resignation: 'It makes one wonder whether authors should be let loose on their plays thirty-odd years later. We now have a different play, a "new" *Godot*, which can be regarded in some important respects as an impoverishment of the original. . . . As a performance piece, as live theatre, I must regard it as an aberration for the most part; but for Beckettian scholars it is invaluable.'

The essays by Katharine Worth and Charles R. Lyons examine an impressive number of plays from *Krapp's Last Tape* (1958) to *What Where* (1983). Worth's discussion concentrates on the decade from 1958 through 1969, which saw Beckett's theatre rise to 'the extraordinary concentration achieved in *Happy Days*' and then fall to the minimalist absolute of *Breath* with its 'wordless image of light playing on a rubbish heap between the cries and the indrawing and exhalation of breath which marks the course of a human life'. Lyons' essay focuses on the later ten-year period from *Not I* to *What Where*. Lyons goes to interesting and revealing lengths to distinguish this late drama from the prose texts. He remarks, for example: 'The writer-protagonists of the trilogy produce daily pages, but each day's work is discrete and contributes to the text as a sequentially written whole. When Beckett's dramatic figures tell stories, the present recitation seems to be a variation of a discourse spoken periodically.'

James Acheson's essay concentrates on two plays written during the decade Lyons is concerned with: *That Time* and *Footfalls*. His approach is quite different from either Worth's or Lyons' as he engages in a subtle form of literary rapprochement. By using Beckett's 'shape of ideas' notion, he skilfully juxtaposes *That Time* with Wordsworth's 'Tintern Abbey' and *Footfalls* with T. S. Eliot's *Four Quartets*. In the course of discussing how the Wordsworth and Eliot texts help explain the structure of Beckett's two plays, he is careful to point out decisive differences, especially in world view.

Dougald McMillan closely examines the unpublished and jettisoned drama which preceded *Endgame*, *Krapp's Last Tape* and *Not I*. He convincingly finds the seeds of these three finished plays in the series of aborted and abandoned texts from 'Human Wishes' through to 'Kilcool'. The inadequacy of language and the centrality of mime are primary concerns. McMillan is genuinely effective in commenting on the three finished works themselves; thus he revealingly describes *Krapp's Last Tape* as 'primarily a mime play performed to an accompanying monologue'.

The remaining essays are concerned with the later fiction. Rubin Rabinovitz ends his discussion of the first gathering of brief texts which followed the novel-length *How It Is* with this suggestive paragraph: 'What is at first so striking about the works of this period is how much has been removed: the house of fiction, it seems, has been razed. But if so, a new structure has been built in its place: simple in shape, economically constructed and – given its modest dimensions – very spacious on the interior.' Rabinovitz, with the same ingenuity and scrupulous attention to sources displayed in his *The Development of Samuel Beckett's Fiction* (1984), uncovers echoes from Vigny, Lamartine, Coleridge, Tennyson and Thomas Gray, amongst others, in his examination of the fiction of the 1960s.

Brian Finney takes over where Rabinovitz leaves off as he looks closely at a number of the texts completed after *The Lost Ones*. He explains persuasively in his opening paragraph: 'These are not abandoned longer works, nor works-in-progress. They are *sui generis*. In them Beckett has created a new subgenre to suit his imaginative needs. In the process of doing so he has pushed back the frontiers of postmodernist fiction in a highly original manner.' He neatly explains the workings of intertextuality in *Company*, which abounds in frequent quotations from his own and other writers' work. He offers a tidy distinction between two later texts: 'Where *Ill Seen Ill Said* is about the workings of the imagination, *Worstward Ho* is about the inadequacy and treachery of language.' He sees the narrator of the latter as striving towards 'a literature of the unword'.

The remaining essays offer close readings of these last three works. Kateryna Arthur usefully counterpoints *Company* with the earlier *Texts for Nothing*. With some help from the theories of Gilles Deleuze and Felix Guattari, expressed in their *Anti-Oedipus*, she makes a number of interesting remarks about the 'scripsophrenia' of Beckett's 1980 text.

Nicholas Zurbrugg concentrates on *Ill Seen Ill Said*, which appeared a year after *Company*. He gracefully weaves Proust and Eluard in and out of his discussion. (Beckett, of course, wrote a monograph on Proust and did a number of Eluard translations.) Just as Brian Finney was able to juxtapose *Ill Seen Ill Said* with *Worstward Ho*, so Zurbrugg tries to reconcile these two late texts in the final pages of his essay.

Enoch Brater moves towards a full-scale discussion of *Worstward Ho* by way of *All Strange Away* and, predictably, *Ill Seen Ill Said*. His reading of *All Strange Away* depends crucially on Rimbaud's 'Voyelles'. (One should recall at this point Beckett's spirited early translation of 'Le Bateau ivre'). After distinguishing *Worstward Ho* from earlier works in the way that it makes 'the language the story, and not the vehicle for a story, Brater elegantly classifies this late text: '*Worstward Ho* is a communion in words, what writing, for better or worse, has always been all about.'

Texts for Company, which brings together gifted critics from the far reaches of the English-speaking world, offers some of the soundest readings we have of Beckett's fiction and drama of the past quarter century. Seminal late works like *Company*, *Worstward Ho*, *Ill Seen Ill Said* and *Catastrophe* are here examined in depth and illumined from a variety of angles. The essays themselves are carefully stitched together by a deft editorial hand. *Texts for Company*, along with several other announced volumes (such as Enoch Brater's *Beckett at Eighty/Beckett in Context*) and a variety of international conferences (such as the August 1986 gathering at the University of Stirling), will honour Samuel Beckett on his eightieth birthday. If the essays which follow this foreword set the tone for the celebration, Beckett should have a memorable birthday indeed. *Venit, expectavit, scripsit scribitque in saeculum.*

MELVIN J. FRIEDMAN

Preface

Beckett's Later Fiction and Drama is dedicated to Samuel Beckett in honour of his eightieth birthday. All thirteen of its essays are published here for the first time. We decided to focus the collection on Beckett's later fiction and drama – his fiction since *How It Is* (first published in French in 1961) and his drama since *Endgame* (also first published in French, in 1957) – because his recent work has to date received relatively little critical attention.

The essays in this collection are offered as 'company' to the reader who is attracted to Beckett's recent work, but feels he would like some help in coming to terms with it. The first seven survey Beckett's fiction and drama over the past twenty-odd years, and provide a context within which to view the remaining essays, which concentrate on individual texts.

In preparing the volume we have incurred a debt of gratitude to Professor Melvin J. Friedman of the University of Wisconsin–Milwaukee, Professor A. N. Jeffares of the University of Stirling and Professor Bruce King of the University of North Alabama. We should like to take this opportunity to thank all three most sincerely for their help, encouragement and advice.

JAMES ACHESON
KATERYNA ARTHUR

Acknowledgements

The editors and the publisher are grateful to Faber & Faber Ltd, and Grove Press Inc. for permission to reprint the extracts from the published works of Samuel Beckett, and to John Calder (Publishers) Ltd for permission to reprint extracts from the following Beckett works: *Collected Poems in English and French, Collected Shorter Prose 1945–1980, Company, Disjecta: Miscellaneous Writings and a Dramatic Fragment* (ed. Ruby Cohn), *How It Is, Ill Seen Ill Said, Molloy/Malone Dies/The Unnamable, Proust/Three Dialogues: Samuel Beckett and Georges Duthuit, Watt* and *Worstward Ho*. The editors and the publisher are also grateful to Mr Beckett, the Dartmouth College Library, the University of Reading Library and the Board of Trinity College, Dublin, for permission to print extracts from his unpublished works.

Notes on the Contributors

James Acheson is Senior Lecturer in English at the University of Canterbury in Christchurch, New Zealand. He has published articles on Beckett in such journals as *Contemporary Literature*, the *Journal of Beckett Studies* and *Critical Quarterly*, and is writing a book on Beckett's early fiction and drama. A member of the Editorial Board of the *Journal of Beckett Studies*, he is currently coediting a special Australasian issue with Colin Duckworth.

Kateryna Arthur is Lecturer in Human Communication at Murdoch University, Western Australia. She was previously Tutor in English at the University of Melbourne. She has published articles on Beckett, Mikhail Bakhtin and Australian literature in such journals as *AUMLA* and *Westerly*, and is currently working on two books: one on Beckett, T. S. Eliot and Dante, and the other on pioneering perceptions of the Australian landscape.

Enoch Brater is Associate Professor in the Department of English and Theater at the University of Michigan. He has edited *Beckett at 80/Beckett in Context* and has written *Beyond Minimalism: Beckett's Late Style in the Theater*, as well as a wide range of essays on modern and contemporary drama. Dr Brater is a member of the Editorial Boards of *Comparative Drama* and the *Journal of Beckett Studies*.

Colin Duckworth is Professor of French at the University of Melbourne. He is author of *Angels of Darkness: Dramatic Impact in Beckett and Ionesco* and editor of the variorum edition of Beckett's *En attendant Godot*. He has directed several of Beckett's plays in London, Auckland and Melbourne, and is a member of the Editorial Boards of *Australasian Drama Studies* and the *Journal of Beckett Studies*. Recently he was made a Commandeur dans l'Ordre des Palmes Académiques by the French Government.

Martin Esslin, Professor of Drama at Stanford University, was Head of BBC Radio Drama from 1963 to 1977. He is author of *The Theatre of the Absurd*, *Brecht: a Choice of Evils*, *Pinter the Playwright*, *Artaud* and *Mediations: Essays on Brecht, Beckett and the Media*, and has edited *Samuel Beckett: a Collection of Critical Essays* in the Twentieth Century

Views Series. Professor Esslin is a member of the Editorial Boards of a number of journals, including the *Journal of Beckett Studies*.

Brian Finney is Senior Lecturer in Literature in the Department of Extra-Mural Studies at the University of London. He is author of *Since How It Is: a Study of Beckett's Later Fiction, Christopher Isherwood: a Critical Biography* and *The Inner Eye: British Literary Autobiography of the Twentieth Century*, and editor of two volumes of D. H. Lawrence's shorter fiction.

Melvin J. Friedman is Professor of English and Comparative Literature at the University of Wisconsin–Milwaukee. He is author or editor of more than a dozen books on such writers as Samuel Beckett, Flannery O'Connor, William Styron and Eugene Ionesco. His most recent edition, *Critical Essays on Flannery O'Connor*, was published by G. K. Hall in 1985. Professor Friedman was founding editor of *Wisconsin Studies in Contemporary Literature* and of *Comparative Literature Studies*, and now serves on the Editorial Boards of such journals as *Contemporary Literature*, the *Journal of Beckett Studies*, *Studies in American Fiction*, *Studies in the Novel* and *International Fiction Review*.

S. E. Gontarski is Associate Professor of English at Georgia Institute of Technology. He is author of *Happy Days: a Manuscript Study, The Intent of Undoing in Samuel Beckett's Dramatic Texts* and *Samuel Beckett: Thirty-five Years of Criticism (1951–1986)*. Professor Gontarski is coeditor of *Samuel Beckett: Humanistic Perspectives* and Editor of the *Journal of Beckett Studies*.

Charles R. Lyons is Professor of Drama and Comparative Literature at Stanford University, where he chairs the Department of Drama. He is author of *Bertolt Brecht: the Despair and the Polemic, Shakespeare and the Ambiguity of Love's Triumph, Henrik Ibsen: the Divided Consciousness* and *Samuel Beckett*, as well as numerous articles on drama. Professor Lyons, who has held both Guggenheim and NEH fellowships, is on the Editorial Boards of *Comparative Drama, Literature in Performance* and *Theatre Journal*.

Dougald McMillan is Publisher of Signal Books and former President of the American Samuel Beckett Society. He is author of *Transition 1927–1938*, coeditor of *Samuel Beckett: the Art of Rhetoric* and coauthor of *Beckett in the Theatre*. Currently he is preparing an edition of Beckett's directorial notebooks and production materials on *Waiting for Godot*. Dr McMillan is a member of the Editorial Board of the *Journal of Beckett Studies*.

Rubin Rabinovitz is Professor of English at the University of Colorado, Boulder. He is author of *The Reaction Against Experiment in the English Novel, Iris Murdoch* and *The Development of Samuel Beckett's Fiction*. His essays and reviews have appeared in the *Journal of Beckett Studies, Modern Fiction Studies, Twentieth Century Literature*, the *New York Times Book Review, New York Magazine, Byte*, and in other publications.

Robert Wilcher is Lecturer in English at the University of Birmingham. He is the author of *Andrew Marvell*; he has published articles on Beckett in the *Journal of Beckett Studies* and *Critical Quarterly*, and a wide range of articles on other authors.

Katharine Worth is Professor of Drama and Theatre Studies at Royal Holloway and Bedford New College, University of London. She is author of *Oscar Wilde, The Irish Drama of Europe from Yeats to Beckett* and *Revolutions in Modern English Drama*, and editor of *Beckett the Shape Changer*, a collection of essays on Beckett. Professor Worth has produced a number of Beckett's plays for stage, radio and television. Her most recent study, *Maeterlinck's Plays in Performance* (accompanied by slides), was published in 1985. She is now working on a critical edition of Yeats's *Where There Is Nothing* and *The Unicorn from the Stars*.

Nicholas Zurbrugg is Senior Lecturer in Comparative Literature at Griffith University in Brisbane, Australia. He is the author of *Beckett and Proust* and has published articles on Beckett in such journals as the *Yearbook of Comparative and General Literature, AUMLA* and the *Journal of Beckett Studies*. Dr Zurbrugg is Editor of *Stereo Headphones*, a journal that has published two works by Beckett, *Rough for Radio* and *As the Story Was Told*.

1

'Out of the Dark': Beckett's Texts for Radio

Robert Wilcher

I

Samuel Beckett's encounter with the medium of radio drama between 1956 and about 1962 has been recognised as an episode of some significance in his development as a writer. Many commentators have observed that the return to English in his first radio play, *All That Fall* (written 1956), signalled both an end and a beginning, after the great central decade of creative activity in French to which we owe his trilogy of novels, *Molloy*, *Malone Dies* and *The Unnamable*, as well as the major stage plays, *Waiting for Godot* and *Endgame*.[1] His second play for radio, *Embers*, has been described as 'the paradigm, for once explicit, of everything Beckett has done since the late 1950s';[2] and a recent study of the drama identifies 'a major transition' in the movement away from 'scenic location' towards the 'non-space or functional space of [his later radio plays] *Words and Music* and *Cascando*.[3] Before embarking on an analysis of the distinctive qualities of the group of texts designed to come 'out of the dark',[4] therefore, it will be useful to place them within the evolution of that lifelong 'work in progress' in which individual items can best be appreciated as parts of a greater enterprise.

Although *All That Fall* was not strictly speaking a commissioned work, Beckett was approached by a representative of the BBC in June 1956 about the possibility of his writing a piece for the Third Programme. By early July he had agreed in principle, and hinted at an idea 'which might or might not lead to something'.[5] In the event, it led with remarkable speed to the completion of his first radio play: the finished manuscript was dispatched on 27 September.

Beckett was urged to follow up the highly successful *All That Fall* (first broadcast on 13 January 1957) with a second play, but in May he informed its producer, Donald McWhinnie, that he could not promise anything in the near future. It was not until February 1959 that he met the request for a new work with *Embers*, which was broadcast on 24 June. In the meantime, however, Beckett's association with the BBC had been flourishing. At his suggestion, readings from *Molloy* and what was later to be entitled *From an Abandoned Work* were broadcast on the Third Programme in December 1957. These proved such a success – both with listeners and with the author – that further readings from *Malone Dies* and *The Unnamable* went on the air in June 1958 and January 1959. It seems likely that *Embers* – both in its subject matter and in its use of the medium – grew out of Beckett's experience of hearing excerpts from the novels transferred from print into sound.

The one major original work of the period between *All That Fall* and *Embers* was also an indirect consequence of the BBC transmissions. McWhinnie had chosen Patrick Magee, the Irish actor who had played the part of Slocum in *All That Fall*, to read the prose texts, and so effectively did his voice convey the quality of the Beckettian narrators that George Devine asked Beckett to supply a stage monologue for Magee as a companion piece to *Endgame*, the premiere of which was being planned for 1958 at the Royal Court Theatre. The result was *Krapp's Last Tape*, first performed on 28 October in a production directed by McWhinnie.

Throughout most of 1959–61, Beckett was occupied with a prose work (*Comment c'est*, completed in 1960) and another stage play (*Happy Days*, completed in 1961).[6] He took time off from his struggles with the French novel to repay a favour to Robert Pinget, who had helped him with the French versions of *All That Fall* and *Embers*. Pinget had responded to the BBC's request for a radio play and Beckett turned his friend's text into English (or rather Dublinese) in what is more of an adaption than a translation. It was broadcast as *The Old Tune* on 23 August 1960.[7]

During another break, this time from the chore of self-translation, he brought to fruition two original projects for radio, one of which he had personally cherished for a number of years. Back in 1957, he had mooted the idea of collaborating with his cousin, the composer John Beckett, who in the interim had furnished music to accompany the broadcast readings from the novels. This idea had apparently been revived by the Radio Drama Department of the BBC in February 1961,[8] but in March John Beckett had been seriously injured in a car accident. According to Deirdre Bair, the project was finally carried through in the autumn of 1961 'in response to a continuing plea from Donald McWhinnie and the BBC for as many radio plays as he could write, and also for John Beckett, as a means to speed his recovery'.[9] *Words and Music*, as the work was called, seems to have issued from the same burst of creative energy that produced *Cascando*, another collaborative undertaking, instigated not by Beckett but by his friend Marcel Mihalovici, the Rumanian-born composer. Mihalovici had written an opera based on the text of *Krapp's Last Tape* in 1960, and when the RTF in France commissioned a musical score for radio from him, he in turn approached Beckett for a script.

Details of the composition of these two pieces for voice and orchestra can be pieced together from evidence in letters and in the various collections of Beckett's manuscripts. On 12 February 1961, Beckett wrote, 'Next job will be with John Beckett – a text-music tandem for the BBC. Beginning to have a few ideas.'[10] Richard L. Admussen records two notes pertaining to *Words and Music* dated 16 February 1961, which he thinks may be a mistake for 1962, since it antedates by nine months the earliest known draft of the play.[11] These notes, however, may well be connected with the 'few ideas' for a 'text-music tandem' reported in the letter four days earlier. Admussen next records a holograph draft of the play, with extensive insertions and deletions, begun on 20 November and finished on 22 November 1961. The text reached the BBC Drama (Sound) Script Library soon afterwards and was entered in their records on 13 December. It was broadcast on the Third Programme on 13 November 1962. *Cascando* was drafted and extensively revised between 1 and 13 December 1961, but Mihalovici's score was not ready for another twelve months and the play was premiered on ORTF (France Culture) on 13 October 1963. The English version was first broadcast by the BBC on 6 October 1964.[12]

Between completing *Words and Music* on 22 November and starting the manuscript of *Cascando* on 1 December, Beckett was busy with another text, later published as *Esquisse radiophonique (Rough for Radio 1)*.[13] A draft of this brief sketch for a radio play (it has never been broadcast) bears the dates 29–30 November 1961.[14] It looks as if it was an attempt to provide a text for the Mihalovici project which was discarded in favour of the slightly different treatment of the same thematic concerns which was to become *Cascando*. Clas Zilliacus makes a good case for seeing it as 'situated halfway between *Words and Music* and *Cascando*' in more than merely a chronological sense.[15] Another sketch for radio cannot be fitted so precisely into a timetable of Beckett's activities. Published in *Minuit* in November 1975 under the title *Pochade radiophonique* and first broadcast in English on the BBC's Radio 3 as *Rough for Radio* on 13 April 1976,[16] it is said to have been written 'in French in the early 1960s' in the prefatory note to the English text (114). Similarities to the pieces on which Beckett is known to have been working towards the end of 1961 make it reasonable to assume that it is closely associated with the group of experiments which turned out to be his final creative involvement with the medium of sound.

II

Immediately prior to the initial enquiry from the BBC in June 1956, Beckett had been engaged on the final revisions to the French *Endgame*. He has said that his earliest excursions into drama – the still unpublished *Eleuthéria* in 1947 and *Waiting for Godot* in 1948–49 – were deliberately undertaken as 'a relaxation' from 'the awful depression the prose led me into'.[17] His third work for theatre, however, was taking him along the same path as the French novels, and the invitation to try his hand at radio may have presented itself as a welcome 'diversion' from what he has described as the 'rather difficult and elliptic' text of *Endgame*.[18] Certainly his first recorded reference to *All That Fall*, in a letter to Nancy Cunard on 5 July 1956, suggests that it was the novelty of the medium itself that had excited his interest: 'Never thought about a radio play technique, but in the dead of t'other night got a nice gruesome idea full of cartwheels and dragging feet and puffing and panting.'[19] That, and the need to compose in English (which may in turn have led him back to the Irish social and linguistic milieu of his childhood for a narrative subject) may account for both the relative expansiveness and 'the slightly old-fashioned air that makes the play something of an exercise in nostalgia'.[20]

All That Fall has the largest cast of any of the published plays, and Maddy Rooney's journey to and from the station at Boghill to collect her blind husband Dan from the Dublin train evokes a historically specific and coherent world of early motor cars, Saturday meetings at the nearby Leopardstown race course and Protestant church services, in stark contrast to Beckett's other work of the 1950s. But although his first venture into radio is to some extent a celebration of the richness of its expressive resources, his lifelong contempt for 'the grotesque fallacy of a realistic art'[21] leads him to mock the very conventions by which the medium imposes an impression of reality upon its listeners. In place of the printed pages of a prose fiction and the human figures moving in space that constitute a stage play, radio offers its consumers a series of auditory effects in time, and, as Martin Esslin has pointd out, 'the slightest verbal, musical or sound hint' acts as a powerful stimulus to the visual imagination.[22] And sure enough – true to his 'nice gruesome idea' – Beckett calls upon a wide range of radiophonic effects to create the detailed 'soundscape' in which Maddy Rooney has her being. The rural chorus of birds and animals and the distinctive noises of donkey and cart, bicycle, motor car and railway engine, with accompanying whinnies, bells, horns, whistles, starter motors, escaping steam and slamming doors, seem designed to run the gamut of radio's descriptive clichés. But working against any illusion of reality that might inhere in the sounds themselves are the careful tactics employed by Beckett to undermine what Zilliacus calls 'acoustic naturalism'.[23] The opening section of animal noises – '*severally, then together*' (12), says the text – is so stylised as to inform the audience simultaneously that the ensuing action takes place in the countryside and that it is being contrived in a studio.[24] Later, as Maddy and Dan struggle homeward, the methods available for establishing the existence of the world the characters inhabit are exposed to scrutiny:

MRS ROONEY: All is still. . . . The wind – [*Brief wind.*] – scarcely stirs the leaves and the birds – [*Brief chirp.*] – are tired singing. The cows – [*Brief moo.*] – and sheep – [*Brief baa.*] – ruminate in silence. The dogs – [*Brief bark.*] – are hushed and the hens – [*Brief cackle.*] – sprawl torpid in the dust (32).

Not only is the logical sequence of sound and comment amusingly reversed, but the passage also plays with the fact that radio has no means of realising the presence of a cow ruminating 'in silence' or a 'hushed' dog.

As this instance demonstrates, however, the sounds of nature and machine take second place to the human voice in radio's expressive armoury. It is chiefly through words that the speaker and the details of scene and event spring into being in the listener's imagination. The golden tassels of 'that lovely laburnum' (14, 36), which mark a stage on Mrs Rooney's outward and return journeys, exist only in her murmurs of appreciation, just as her own physical bulk is created by a vivid simile: 'Oh let me just flop down flat on the road like a big fat jelly out of a bowl and never move again!' (14). Like Beckett's later fictional narrators, and like Estragon and Vladimir or Hamm and Clov, Maddy Rooney is endowed with a self-conscious awareness of her involvement with the artistic medium to which she owes such reality as she has. She interrupts a conversation being carried on among other voices at the station with a speech which operates in two different dimensions. Within the fictional world, she is sarcastically complaining that she and her troubles are being pointedly ignored by Mr Tyler, Miss Fitt and Mr Barrell; but insofar as her words are addressed to the radio audience, she is asserting her role as the play's most important character against the oblivion that threatens to swallow her up whenever she is neither speaking nor being spoken to:

> MRS ROONEY: Do not imagine, because I am silent, that I am
> not present, and alive, to all that is going
> on. . . . Do not flatter yourselves for one
> moment . . . that my sufferings have ceased.
> No. The entire scene, the hills, the plain, the
> racecourse with its miles and miles of white rails
> and three red stands . . . I see it all . . . (25).

Her description of the 'entire scene' – the most elaborate pictorial passage in the play – flaunts the power vested in her to provide or deny visual information to those whose eyes she is as they listen to her voice coming 'out of the dark'.

Most significant of all for Beckett's later use of the medium is his recognition in this first work of its distinctive ability to take us inside the head of another person. Martin Esslin explains how the technical resources of radio have been developed to facilitate this inherent tendency of sound drama:

> Through the use of acoustic perspectives the radio writer and director can clearly convey to the listener with *whose* ears, from which subjective viewpoint, he is witnessing the action, and indeed inside whose mind he is supposed to be. Thus, by the use of stylised and distorted sounds radio can create a subjective reality halfway between the objective events experienced and

their subjective reflection within the mind of the character who experiences them – halfway between waking consciousness and dreamlike states, halfway between fact and fantasy, even hallucination.[25]

The first half of *All That Fall* – consisting of Maddy's encounters with a succession of other characters – exploits the techniques described by Esslin in order to dramatise the plight of the Beckett solitary whose mind is invaded and identity threatened by the surrounding universe of 'extracircumferential phenomena' ('Proust', p. 65). In McWhinnie's production, each meeting was heralded by the distorted sound effect of an approaching vehicle which, as it was brought into acoustic focus, enabled the listeners to share Maddy's experience of the impingement of external reality upon the private world inside her skull. Such narrative impulse as there is derives from the counterpoint between the old woman's laborious and interrupted progress and a rising sense of urgency, which culminates in the panic caused by the lateness of the train: 'Not an accident, I trust!' . . . 'Not a collision surely?' (26).

After the arrival of the delayed train, which McWhinnie perceived to be a climax 'impossible to exaggerate' as a radio event, a 'sound-complex' of 'grotesque fantasy',[26] Maddy is reunited with Dan. The story that Dan has to tell supplies the narrative core of the play's closing movement. What he calls at one point 'my composition' (34) consists merely of an account of the musings that occupied his mind and the physical discomfort that agitated his body while the train was inexplicably at a standstill between stations. 'Say you believe me' (35) he implores his wife when it is over, knowing that he has evaded her anxious appeals: 'Did something happen on the line? [*Pause.*] Dan! [*Brokenly.*] Why won't you tell me!' (31).

Later, as they are nearing home, Dan identifies the music we heard at the very beginning of the play: 'Death and the Maiden' (37). As Maddy weeps – for the old woman playing the same old record all day, for herself and for the little daughter whose loss she lamented earlier – Dan tries to distract her with an enquiry about the text for the following day's sermon. 'The Lord upholdeth all that fall and raiseth up all those that be bowed down',[27] she replies, and *'They join in wild laughter'* (38). The play ends with a partial answer to the narrative question that Dan's 'composition' has failed to satisfy. The boy who usually leads him from the station runs up with news which intensifies the bitter irony of the biblical verse that gives the work its title: 'It was a little child fell out of the carriage, Ma'am. [*Pause.*] On to the line, Ma'am. [*Pause.*] Under the wheels, Ma'am' (39).

This information also casts a sinister light on Dan's reluctance to talk about the interrupted journey and on his earlier, apparently casual, remark: 'Did you ever wish to kill a child? [*Pause.*] Nip some young doom in the bud' (31). But Beckett does not deal in neat narrative solutions, and he leaves his first radio audience to ponder the implications of the boy's words as they listen to the concluding sound effects of wind and rain.

III

Whereas *All That Fall* reworks in sound the material of the early novels and plays – the 'lingering dissolution' (15), as Maddy Rooney calls it, of the human passage from womb to tomb – *Embers* takes up the preoccupations of the later prose, by way of *Endgame* and *Krapp's Last Tape*, and presents the predicament of the artist who is cut off from effective participation in the common round of domestic and social existence by a need of his own nature which cannot be suppressed. Hamm, symbolically blind, describes the way his mind compulsively generates voices to stave off the fear of its own isolation: 'Then babble, babble, words, like the solitary child who turns himself into children, two, three, so as to be together, and whisper together, in the dark' (45). Krapp, alone in a pool of light, spends much of his time on stage listening to a disembodied voice from the past – the voice of one of his former selves recorded on tape. Radio makes the mechanical device for externalising the activity of memory redundant, and *Embers* takes us inside the head of a man who can call up sounds and voices out of the darkness more or less at will.

Since 'the process of imagining and thinking itself' is ultimately 'both the subject-matter and the material from which radio plays are built',[28] the appeal of the new medium must have been irresistible to a writer who was, to quote Hugh Kenner, 'at a crest of preoccupation with the fact that for him to live was to make stories, creating with words beings not himself, but perfecting his own identity in perfecting their words'.[29] The creation of a successor to Hamm and Krapp capitalises on the striking similarity between the resources of a broadcasting studio and the resources of a human mind. As we might expect, however, Beckett does not allow the medium to draw us into the illusion of Henry's internal reality without reminding us first of its essentially illusory nature. When Henry speaks, we might take him to be talking to himself in some supposedly real location, urging his reluctant limbs into motion:

> On. [*Sea. Voice louder.*] On! [*He moves on. Boots on shingle. As he goes.*] Stop. [*Boots on shingle. As he goes, louder.*] Stop! [*He halts. Sea a little louder.*] Down. [*Sea. Voice louder.*] Down! [*Slither of shingle as he sits.*] (93).

But he might equally be understood as a radio actor addressing a sound effects engineer who is slow to pick up his cues.

As the play progresses, however, we come to accept the convention that the sea is 'really' there and that the noise of the shingle, too, indicates 'real' movements in the physical world. Every other sound emanates from within Henry's skull. But the sea – which is to be '*audible throughout what follows whenever pause indicated*' (93) – is much more than an insistent aural backdrop. It performs the role of antagonist, giving the necessary tension of drama to the flow of the monologue. Henry's voice and the other voices and sounds he has at his disposal are primarily a means of drowning out the endless rhythm of the waves. His reminiscences about the death of his father; the story he tells himself about Bolton and Holloway; the conversation he manages to actualise with the remembered voice of his wife, Ada; the hooves, magnified drips, and slamming door; and the comic vignettes of his daughter's piano and riding lessons, each ending in a '*wail amplified to paroxysm*' (99) – all are only temporary respites from the incessant wash of the sea, which he characterises as 'Lips and claws!' (98) and 'this. . . [*Pause.*] . . . sucking!' (101). 'Listen to it!' (98) he cries in horror as it surges inexorably back into acoustic prominence.

But his resources are failing, and his lifelong resistance to whatever the sea may be taken to represent – the demands of life itself, death, nothingness, the unshaped flow of sense perceptions upon which the artist obsessively seeks to impose order or meaning – is coming to an end. Like Krapp, who found he had nothing to say when he sat down to record his impressions of his sixty-ninth year, Henry's creative powers are almost exhausted. Krapp had listened to his thirty-nine-year-old self confidently recording the experience that was to transform his life as a writer – the 'vision at last' – and looking ahead to that distant day 'when my work will be done and perhaps no place left in my memory, warm or cold for the miracle that . . . [*hesitates*] . . . for the fire that set it alight' (60); and had wound on impatiently to the description of a moment with a woman in a punt.

The miraculous fire of the imagination is almost extinguished in Henry, and when his story of Bolton and Holloway falters, he, like Krapp, tries to escape from present consciousness into memories, however painful they may be: 'no good, fire out, bitter cold, great trouble, white world, not a sound, no good. [*Pause.*] Father!' (96). But his father's voice is already beyond recall when the play opens, and Ada warns him that she too will not continue to be available indefinitely. After Ada has withdrawn, the sound-effects facility of his mind ceases to function, and his third attempt to carry on with his narrative reaches the same impasse of unresolved pleading and denial: 'night and the embers cold, and the glim shaking in your old fist, saying, Please! Please! (104).

The image on which the encounter between the two old men comes to rest is one which recurs in the plays of this period: 'Not a word, just the look, the old blue eye . . . fixes Holloway, eyes drowned, won't ask again, just the look, Holloway covers his face' (104). Krapp had been obsessed with 'The eyes [she had]!', and had pleaded 'Let me in' (60) as he bent over the woman in the punt and her eyes opened. The stage play recalls a memory of the individual's yearning to alleviate the human condition of solitude by entering the mystery of another being through the eyes – traditionally the windows of the soul. Henry's story in *Embers* seems to express the artist's terror of allowing the fictive projection of the self (Bolton) to merge with the fictive projection of another being (Holloway), because that would signal the final collapse of his ability to take refuge from loneliness by calling into being independent creatures inside his head. And if his story-telling – the art to which he has devoted his life, like Krapp (and Beckett) – is nothing more than a sophisticated version of the 'babble' of Hamm's frightened child, whispering to itself 'in the dark', then perhaps Ada's verdict on his obsession with the sea sound that drives him to the creation of an alternative order of reality in words is correct: 'It's silly to say it keeps you from hearing it, it doesn't keep you from hearing it and even if it does you shouldn't be hearing it, there must be something wrong with your brain' (100).

Although most, if not all, of the voices and sounds we hear in
Embers are constructions of Henry's mind, the dramatic illusion of a
character with a quasi-realistic temporal, spatial and social context is
maintained. Henry comes over the airwaves to us as a man with a
past that includes relationships – however distorted by memory –
with a father, a wife and a daughter. In the last group of pieces for
radio, Beckett abandons even that degree of compromise with the
'grotesque fallacy of a realistic art'.

IV

As early as *Molloy*, Beckett had invented a surrogate narrator who
dwelt 'deep down', 'somewhere between the mud and the scum',
and who had been afflicted by 'a voice telling me things'.[30] The
later incarnation of this narrator in *The Unnamable* had doubted
the validity of 'all this business about voices', but admitted
that 'Hearing nothing I am none the less a prey to
communications' (338). The speaker of *How It Is*, the prose–poem
that intervened between *Embers* and *Words and Music*, insists from
the very first fragment of his text that he is not to be regarded as the
source of the words: 'I say it as I hear it', he emphasises. What he
hears is nothing more than 'scraps of an enormous tale as heard so
murmured to this mud which is told to me'; and what he murmurs
into the mud is in turn overheard by 'a witness' and entered in a
'ledger' by a 'scribe'. The tale he has to tell is of an unending cycle of
torture in which songs and stories of 'life above in the light' are
extorted from one prone and helpless figure by another.[31]

In the autumn of 1961, Beckett came back to the medium most
suited to the evocation of the inner processes of the writer's art as he
had experienced it and begun to explore it in the prose. The
sound-sources no longer represent fictional characters, whether
present in some audibly realised setting like that of the Rooneys or
activated by memory or imagination like Ada and the wailing Addie;
they are abstracted aspects of the creating mind itself. Each of the
four pieces – 'plays' seems an inappropriate term – opens an
inspection shaft into the writer's 'obligation to express'.[32]

In the first of them, Croak[33] coerces Words and Music into
performing by the threat of his club, just as Bom used pain to wrest
song and speech from Pim in *How It Is*. A minimal narrative context
is retained in the references to the 'stairs' (127) by which Croak

descends from 'the tower' (128), and in the title by which he is addressed by Words – 'My Lord'. As Clas Zilliacus points out, there is just enough here to suggest the world of the chatelain of feudal Europe, commanding a demonstration of lyric art from his minstrels.[34] The artist's latent powers ('cooped up here in the dark' (127)) await release by Croak, whose function it is to propose a theme and force the conceptualising and imagemaking faculty of Words and Music's ripples and floods of emotion into mutual support as they seek to develop it. Each of the three improvisations – on Love, Age and 'the face' – probes further into the mind's recesses, eventually making contact with an image which inspires the combined resources of Words and Music. By way of a deliberately 'cold' description of a woman in orgasm – 'Lily!', cries an anguished Croak (132), remembering a moment like the one contemplated by Krapp – Words is swept from prose into poetry by the currents of emotion he has unexpectedly let loose:

> . . . a little colour comes back into the cheeks and the eyes . . .
> [*Reverently.*] . . . open. [*Pause.*] Then down a little way . . . [*Pause.*
> *Change to poetic tone. Low.*]
> > Then down a little way
> > Through the trash
> > To where . . . towards where . . .
> > (133).

With Music's assistance, he articulates the self's quest for communion with the self of another – in at the eyes and down 'through the trash', 'through the scum', 'To where one glimpse / Of that wellhead' (133–4), the inaccessible place where Molloy had his dwelling, 'somewhere between the mud and the scum' (14) of that bodily tenement which the Beckettian mind has always viewed with such contempt. Croak, that part of the artist's consciousness which lives (as a recurrent phrase in *How It Is* has it) 'above in the light', drops his club and shuffles away in silence – recoiling in horror or awe from the memories that lie in wait for those who dare (or are compelled) to make such descents into the darkness. But Words, the mind's capacity to handle concept and image, is untouched by the pain of individual experience and registers with a deep sigh the satisfaction that accompanies the successful fusion of idea and emotion in a work of art.

In the three remaining French texts for radio, Beckett pursues other insights into the writer's predicament. *Rough for Radio II* distributes Croak's role amongst an Animator, a Stenographer, and a character named Dick, whose mute presence only makes itself audible in the swish and thud of the bull's pizzle with which he extorts speech from the cowering figure of Fox.[35] The tormentors are themselves bound by a series of 'standing exhortations' (116) drawn up by some nameless authority, and their one hope of release lies in the murmured narrative of their victim. As the Animator puts it, echoing those earlier narrators of *The Unnamable* and the *Texts for Nothing*:

> Of course we do not know, any more than you, what exactly it is we are after, what sign or set of words. But since you have failed so far to let it escape you, it is not by harking on the same old themes that you are likely to succeed . . . (122).

The two brief movements of *Rough for Radio I*, similarly, dramatise public and private facets of the artist's dilemma. In the first, 'He' meets his 'debts' (107) by permitting – not inviting – an inquisitive visitor into the studio where the raw materials of his art are constantly available at the turn of a knob. There are no sound effects apart from the click which switches on the faint strains of a voice and an orchestra; and the radio listener's appetite for visual stimulation is teased by the most meagre and incongruous fare: 'May I squat on this hassock?' (107), 'Are these the two knobs?' (108), and 'To the right, madam, that's the garbage' (109). The visitor who comes prying into the nature of the artistic process remains unenlightened – 'It's unthinkable', 'It's unimaginable', 'It's inconceivable' (107–8) are her responses to such information as he can give her – and she departs with little more than an impression of the cold, dark and troubled solitude to which the artist's 'needs' have consigned him.

The '*Sound of curtains violently drawn, first one, then the other, clatter of the heavy rings along the rods*' (109) inaugurates the second movement, in which the restraint that has characterised the piece so far gives way to the '*shrill*', '*agitated*' and '*vehement*' (110–11) tones on onesided telephone calls punctuated by the familiar radio noises of dialling and ringing, and of a receiver repeatedly picked up and slammed down. The speaker – now named Macgillycuddy, as if in extravagant compensation for his earlier anonymity – makes several urgent attempts to inform 'the doctor' that the Voice and Music on his two channels seem to be both 'ending' and 'together'. Each of these developments causes him consternation, and as the two sounds fade out simultaneously, he is left to wait bleakly in the ensuing silence for a promised consultation at noon on the next day.

Cascando marks the furthest refinement of Beckett's work on radio. Sound effects have been completely eliminated, leaving only the two speakers and Marcel Mihalovici's score to interact with each other and the surrounding silence. No location of any kind is evoked in the words of the Opener, who regulates the flow of Voice and Music without any resort to the fictions of clubs or bull's pizzles or knobs. The only indications of anything external to this studio of the mind are the opening allusion to 'the month of May' (137), later elaborated as 'the reawakening' (141) and the 'long days' (142), in ironic counterpoint to the play's journey towards dissolution; and the Opener's indifference to the taunts of a public somewhere out there that regards his work with incomprehension (like the visitor in *Rough for Radio I* and Ada, in *Embers*, who could only interpret Henry's compulsive need to tell stories as evidence of 'something wrong' with his brain):

> They say, He opens nothing, he has nothing to open, it's in his head. They don't see me, they don't see what I do, they don't see what I have, and they say, He opens nothing, he has nothing to open, it's in his head.
> . . .
> They say, That is not his life, he does not live on that. They don't see me, they don't see what my life is, they don't see what I live on, and they say, That is not his life, he does not live on that. [*Pause.*]
> I have lived on it . . . till I'm old (140).

The artist who has spent a lifetime trying to heave up from the 'heart-burning glut of words' within him what the narrator of *Texts for Nothing* called 'the right ones, the killers',[36] the perfect combination that would finally lay to rest the 'obligation to express', is no longer troubled by those who can discern nothing more than the obsessions of a madman in what he 'opens' or lays bare in his writing, or by those who are skeptical about the power of his artistic calling to sustain him over the years. The equanimity with which he shrugs off these slurs on his art and his life goes with a recognition that the two cannot be disentangled and an acceptance of that imminent merging and cessation of Voice and Music which drove

Macgillycuddy into a panic: 'From one world to another, it's as though they drew together. We have not much further to go. Good' (141).

Voice has two separate functions, distinct from that of Opener, though all three project the operations of a single mind. Whereas Opener relates to an external world where other minds pass judgement on the activity he mediates, Voice belongs exclusively to that inner world where the mystery of the creative process takes place. It is both the source of the story and aesthetic intelligence that keeps watch over the flow of words, narrating the endeavour of the latest Beckett solitary – 'Woburn . . . same old coat' (137) – to cut loose from the shore to which Henry was confined and launch out on the open sea under a starlit sky, and urging itself forward with the conviction that this time 'it's different. . . I'll finish it' (137).[37] As Voice grows in assurance that the story of Woburn is 'the right one . . . this time. . . I have it. . . we're there. . .' (143), Opener's final 'Good!' (144) endorses the mutual efforts of Voice and Music in strong contrast to Henry's bitter 'No good' (95) when his story of Bolton and Holloway broke down. A formal conclusion is not reached within the text, but Voice's urgent appeals – 'just a few more . . . don't let go . . . Woburn . . . he clings on . . . come on . . . come on' (144) – are still affirming the rightness of that unachievable quest for the perfect story, in spite of all 'they say', as the silence that engulfs all radio drama, and is perhaps its most eloquent metaphor for the void against which identity seeks to define itself through art, closes in.

V

Samuel Beckett has not returned to sound drama since the series of experiments that culminated in *Cascando*. His six radio plays, however, offer one of the clearest demonstrations of the rigour with which he has pursued, in medium after medium, the principle enunciated in 'Proust': 'The only fertile research is excavatory, immersive, a contraction of the spirit, a descent' (65). And of all the media he has explored and tested during his long career, radio's capacity to transmit disembodied voices 'out of the dark' to an audience of solitary listeners perhaps comes nearest to fulfilling the austere Beckettian dictum that 'art is the apotheosis of solitude' (64).

Notes

1. In fact, Beckett had returned to English a year or two before with *From an Abandoned Work* (in Samuel Beckett, *Collected Shorter Prose 1945–80* (London: John Calder, 1984) pp. 129–37.) For dates of composition see Richard L. Admussen, *The Samuel Beckett Manuscripts: a Study* (Boston: G. K. Hall, 1979) pp. 18 and 54.
2. Hugh Kenner, *A Reader's Guide to Samuel Beckett* (London: Thames & Hudson, 1973) p. 166.
3. Charles R. Lyons, *Samuel Beckett* (London: Macmillan, 1983) pp. 144–5.
4. Samuel Beckett, in a letter to his American publisher, Barney Rosset, 27 Aug. 1957. Quoted by Clas Zilliacus in *Beckett and Broadcasting* (Abo: Abo Akademi, 1976) p. [i].
5. Quoted by Martin Esslin in 'Samuel Beckett and the Art of Broadcasting', *Encounter*, 45 (1975) 39. This article is the source of the information about Beckett's dealings with the BBC in what follows.
6. See Admussen, pp. 32–5 and 55–6.
7. Samuel Beckett, *Collected Shorter Plays* (London: Faber & Faber, 1984) pp. 175–89. All quotations from the plays discussed in this essay (apart from *Endgame*) are from this edition. Quotations from *Endgame* are from the Faber & Faber edition (London, 1958). Page numbers are given in the text.
8. Esslin, 41–3.
9. Deirdre Bair, *Samuel Beckett: a Biography* (London: Jonathan Cape, 1978) p. 541.
10. Quoted in *Beckett and Broadcasting*, p. 99.
11. Admussen, p. 94.
12. Details of dating are from *Beckett and Broadcasting*, pp. 99, 118–19, 122 and 131.
13. *Esquisse radiophonique* ws first published in *Minuit*, 5 (Sept. 1973) 31–5. It first appeared in English as 'Sketch for Radio Play' in *Stereo Headphones*, 7 (Spring 1976) 3–7. It appears in Samuel Beckett, *Ends and Odds* (London: Faber & Faber, 1977) pp. 85–91, as *Radio I*; but in Beckett's *Collected Shorter Plays*, pp. 105–11, its title is *Rough for Radio I*.
14. Admussen, p. 47.
15. *Beckett and Broadcasting*, p. 122.
16. *Minuit*, 16 (Nov. 1975), 2–12. In 'Beckett's *Rough for Radio*', *Journal of Modern Literature*, 6 (February 1977) 97, Martin Esslin reveals that Beckett's English translation of *Pochade radiophonique* was originally entitled *Radio II*, but that Beckett altered it to *Rough for Radio* to avoid confusion over the fact that it was to be broadcast on Radio 3. The play appears in *Ends and Odds*, pp. 93–104, as *Radio II*, and in Beckett's *Collected Shorter Plays*, pp. 113–24, as *Rough for Radio II*.
17. Quoted in Bair, p. 361.
18. Quoted in Bair, p. 464.
19. Quoted in Bair, p. 474.
20. John Fletcher and John Spurling, *Beckett: A Study of his Plays* (London: Eyre Methuen, 1972) p. 83.
21. Samuel Beckett, 'Proust' (1931), in *Proust/Three Dialogues with Georges*

Duthuit (London: John Calder, 1965) p. 76. All quotations from 'Proust' are from this edition; page numbers are given in the text.

22. Martin Esslin, 'The Mind as a Stage', *Theatre Quarterly*, 1, no. 3 (1971) 5.

23. *Beckett and Broadcasting*, p. 62.

24. This effect was reinforced in the original BBC production, in which the director, Donald McWhinnie, decided to get human beings to impersonate the various animals rather than using naturalistic recordings. See Donald McWhinnie, *The Art of Radio* (London: Faber & Faber, 1959) pp. 133–4.

25. 'Samuel Beckett and the Art of Broadcasting', 40–1.

26. McWhinnie, pp. 146–7.

27. Psalm 145.14.

28. Esslin, 'The Mind as a Stage', 8.

29. *Samuel Beckett: a Critical Study*, p. 168.

30. Samuel Beckett, *Molloy/Malone Dies/The Unnamable* (London: Calder & Boyars, 1959) pp. 14 and 176. Further page references to this edition will be included in the text.

31. Samuel Beckett, *How It Is* (London: Calder & Boyars, 1964) pp. 29, 20, 88, 79.

32. Samuel Beckett, 'Three Dialogues with Georges Duthuit' (1949), in *Proust/Three Dialogues with Georges Duthuit* (London: Calder, 1965) p. 103.

33. Croak's name perhaps indicates his descent from the narrator of *From an Abandoned Work*, who had a 'sore throat' caused by 'All this talking, very low and hoarse'. See Samuel Beckett, *Collected Shorter Prose 1945–1980* (London: John Calder, 1984) p. 132.

34. *Beckett and Broadcasting*, pp. 105–6.

35. The situation is similar to that described in *How It Is*: 'all alone and the witness bending over me . . . and the scribe . . . keeping the record' (p. 88).

36. Samuel Beckett, 'Text for Nothing VI', in *Collected Shorter Prose 1945–1980* (London: John Calder, 1984) p. 91.

37. Compare the similar voyages to oblivion at the end of *Malone Dies* and the novella, *The End*.

2

Past into Future: *Krapp's Last Tape* to *Breath*

Katharine Worth

Krapp's Last Tape opens with a strange stage direction: '*A late evening in the future*' (55).[1] A disconcerting direction for a play so taken up with the past, a memory play if there ever was one, we might say. In terms of realism what the audience sees is an old man, looking back from the present, the time we are in ourselves. There does not seem to be much sense of the future in the scene as sixty-nine-year-old Krapp, nearsighted and hard of hearing, fumbles for the tape of his choice and sits back to hear the '*Strong . . . rather pompous*' (57) voice of his thirty-nine-year-old self passing judgement on a Krapp still further back: 'Just been listening to an old year, passages at random. I did not check in the book, but it must be at least ten or twelve years ago. At that time I think I was still living on and off with Bianca in Kedar Street' (58).

It is, however, 'a late evening in the future'. Commentators have pointed out that in 1958 when the play was written it would not have been possible for Krapp to play tapes recorded thirty years back, tape recorders not having been around then: Beckett forestalled ironic comments on the point by setting the play in the future. But the implications of the setting go beyond that. If Krapp has not yet reached in reality the space occupied by the clownlike figure on the stage, this is some other dimension where, by some magic, past and future meet in a long moment of insight. The little pool of '*strong white light*' (55) on the dark stage where Krapp sits at his table is to become by the end of the play a place for movement away from attitudes of the past. In a situation so restricted that there seems no room at all for change, it is on change of a creative kind that the emphasis falls.

Krapp's Last Tape (1958) sets a pattern for two major plays that followed, *Happy Days* (1961) and *Play* (1963), and for the tiny 'dramaticule', *Come and Go* (1966). In them all Beckett turns the stage into a domain of the inner self, using basic elements of theatre – light and dark, stage groupings, sound – to create compelling images of the mind continually reshaping its past and confronting its future. Memory in these memory plays is an active and creative force, not just passive reverie.

In contrast, two plays written around the time of *Krapp's Last Tape*, *Rough for Theatre I* and *Rough for Theatre II* as they are now called,[2] deal with characters who fail to achieve change. These really are the plays of impasse that *Play* and the others look on the surface to be. More discursive, perhaps more provisional, they look back to earlier plays and are full of hints for plays to come. Though the characters are inhibited from reaching for it, each play is concerned with the future as well as the past. In one a promising new symbiosis is contemplated between two beings with complementary deficiencies; in the other the past is reviewed with a more sinister question in mind: whether or not the character under review should take steps (literally) to end it all. But neither piece achieves a stage image of sufficient force to involve us with the characters' irresolutions and obscure shifts of mood as we become involved with the finest shades of feeling in *Krapp's Last Tape* or *Happy Days*. The characters of the two *Rough for Theatre* plays seem in a way to be too free. It is when he traps his people in islands of dark or light, in a mound, in urns, that Beckett is able to give the audience the freedom of the city, the hidden domain of the solitary mind.

The sequence of plays I am considering ended in 1969 with the miniscule *Breath*. The play that opened it, *Krapp's Last Tape* (28 October 1958, Royal Court Theatre, London), was written in English, very fast, with much revision. In the three weeks of its composition, S. E. Gontarski points out, it went through seven distinct stages, at first sharing an incubation period in the same rich notebook with the 'Winnie-Willie Notes', nucleus of *Happy Days*. By the time of the first typescript version (there were four in all) Beckett had still not committed himself to an opening stage direction or a description of setting: all was open, nebulous.[3]

When a stage direction did appear it was startlingly precise. The action was set in April 1986, the date of Beckett's eightieth birthday,[4] the very event to which this volume pays tribute. The time shifts in *Krapp's Last Tape* acquire a strange new resonance when we think of Beckett in 1958 envisaging a future that has become his present in a very special sense: wherever his writings are known, 1986 is Beckett's year.

Twenty-eight years separate Beckett from the self that penned
Krapp, just about the distance between stage Krapp and his younger
self. So we may see Beckett arriving at Krapp by projecting himself
on tape into the future, envisaging with dry humour, some
sympathy, some revulsion and sadness, what it might be like in that
distant time. Such projections involve stocktaking: from what the
life has been up to then, the lines of the future emerge. Middle age is
the classic time for such operations: in March 1958 when he wrote
Krapp's Last Tape Beckett was approaching his fifty-second birthday,
and no doubt had some fellow feeling with Krapp who records on
his thirty-ninth birthday that he has just celebrated another 'awful
occasion' (57). The autobiographical allusions in the play were
toned down in later drafts (a customary procedure in Beckett's
revisions). 'April 1986' became 'the eighties' and in the final version
simply 'in the future'. This was all part of a subtle distancing process
from which Krapp emerges powerfully self-standing and free of his
author, despite the personal note in Beckett's thoughts about
ageing.

Another distancing technique was to invest stage Krapp with
exaggerated clownlike characteristics: purple nose, white face, dirty
white boots, a proneness to slip on banana skins. These effects too
were toned down in later productions after Beckett had come to find
them overdrawn, but a touch of the clown can bring the right kind of
hardness into the portrayal of Krapp. He is not to be seen as totally
pathetic but as one who uses trouble as a clown does, getting the
most out of what goes wrong, alert to possibilities for humour and
delight in the most dire circumstances. Max Wall, who has well
brought out this aspect of Krapp, found his own music hall routines
a good preparation: his manic musical Professor, for instance,
relishing the word 'stool',[5] could almost be a rehearsal for Krapp's
lovingly long-drawn-out enunciation of 'spool' ('Happiest moment
of the last half million' (62)).

Thirty-nine-year-old Krapp has not gone as far on the road to
buffoonery as his later self, would indeed not think of himself as a
buffoon at all. But from the farther perspective he can look it: a
'stupid bastard' he seems to old Krapp, throwing away the pleasure
of life for his 'homework': 'Everything there, everything on this old
muckball, all the light and dark and famine and feasting of . . .
[*hesitates*] . . . the ages. [*In a shout.*] Yes. [*Pause.*] Let that go. Jesus!
Take his mind off his homework. Jesus!' (62).

The past holds all the joy, it seems. 'What's a year now?', says sixty-nine-year-old Krapp as he sets about recording a new 'awful occasion'. The answer he gives himself – 'The sour cud and the iron stool' (62) – is a bleak image of the shrunken life of age. Lyrical love has been reduced to occasional visits from Fanny, 'bony old ghost of a whore' (62), and everything appears to be on a declining note. The table where the work on the tapes is done is a little island of light in a darkness which is waiting to encroach on the light;[6] as in the hymn Krapp quavers out: 'Now the day is over, Night is drawing nigh-igh' (62).

Martin Held, for many people the most deeply convincing of many fine Krapps, was directed by Beckett (in the 1969 production with the Schiller-Theater Werkstatt), to look apprehensively into the dark, as if, in Beckett's words, 'Old Nick's there'. Death is waiting behind him and, says Beckett, unconsciously he is seeking it: 'He's through with his work, with love and with religion.'[7]

Yet this is not all the play tells us. Krapp in old age is a humourist still, more so in fact than in his palmier days. He can enjoy a sardonic joke with himself about the slow sales of his books: 'Seventeen copies sold, of which eleven at trade price to free circulating libraries beyond the seas. Getting known'. (62). And his ironic wit plays over the lapses into pomposity of his younger self. He seems to have freed himself from all that, which must be counted a gain. A gain too is the perspective he has achieved on his life. His earlier self was seeking just that perspective: the whole laborious business of the tape recordings – the 'retrospects' and 'P.M.s' – has been a kind of endless stocktaking, an examination of experience in an attempt to value it properly – and to preserve it. It was so for middle-aged Krapp, as he tells us at the opening of the Spool 5 recording: 'Sat before the fire with closed eyes, separating the grain from the husks. Jotted down a few notes, on the back of an envelope' (57). A moment later he expands on the theme: 'The grain, now what I wonder do I mean by that, I mean . . . [*hesitates*] . . . I suppose I mean those things worth having when all the dust – when all *my* dust has settled. I close my eyes and try to imagine them' (57–8).

The dust is far from having settled as he says this. He is in the thick of experience, cannot yet fully separate the grain from the husks, though he intuits what the 'grain' will prove to be, giving, for instance, great care and feeling to his account of his mother's death: the 'small, old, black, hard, solid rubber ball' he was holding in his hand when the blinds went down, will be remembered 'until my dying day' (60). The same loving care is given to the episode of the girl in the punt. Though in the course of it he breaks off the relationship – 'I said again I thought it was hopeless' – he also communicates with great poetic force the sense of ecstasy, the lovers lying together, drifting on the water, his face in her breasts, her eyes opening suddenly against the glare of the sun to let him in, while under them 'all moved and moved us, gently, up and down, and from side to side' (61).

He could not hold onto that ecstasy in physical reality: who can? But he can record it, with power and feeling, for the future: as he says, he is looking 'back on the year that is gone, with what I hope is perhaps a glint of the old eye to come' (59). It is an inspired moment. Others are less so: he has recorded some experiences the future self will not want to hear of – speculations about the dark, imagery of storm and lighthouse, all that is abstract. Beckett enjoys himself with the opportunities offered by the tape recorder – a new instrument to him then[8] – to externalise old Krapp's mental responses in violent switchings off and rewind and replay operations – accompanied by curses. It is amusing and of course sad too, for the old man is so alone with his tapes and his booze: his *'wearish'* (55) state makes a painful contrast with the rich sensuousness of the past when he returns to the one place in the recording he cherishes: the story of the girl in the punt, and the moving waters.

For some the effect is overwhelmingly melancholy. Here much may depend on the actor: Patrick Magee (for whom Beckett wrote the part), though colourful and flamboyant vocally, had a strong pull to the elegiac, whereas Martin Held conveyed more of the ordinary, purposeful life of choice and decision that continues from one tape to the next. It is in essence the same life, centred on the activity of 'sifting' (the word used in *Play*), of finding the right words to record experience, of revising – endless revising – and replaying. A writer's life, in short, for that is what Krapp is, as the old rather than the middle-aged self makes clear in the joke about 'getting known'.

And it is not all looking back. Listening to Krapp on Spool 5 provides the impetus for making the new recording on the sixty-ninth birthday. It is Krapp's 'Last Tape' which, as has been said, might suggest that death is approaching very fast, and that he will not make another. However, it could equally mean the last one before the next one, and that is how it seems to me, for old Krapp has a will to continue at least as strong as his wish to be done with it all. He records on the 'last' tape how he crawls out to sit shivering in the park 'drowned in dreams and burning to be gone', but the life force drives him still: 'Be again in the dingle on a Christmas Eve, gathering holly, the red-berried. [*Pause.*] Be again on Croghan on a Sunday morning, in the haze, with the bitch, stop and listen to the bells . . . Be again, be again' (63). If the price is to relive the 'old misery', so be it: there is pain in the recording and listening process but it brings the past into the future, fresh and new, to be experienced as if for the first time – the process of art, in fact.

Krapp sees his future with a clarity that eludes the characters in *Rough for Theatre I.* James Knowlson has shown that this play originated in an English version, 'The Gloaming', written in 1956.[9] It has the distinction of being Beckett's first stage play in English, following (and perhaps encouraged by) the radio play, *All That Fall* (1957), which broke the French theatrical mould established with *Godot.* 'The Gloaming' was not published nor produced by a French version, *Fragment de théâtre*, appeared in 1974 (in *Minuit* 8) and in 1976 *Theatre I*, described as a translation from the French by the author, was published in *Ends and Odds.*[10] *Rough for Theatre I* thus has a curious bilingual background: in its passage from 'The Gloaming' it was severely cut, especially, as with *Krapp*, where autobiographical reference was too overt.

The play has obvious, perhaps too obvious, links with *Endgame* (as with Yeats's *The Cat and the Moon*, a prototype for both). Again a lame man and a blind man are preoccupied with the idea of symbiotic relationship, but in this play no connection is made: the afflicted pair discuss the possibility of a partnership but cannot achieve it. Something keeps them apart, though they can see clearly enough the advantages of teaming up:

> B: . . . And if you care to push me about I shall try to describe the scene, as we go along.
> A: You mean you would guide me? I wouldn't get lost any more?
> B: Exactly. I would say, Easy, Billy we're heading for a great muckheap, turn back and wheel left when I give you the word (70).

The 'muckheap' prompts thoughts of Krapp and his speculations on 'this old muckball' (62), but whereas for Krapp the muckball is associated with feasts as well as famine, for A and B the prospect is greyer:

A: Will it not soon be night?
    [*B looks at sky.*]
B: Day . . . night . . . [*Looks.*] It seems to me sometimes the earth
    must have got stuck, one sunless day, in the heart of winter, in
    the grey of evening (72).

At the time he was writing 'The Gloaming' Beckett was
experiencing acute frustration over the failure of *Fin de partie* to find a
theatre in Paris. Finally Roger Blin's production had to open in
London, playing at the Royal Court Theatre (3 April 1957) to an
audience who would obviously experience difficulty with such a
text delivered in French: Beckett said it was like 'playing to
mahogany, or rather teak'.[11] There is a connection here with the
play that became *Rough for Theatre I*, for the sense of a future that
cannot be realised is strong in its dramatic action. Inevitably,
perhaps, no stage image is created equal in power to the closed room
of *Endgame* or the tape recorder of *Krapp's Last Tape*. Only at the end
of the play do we move towards a strongly expressive image, when
A finally responds to B's seductive invitation to become his partner
by stooping down with hands clasped on the cripple's rug, saying
he could stay like that for ever 'with my head on an old man's
knees' (72). 'Knee', B corrects him (he has only one leg); the rough
joke is followed by a rough pushing of the blind man so that he falls
to the ground. A tries to hold on to a consoling vision, the sound of
the harp he used to play, but B mockingly demolishes it, drawing a
picture of a future in which some other old man will 'come out of his
hole' (73) to find A playing the mouth organ and talking of the little
fiddle he used to have. He drives the point home by poking A in the
back with the pole he uses to push his wheelchair, a final taunt
which goads A to violent action: he seizes the pole and 'wrenches it
from B's grasp' (73), leaving the one-legged man helpless. On this
rather grim note the curtain descends.

The play opens with a vision of the future: B comes on to the
sound of A's fiddle exclaiming 'Music. [*Pause.*] So it is not a dream
At last.' (67). It ends with the characters still unable to move
forward, each worse off than in the fuller time gone by, when they
had the support of a woman: 'You yours to lead you by the hand and
I mine to get me out of the chair in the evening and back into it again
in the morning . . .' (69). The difficulty of making an 'about-turn'
(B's phrase) proves too great for the reduced powers of the two who
are both, in their different ways, in the dark; A involuntarily and B,

it seems, of his own choice: 'I sit there, in my lair, in my chair, in the dark, twenty-three hours out of the twenty-four. [*Violently.*] What would you have me observe?' (69).

B poses a choice at the start. Should he go back to his 'hole', accepting that 'the mystery is over', or should he venture on change by teaming up with A, 'join together and live together till death ensue?' (67). The choice is not made and though the violent business with the pole seems to promise some new turn, what it will be is obscured from us – as his own immediate future in the theatre was from the author of the still unplaced *Fin de Partie*. Yet the dialogue between A and B is full of interest: many intriguing echoes. and anticipations of plays to be are heard: A cannot go without his 'things', for instance, even though they are no good to him, a curious prelude to Winnie's precious bag of things in *Happy Days*. While the curtain line points even further ahead: B's 'Eh Billy?' (73) anticipates *Eh Joe* in its taunting note as well as in its verbal closeness. Like Joe, A is left by the mocking voice with thoughts of a future that can only repeat in attenuated form the movements of the past.

Thoughts of suicide surface momentarily in *Rough for Theatre I*: B asks A, 'Why don't you let yourself die?' and is told, with a wry, punning wit (enough in itself to explain why it could never happen), that A has never been unhappy enough: 'that was always my unhap, unhappy, but not unhappy enough' (68).

In the other play of the period which was not produced and remained unpublished for years, *Rough for Theatre II*, suicide appears to be a more serious possibility. The stocktaking conducted by the two assessors, A and B, threatens a no-future rather than the disconcertingly open one of *Rough for Theatre I*. 'Let him jump, let him jump' (86), says the hardhearted B of the mute subject of their investigation, C, who is standing throughout by the open window as if ready at any moment to throw himself out.

Rough for Theatre II was first written in French in August 1958, shortly after *Krapp's Last Tape* had been finished.[12] Beckett made several stops and starts on the text but was always clear about the stage image: a diagram of the set in the original manuscript shows the scene as it was to remain: the high double window upstage centre, open on to a bright night sky; downstage the two identical tables and chairs facing each other symmetrically, each with its lamp, one with a briefcase 'crammed with documents' (77). There are anticipations here of a much later play, *Ohio Impromptu* (1981), which has two figures sitting at a table, one reading a 'story' of a life from a book, the other listening mutely; mirror images of each, with their white hair, black coat and shared black hat, they form a strange symmetry with each other and with the white table and chairs.

There are touches of that mesmeric strangeness about *Rough for Theatre II*, though it is a play of curiously mixed mood, leaning to farce and replete with puns and gags. Like B in the earlier play, A in this one sounds a note of mystery at the start: 'I still don't understand. [*Pause.*] Why he needs our services. [*Pause.*] A man like him. [*Pause.*] And why we give them free. [*Pause.*] Men like us. [*Pause.*] Mystery' (77).

They are C's servants but also his judges, weighing up the quality of the life recorded in the briefcase documents, their function, as A puts it, to 'sum up and clear out' (77). What they find from their 'sources' is that C is culpably negative and deficient in optimism. 'To hear him talk about his life after a glass or two', says one, 'you would have thought he had never set foot outside hell' (80). It all adds up, as B sees it, to a cast iron case for letting him jump: the evidence is 'Tied together like a cathedral'. 'And his sense of humour? Of proportion?', asks A. 'Swamped', says B, tersely (78).

Clearly Beckett is enjoying a joke against himself. With sense of humour far from swamped, he accumulates the hearsay and circumstantial evidence that suggests it ought to be. Everything is comically exaggerated, as in the list of C's psychosomatic illnesses, which includes irrational fear of vipers and pathological horror of songbirds, as well as rather more common complaints like sick headaches and eye trouble. He has fun, too, with designing droll Happy Families names for the witnesses: Mrs Aspasia Budd-Croker, button designer; Mr Moore, light comedian, c/o Widow Merryweather-Moore, All Saints on the Wash.

But there are also moments in the play which suggest a more serious connection between C and his assessors. Some obscure inner conflict is being expressed, we may assume, in shifts of tone such as B's outburst when confronted with the notion that there might be 'positive elements' in C's character: 'Positive? You mean of a nature to make him think . . . [*hesitates, then with sudden violence*] . . . that some day things might change? Is that what you want? [*Pause. Calmer.*] There are none' (80).

Positive and negative forces alternate in a long drawn-out comic business with the two lamps which go on and off with manic independence as the assessors look into the 'Slim file' (82) of C's confidences about himself, discovering major fuse points on the phrases, '. . . morbidly sensitive to the opinion of others', and 'I was unfortunately incapable . . .' 'Mysterious affair, electricity' (83), says A, clearly speaking of more than the farce: he is interested in the 'spark' he thinks C has in him still, and B terminates the horseplay – 'This gag has gone on long enough for me' (84) – by moving closer to scrutinise C's expression (invisible to the audience). It is glum, we are told: he has lost 'that little smile' (85). One of the caged birds is dead, the other sings on regardless, shocking B, and drawing from A a characteristic comment on the great gap between '[a]ll that splendour' (the beauty of the birds) and the unavoidable facts of physical existence: 'And to think all this is organic waste.' (88).

The assessors are themselves almost ready to jump out of the window now, the fate that C seemingly cannot avoid, in the light of their verdict: 'A black future and an unpardonable past' (86). The play ends with A raising his handkerchief timidly to C's face, as if to wipe tears away. In this version C is denied the benefit of the original French, where 'avenir noir' appears as 'avenir d'encre',[13] postulating a rather more hopeful, writer's future. In English the jokes about impasse and depression turn sour, despite the intermittent hilarity, and it is hard to feel involved with C's fate when he is kept so far away from us.

When the suicide motive reappears in a new play, it is a very different matter. No difficulty about becoming involved with the fate of Winnie and Willie in *Happy Days* (Cherry Lane Theatre, New York, 17 September 1961). From the moment Winnie opens the play with her sublimely incongruous 'Another heavenly day' (9), going from prayers to tooth brushing and then to rumination on 'poor dear Willie' (10), she holds our attention, imposing a rhythm and focus which gives every smallest move of hers compelling interest.

A powerful scenic image aids the extraordinary concentration achieved in *Happy Days*, a concentration which keeps us intent and keyed up even when Winnie, buried up to her neck in the second act, has only her facial expression and voice to move us by. Under a harsh, inescapable light, ruled by an inescapable bell, the so-ordinary middle-aged blonde is trapped in the earth which, as she says, is 'very tight today' (23). Yet she succeeds in rising above it – for such is at least one implication of the strange, symbolic structure in which she is encased. The low mound that rises out of the scorched grass and has Winnie at its exact centre can be seen in many ways: as a burial mound, no doubt, and also its opposite, an erotic zone (Winnie tends to see herself as a Queen of Love). Simply by raising her up as it does, however, it also makes the suggestion that there is something lofty about Winnie.

The word may seem an odd one for a woman in some ways so down to earth (only too literally). She is capable of coarseness, as when she enjoys the pornographic postcards that Willie hands her, uttering suitably shocked expressions of disapproval the while: 'Heavens what are they up to. . . . No but this is just genuine pure filth. . . . What does that creature in the background think he is doing?' (16–17). Yet though she joins with Willie in this unsavoury pleasure, she is really far above him, as the metaphysical mound implies. Originally Beckett had thought of stressing the comparison even further in a more broad and farcical way: in a first version the mound was to have had ledges and the opening scene would have shown Willie (then called Tom) sitting on the lower ledge, in striped pyjamas, 'leaning forward and exposing bare flesh around his midriff'.[14] This was abandoned in favour of the scene as we have it: Willie visible only intermittently, behind the mound, showing parts of himself (bald head, hairy forearm) in broad comic style.

Willie is more mobile than Winnie but also more passive: as in the *Rough for Theatre* plays, freedom from creative pressure appears to bring with it depressive moods, even suicidal inclinations. The revolver has sinister significance for Willie, as Winnie reminds him: 'Remember how you used to keep on at me to take it away from you? Take it away, Winnie, take it away, before I put myself out of my misery' (26). 'What a curse, mobility!' (35), she says, perhaps a trifle complacently, as she watches him crawling back into his hole. He is of the earth, earthy; an 'old turtle', as Beckett described him, whereas Winnie is associated with air and fire.[15] The allusion to Shakespeare's Cleopatra adds a grace note to the subtle harmony of literary quotation which is one of Winnie's chief means of rising above the limitations and erosions of the earthy state. Humour is another, sometimes applied to her own literary leanings, as in the delicious 'what is that unforgettable line?' (37). Perhaps feeling for Willie is yet another. He is certainly important to her as a listener: one of the malign changes in the second act which make her later condition so overwhelmingly tragic is the breakdown of even the minimal response she had from Willie in Act 1: 'May one still speak of time? (*Pause.*) Say it is a long time now, Willie, since I saw you. (*Pause.*) Since I heard you' (37).

Yet even when everything deserts her – no hands for the parasol, or the bag, or the revolver conveniently placed on the mound beside her, no movement except in the face – she continues to construct her airy world of the mind. The immense energies of the first act are depleted, of course. Ruby Cohn has spoken of the 'white voice' that Beckett required from Eva Katherina Schulz playing Winnie in the 1971 production at the Schiller Werkstatt in place of the many-coloured vocal tone called for in the first act.[16] All Winnies must become blanched and drained when the earth has them so clenched: the contrast is sad but it brings out the almost infinite variety of the earlier self-projection. It has taken many forms in the theatre: the gallantry which was emphasised by Brenda Bruce, the first English Winnie; the steely manners of Madeleine Renaud, Peggy Ashcroft's homelier poignancy; the tragic grandeur of Billie Whitelaw. All – along with other memorable Winnies – have projected the remarkable sense of ebullience that allows the character to rise above herself: 'Is gravity what it was, Willie, I fancy not. (*Pause.*) Yes, the feeling more and more that if I were not held – (*gesture*) – in this way, I would simply float up into the blue' (26).

Though in the second act she loses the stimulus of Willie's responses (minimal as they were), Winnie remains creative. She continues to compose and edit stories. 'Gently, Winnie', she warns herself on coming to 'Suddenly a mouse –' (41) in the story of Mildred and the doll. And it is now, when the earth hardly allows her to do more than breathe, that she succeeds in summoning up Willie to crawl to her in full wedding kit, a journey we know full well he could not have made without her.

How this event will turn out we cannot tell: Winnie's reactions to Willie at close quarters suggest some traumatic possibilities: 'Don't look at me like that! . . . Have you gone off your head, Willie?' (47). He is 'dressed to kill' (45), the revolver is at hand, the old question of suicide is perhaps surfacing (though some have thought the threat is aimed at Winnie). But whatever the dark notes, an amazing thing is happening. At last Winnie is able to sing the song we have been waiting all the play to hear. And though it is certainly an ambiguous confrontation on which the curtain descends – the two exchanging a long look following the last of many repeated directions for 'Smile off' (48) – yet we must surely feel it is an achievement. Something new has come about in this extreme situation of stasis: the audience is left looking forward, questioning what will happen, recognising the creative energy that has drawn the vanished past into the

compelling image there before us. Against all the odds, Winnie
takes us with her into the future.

The future becomes terrifyingly fused with the past in Beckett's
next exploration in stocktaking, *Play* (Ulmer Theater, Ulm-Donau, 14
June 1963, as *Spiel*). It rests on an idea he had thought of using in
Krapp's Last Tape: in an early draft Krapp was to have tried to move
away from the lighted zone round his table only to find himself
pursued by the light. The suggestion here of a conflict 'between
Krapp and some force outside himself represented by the light'[17]
was developed in the tense relationship of *Play* amongst the three
heads in urns and the spotlight on which they are dependent for
speech. 'Get off me! Get off me!' (16) shrieks W1, as the spot moves
from one urn to another, inexorably lighting whatever head it wants
to hear, drawing out of them confessions of misery, guilt and
resentment. This light seems to be weaving its own drama out of the
trio's individual memories of the sorry adultery they acted out – in
'play', as it seems to them in the second half, when they are forced to
think back over their affair with changed feeling.

The play opens on an agitated confessional note, but only as a
brief babble of sound, before the voices switch to the narrative set
back in the 'play' time when they acted out their spiteful sexual
comedy, unaware that they were under the spotlight. Blithely (it
really seems the word), W1, W2 and M recapitulate the sorry drama,
each seeing him or herself as the put-upon victim, each aiming to
put down the others with gibes and taunts that do indeed have the
effect of turning their affair into a play – a comedy such as any
theatre audience can enjoy, full of droll repartee and catty comment:
'Her photographs were kind to her. Seeing her now for the first time
full length in the flesh I understood why he preferred me' (148); 'She
had a razor in her vanity bag. Adulterers, take warning, never
admit' (150). These tart, funny lines fall from lips which scarcely
seem living flesh. Some memorable production pictures (from the
National Theatre, London, for instance) show how the
extraordinary effect that Beckett called for can be realised; flaking,
peeling faces, 'so lost to age and aspect as almost to seem part of
urns' (147). The three nameless heads protruding from their
shadowy funereal urns, look as dead as dead can be: and it is a dead
past they tell of, in their amusingly 'dead' language ('Judge then of
my astoundment . . .' (149)). What room for change is here?

Yet the play is built upon the idea of change. It begins towards the
end of the comedy sequence when the style moves away from the

affected histrionics to the lyrical and serious. The surface of the narrative cracks, deeper feeling begins to force its way through: 'I made a bundle of his things and burnt them. It was November and the bonfire was going. All night I smelt them smouldering' (151).

It is a prelude to the descent into emotional depths which comes about when the spotlight switches off and after a brief blackout, a new sequence begins, with light and sound at half strength and style correspondingly lowtoned. 'When first this change' (152): M's line gives us the *leitmotif*. They are aware of the spotlight now and of the demands it seems to be making on them, though resentfully. 'Give me up as a bad job', shouts W2, 'Go away and start poking and pecking at someone else' (152). Grim conscience is at work, mixing with muddy remains of former confidence and with finer feelings, as in M's revelation of his romantic yearnings: 'Never woke together on a May morning, the first to wake to wake the other two. Then in a little dinghy –' (156). Critics have sometimes joined the stage victims in feeling that the spotlight's operation is mechanical and arbitrary: 'Mere eye' (157). Even M, who thinks the dark they all long for might somehow be 'worse' (157), shares the fear that there is no meaning in what is happening: 'There is no future in this' (153).

But there is a future: paradoxically, it is the extraordinary *aria da capo* which takes the action back to the starting point, playing it all through again word for word. Is this, then, the signal that the play is about the impossibility of change? Its production history and Beckett's revisions show him offering a choice between a repetition which is 'an exact replica' (160) of the first round and one with variations: in London and Paris, he comments in his note on the Repeat, they opted for 'deviations from the first statement' (160). He also remarks that the spotlight is not to be thought of as a totally detached 'unique inquisitor' (158), but as itself a victim.

There is room here for a question mark about the future, such as can be raised by the journey the play makes in the theatre: it is usually an exhilarating, not a depressing one, in my experience. Unlike the doomed trio in Sartre's *Huis clos*, the figures of *Play* have already shown capacity for change, though, as Voice in *Cascando* says of his invented character, Woburn, 'not enough' (137). Whether they can go any further is veiled from us: what is certain, however, is that the audience itself is changed. The laughter that greets the first round always dies down once the dip into purgatory has been experienced. It is an extraordinary thing to be in an audience which has been relishing the comedy, as at a particularly funny production at the Royal Court in 1976, and feel the response completely altered in the Repeat. The words remain unchanged but the audience has seen the future, seen behind the jokes and along with the characters (and the author) is rewriting the past.

In the tiny play, *Come and Go*, future and past merge again, but this time softly and poignantly in the image of three women sitting on the bench which is the log of the long-ago 'playground at Miss Wade's' (194), as well as the place where they murmur confidences about the dark future. Again the audience is provoked into making its own deductions: as James Knowlson has shown, Beckett very deliberately excised all the detail he had originally supplied in an early draft, 'Good Heavens!', where he made it clear that the future held only death.[18] Probably the audience fill in along that line for themselves, supplying terminal cancer or some such ordinary horror in the spaces where the two women whisper to each other about the absent one, who leaves the gentle circle of light while her fate is revealed. What we see, however, has to be set against what we imagine being said in those silences. And what we see is a joining of hands – in an intricate pattern laid down by Beckett – which suggest that the three faded flowers, Vi, Ru and Flo, are forever joined in some pattern which is beyond their view or ours. 'I can feel the rings' (195), Flo's closing line, contradicts what we see – hands (picked out by the light) with no rings apparent – drawing attention to possible fantasies and failures in their lives (failure to achieve marriage, for instance), but also to the sense of this invisible pattern which is being woven out of their past and their future.

The sense of life's sad transience which suffuses *Come and Go* is felt again, mixed with a more caustic note, in the 35 seconds' *Breath* (Eden Theater, New York, 16 June 1969): it crystallises past, present and future in the wordless image of light playing on a rubbish heap between the cries and the indrawing and exhalation of breath which marks the course of a human life. The final cry indicates life continuing, though whether that is for the good no one knows. Kenneth Tynan tried to make it seem so by adding naked bodies to the rubbish heap (*Breath* was given to him for his review, *Oh! Calcutta!*) but Beckett stamped on that particular extension.[19]

The human span may be, as the last two pieces suggest, pitiably short, but *Krapp's Last Tape* and the other plays here discussed show Beckett's art opening up great vistas of possibility in situations of grotesque limitation. 'There is no future in this' is a line that is not endorsed by the plays nor, most certainly, by the theatre, which will be taking them into the future far beyond any date that could have been envisaged when the old age of Krapp was planned.

Notes

1. All quotations from the plays discussed in this essay, apart from *Happy Days*, are from Samuel Beckett, *Collected Shorter Plays* (London: Faber & Faber, 1984). All quotations from *Happy Days* are from the Faber & Faber edition (London, 1976). Page numbers are given in the text.
2. They were known as *Theatre I* and *Theatre II* when first published in *Ends and Odds* (N.Y.: Grove Press, 1976). The change of title brings them into line with *Rough for Radio I* and *Rough for Radio II*, also in *Collected Shorter Plays*.
3. S. E. Gontarski, 'The Making of *Krapp's Last Tape*', in *Theatre Workbook 1*, ed. James Knowlson (London: Brutus Books, 1980) pp. 14–23. See also for references to Beckett's production notes on *Krapp's Last Tape*.
4. Deirdre Bair records in her *Samuel Beckett: a Biography* (London: Cape, 1978) p. 3, that Beckett's birth certificate gives 13 May 1906 as his date of birth, but Beckett himself has maintained that he was born on Good Friday, 13 Apr. 1906.
5. Max Wall's classic piano playing routine has his comical Professor study the piano stool as a prelude to his performance, exclaiming 'stoool' with the utmost relish. (See *Theatre Workbook 1*, p. 112).
6. The interplay of light and dark in *Krapp's Last Tape* and other plays has intricate symbolic significance for Beckett, which James Knowlson has discussed in his *Light and Darkness in Beckett's Theatre* (London: Turret Books, 1972).
7. 'Martin Held Talks to Ronald Hayman', *Times Saturday Review*, 25 Apr. 1970.
8. Beckett's interest in tape recorders was stimulated by the first production of *All That Fall*, broadcast on the BBC Third Programme, 13 Jan. 1957. (See Martin Esslin, 'Samuel Beckett and the Art of Broadcasting', *Encounter*, 45 (Summer 1975) 40).
9. James Knowlson and John Pilling, *Frescoes of the Skull: the Later Prose and Drama of Samuel Beckett* (London: John Calder, 1979) p. 229. Hereafter cited as *Frescoes*. The manuscript of 'The Gloaming' held in Reading University Library is dated Dec. 1956.
10. *Minuit*, 8 (Mar. 1974) 65–72; *Ends and Odds*, pp. 71–80.
11. 'On *Endgame*', [extracts from correspondence with Director Alan Schneider, 1955–8], in Samuel Beckett, *Disjecta: Miscellaneous Writings and a Dramatic Fragment*, ed. Ruby Cohn (London: John Calder, 1983) p. 108.
12. See Richard L. Admussen, *The Samuel Beckett Manuscripts: a Study* (London: George Prior, 1979) p. 112. The French original, *Fragment de théâtre II*, appears in Samuel Beckett, *Pas suivi de quatre esquisses* (Paris: Minuit, 1978) pp. 37–61.

13. *Pas suivi de quatre esquisses*, p. 55.
14. *Happy Days: a Bilingual Edition*, ed. James Knowlson (London: Faber & Faber, 1978) p. 129.
15. See Ruby Cohn, *Back to Beckett* (Princeton University Press, 1973) pp. 190–1.
16. Ruby Cohn, *Just Play: Beckett's Theater* (Princeton University Press, 1980), p. 254.
17. S. E. Gontarski, op. cit., p. 14.
18. *Frescoes*, p. 121–2.
19. *Frescoes*, p. 127.

3

Towards the Zero of Language

Martin Esslin

I

Beckett's theatre has always been primarily a theatre of images: the waiting figures on the lonely road; the blind master enthroned in the centre of his circular room with its eye-windows, his aged parents peering from their dustbins; the old man bent over his tape recorder; the woman sinking deeper and deeper into the earth; the dead faces protruding from their funerary urns; the lonely mouth suspended in the dark void, babbling away; the woman pacing to and fro, to and fro, with shuffling gait; the old man's whitehaired face emerging from the gloom, listening to his own thoughts; the old woman rocking herself into nonexistence; the miserable figure being arranged upon its pedestal – all these images, unforgettable once seen, encapsulate the essence of the meaning of whole plays more efficiently and more lastingly than even the most poetic or significant lines of dialogue.

Indeed, in Beckett's drama the image tends to override the words: 'Yes, let's go' are the last words spoken in *Waiting for Godot* but the action, the final image is 'They do not move.' Clov has said that he intends to leave at the end of *Endame* but here too the image is of his standing there without moving.

When Billie Whitelaw anxiously inquired about the meaning of the words she was to speak in *Footfalls*, Beckett replied with a postcard reassuring her that the words were not the most important element of the play. What mattered was the pace, the rhythm, the words were merely 'what pharmacists call the excipient'.

The *image* that sums up the meaning of the play does, of course, comprise more than its merely visual aspects: sound plays an essential part, whether it is the sound of the words, their low murmuring, their rhythm and pace, the shifting sources from which they emanate; or natural sounds like the shuffling of feet in *Footfalls*, the strident ringing of the alarm bell in *Happy Days*, to cite but a few striking examples.

And, to be sure, from the very beginning of his career as a dramatist Beckett experimented with *Acts Without Words*.

II

This striving for the concision of the image which compresses a large number of signifiers into a single frame, so that they can all be perceived in an instant, can be seen as part of Beckett's conviction that economy is the essence of art, that cramming a large amount of inessential information into a story or play, the description of illustrative incidentals, is a waste of the reader's or spectator's time and hence, apart from everything else, bad manners. But, above all, there is Beckett's love-hate of language itself. 'As we cannot eliminate language all at once, we should at least leave nothing undone that might contribute to its falling into disrepute. To bore one hole after another in it, until what lurks behind it – be it something or nothing – begins to seep through' he wrote (the original is in German) in his letter to Axel Kaun, dated 9 July 1937.[1] And he added:

> Is there any reason why that terrible materiality of the word surface should not be capable of being dissolved, like for example the sound surface . . . of Beethoven's seventh Symphony, so that through whole pages we can perceive nothing but a path of sounds suspended in giddy heights, linking unfathomable abysses of silence? . . . On the way to this literature of the unword, which is so desirable to me, some form of Nominalist irony might be a necessary stage. But it is not enough for the game to lose some of its sacred seriousness. It should stop.[2]

This skepticism towards language informed Beckett's writing even in the period after the war, when his fiction poured out of him in verbal profusion as a series of internal monologues of relentless momentum. That he was fully aware of the contradiction between his disgust with language and his use of it, emerges from his answer to Niklaus Gessner, the author of one of the earliest critical examinations of Beckett's language,[3] when he drew his attention to it: 'Que voulez-vous, Monsieur? C'est les mots, on n'a rien d'autre.'

Beckett's steadily increasing interest in drama, as against narrative fiction, may well have been due to his desire to escape from the linearity of discursive speech into the multidimensional semiotic field of the image, with its immense potential of nonverbal signification.

Even Beckett's narrative fiction concentrated, from *How It Is* onwards, more and more upon the delineation of an image rather than the reproduction of an unceasing internal monologue shifting from narrator to narrator. Increasingly the voice of his narrative prose became that of an artist striving to delineate a visual image with words – in *The Lost Ones*, the cycle of fragments around *Imagination Dead Imagine*, *Ping*, *Still* and *Lessness*, or, later in *Ill Seen Ill Said*.

III

Increased preoccupation with the stage confronted Beckett with the problem of the need to realise his images as fully, as near to his original vision, as possible. More than once he was appalled at the failure of directors to reproduce the images he had in mind. There was only one way out – he might have to direct his own plays.

Yet stage productions are ephemeral. The image, however faithfully it represents the author's original vision, only has a brief, fleeting existence. The writer's, the painter's work, once fixed, can endure. Not so that of the playwright, even if he himself realises his vision. Here the mechanically recorded media – radio, the cinema and television offered a way towards preserving dramatic performances in a more permanent form.

Beckett had been involved with BBC radio since 1957 (his fascination with the technique of tape-recording which he encountered in that connection, led to his writing *Krapp's Last Tape*), and he had written a number of radio plays for the BBC. Even though radio is so verbal a medium, he was impressed by its ability to preserve, in the final recording, the author's original concept down to the slightest inflection, the smallest pause. And even on radio the use of music allowed him to counterbalance the verbal element, notably in *Words and Music* where the music itself becomes a major character, expressing itself fully without the use of words.

Yet, as far as the realisation of the poet's visual imagination itself was concerned only the cinema and videotape recording could guarantee the permanence of that authentic vision in its integrity. Hence Beckett's interest when his American publisher, Barney Rosset of Grove Press, who had ventured into film distribution, asked him in 1963 to write a short film to form part of a triptych of short features by the star dramatists of the Grove Press. (Ionesco and Pinter wrote the other segments that were, however, never produced in the framework of this project. Rosset's film venture had run into difficulties before shooting could start.)

Film which was shot in New York in 1964, directed by Alan Schneider and with that veteran master of silent film comedy, Buster Keaton, in the principal role, is almost entirely wordless. In this respect it is linked directly with the *Acts Without Words*.

The script of *Film* clearly states its theme, one of Beckett's principal preoccupations, viz. the fact that human consciousness is inevitably divided – into a stream of thoughts on the one hand, and a perceiver of this internal monologue on the other. Quoting Bishop Berkeley, Beckett states this at the opening of his script with, for him, exceptional directness:

Esse est percipi.

All extraneous perception suppressed, animal, human, divine, self-perception maintains in being.

Search of non-being in flight from extraneous perception breaking down in inescapability of self-perception.

No truth value attaches to above, regarded as of merely structural and dramatic convenience.[4]

The film shows the protagonist, in his form as an observed object – O – in flight from a pursuer, who in the final shot turns out to be his own organ of self-perception, his (inner) eye (or essential 'I'?). It shows O hurrying through a New York street, encountering some passers-by, then hurrying upstairs to his room, where he frantically tries to exclude all perceivers, dog, cat, goldfish, parrot, even a picture representing God's all-seeing eye. He even tears up all photographs of himself that he carried with him in his briefcase. Finally, alone in his rocking chair, O expects the ultimate bliss of non-perceivedness, hence non-being. But now the camera has become E, the observing inner eye of the split protagonist. E stares at O, O at E, whom we now see as 'O's face . . . but with a very different expression, impossible to describe, neither severity nor benignity, but rather acute *intentness*'.[5]

Although Beckett came to New York to be present while the film was being shot, Alan Schneider was in charge and the discrepancies between the original script and the finished work show that, through various difficulties during the course of production, Beckett's original vision had not been fully realised.

Film was soon followed by Beckett's first work for television, *Eh Joe*, which he wrote for the BBC in 1965.[6]

Eh Joe is a brilliant televisual conception: the play could not work as well in any other medium. Here the camera itself is made the second character. The voice of the unseen woman is, in fact, made palpable through the camera. The voice, which Joe, the elderly man huddled on his bed hears inside his head, is the voice of a woman who reminds him how cruelly he treated the women in his life, driving one of them to suicide. As the voice becomes more and more insistent, the camera relentlessly moves closer and closer to Joe, until, in the final shot all we see are Joe's horrified eyes in an immense close-up.

Yet here, too, as so often in Beckett's career as a dramatist, the final realisation did not entirely match Beckett's original vision of the play.

From the very beginning Beckett had increasingly become involved in the production process of his plays, so that, it became more and more frequent that, although a director had signed for the production, Beckett himself had effectively been in charge.

From this to his becoming, openly and officially, the director of his own plays, with, at last, complete control over their realisation, there was only a small step. More and more he was pushed towards taking this final step – very painful though it must have been for so shy a man.

When an offer came from Germany, he could not resist availing himself of it: in the autumn of 1967 Beckett undertook to direct a production of *Endgame* for the studio of the Schillertheater in West Berlin. He liked the lavish technical assistance offered by the highly subsidised German theatre. There followed productions at the Schillertheater studio of *Happy Days* (17 September 1971), *Krapp's Last Tape* (1973) and in the Schillertheater's large auditorium of *Waiting for Godot* (8 March 1975).

In the spring of 1976 Beckett directed the world premiere of

Footfalls at the Royal Court Theatre in London. By this time he had gained full confidence in his skill as a director and made frequent use of it.

IV

It is this confidence in his ability to realise his own vision with the utmost precision which shines through the group of television plays he wrote between 1975 and 1982: *Ghost Trio* (written 1975); . . . *but the clouds* . . . (1976); *Quad* (1982) and *Nacht und Träume* (1982). Here the televisual image, firmly fixed once and for all, can embody and preserve the poet's imagery without having to rely on language as its primary medium, and, in the end, even enable him to dispense with it altogether.

In *Ghost Trio*, written ten years after *Eh Joe*, there is still a woman's voice. But it is no longer an interior voice. It is external to the action, objective, no more than an announcer. It greets the viewer with: 'Good evening. Mine is a faint voice. Kindly tune accordingly.'[7] Having thus warned the public not to turn up the volume knob, the voice gives a faintly ironic, self-parodying description of the by now familiar Beckett room – grey, bare, bereft of colour, with the pallet by the window. Each item that is described is shown, as though we were watching a real estate agent's demonstration of a dwelling and its inventory. This first of the three sections of the script, (marked by Roman numerals I to III), concludes, after we have been shown the external elements from which the image we are being offered will be built up, with the introduction of the protagonist: 'Sole sign of life a seated figure'[8] an old man bent over an object at first difficult to identify. In section II the voice announces and introduces the actions of this figure (referred to in the script as F) as he goes to the door to listen if someone is coming, to the window, the mirror, the pallet, and the door again.

In the third section, the voice, having fulfilled its function of introducing the image, vanishes altogether. We have reached the stage of complete wordlessness and we realise that the first two sections merely served to set the scene, to prepare us for the unfolding of the wordless action, the image itself.

The old man thinks he can hear someone coming, his expectation is disappointed, when he opens the window to look out, there is only the rain outside. He goes to the mirror and for the first time we see his face and get a close-up of his haggard features. But then footsteps are heard outside in the corridor, there are knocks on the door, the door opens: outside there stands a small boy dressed in an oilskin against the pouring rain: *'Boy shakes head faintly. Face still, raised. 5 seconds. Boy shakes head again. Face still, raised. 5 seconds. . . . Boy turns and goes. Sound of receding steps.'* [9] The door closes, the old man remains seated, we have gradually realised that the music we have been hearing – passages from the Largo of Beethoven's fifth piano trio, the 'Ghost Trio' – emanates from the object over which he has been bent – a cassette player. *Ghost Trio* ends with the old man raising his head and a second close-up of his ravaged face. The camera takes another last general view and then the image fades.

Ghost Trio, originally entitled *Tryst*, displays some intriguing parallels to *Waiting for Godot* – the little boy who shakes his head to indicate that the expected person, with whom the tryst – or rendezvous – of the original title was to be, would not be coming, except that in this case the tryst seems to have been with a woman, that 'lost one' who haunts so many of Beckett's works.

What is striking in *Ghost Trio* as well as its companion piece . . . *but the clouds* . . . is the technique of first demonstrating and verbally introducing the ingredients from which the image is built up, after which the image is, wordlessly, left to speak for itself. This is almost reminiscent of the Elizabethan technique of preceding a play with a mimed enactment of its 'argument', except that here the order is reversed – the argument is verbal, the play itself a mime.

In . . . *but the clouds* . . . the voice which instructs the viewer is in the first person singular. It is the voice of an old man who is shown in his daily round of arriving home in the evening after having roamed the roads all day, shedding his greatcoat, donning his nightshirt and then settling down to try and evoke the image of a long-lost love. Then emerging again from his sanctum in the morning, changing his nightshirt for his greatcoat and hat, and leaving to roam the back roads once more, and so on and on. . . . The image on the screen is that of a circle of light surrounded by darkness, into which the man enters from the left (West), exits to the right (East) to change his clothes, and retires to his sanctum in the centre, back (North). When he is seen trying to remember the beloved face the old man sits in Belacqua's foetal position, his head between his knees. The voice demonstrates the moves, talks the viewer through them, as it were, like an air controller talking a pilot through a manoeuvre. This, although clearly the voice of the

protagonist, is not an internal monologue, it is the voice of someone
who is demonstrating a situation and providing a *mode d'emploi* for
viewing a visual experience.

We are shown four possible variants of what could happen in
response to the man's begging for the woman's image to appear: she
might appear and be gone almost instantly; she might appear and
linger a moment; she might appear and her lips might be moving
soundlessly; or indeed, fourthly, she might not appear at all – the
most frequent case.

After all the moves have been named and demonstrated the final
image develops in silence, except that, when, at the climax the
woman's face appears superimposed on the screen and we see her
lips move we hear the old man's voice repeating the lines the lips are
obviously forming, lines from Yeats' poem 'The Tower':

> . . . but the clouds of the sky
> When the horizon fades;
> Or a bird's sleepy cry
> Among the deepening shades.

The reference here clearly is to the preceding lines of the poem –
they are not quoted, Beckett seems to presuppose that they are
known to his ideal viewer – the lines which speak of

> The death of friends, or death
> Of every brilliant eye
> That made a catch in the breath . . .

that now seem 'but the clouds of the sky . . .'.

Beckett was directly involved in producing both these short
television pieces twice – for the BBC and for the Süddeutscher
Rundfunk, Stuttgart. There are differences between the two
versions, the German ones are later and perhaps incorporate some
of Beckett's own second thoughts about the first versions. Perhaps
they are closer to the definitive images he was striving for. (In . . .
but the clouds . . . there is also a textual difference: a much longer
passage from Yeats' poem is quoted at the end, unfortunately in a
translation so imperfect that it is hardly discernible whether what
we hear is poetry or prose).

What is striking about these two works – one hesitates to call them
plays (although *Ghost Trio* and . . . *but the clouds* . . . are both

subtitled 'A play for television') is precisely that they have ceased to exist as works of literature. The script has become little more than a mere technical notation of camera positions (diagrams) and indications of timing. The lines of text that remain are a relatively insignificant ingredient. And this residual text merely serves to instruct the viewer, to teach him how to look at and contemplate the actual, wordless visual experience. In *Ghost Trio* music also plays a vital part, it alone depicts the internal aspect of the protagonist's experience: the ebb and flow of his stream of *emotional* consciousness. Yet even this comes, strictly speaking, from the outside: F, the figure, is listening to a recording which he switches on and off, winds backwards and forwards – and if his emotion matches the music, that is merely because he internalises this external sound.

In . . . *but the clouds* . . . , quite analogously, the only hint at a verbal inner monologue is a quotation from a remembered pre-existing literary text, lines from the poem by Yeats.

In Beckett's next two television pieces the verbal element has finally reached the point of zero. Both were written by him for Süddeutscher Rundfunk and also directed by him.

In *Quadrat I & II* (1981 – the production started on Beckett's 75th birthday, 13 April 1981 – the original typescript in English is titled *Quad*)[10] the script is basically a diagram and a string of what looks like mathematical formulae.

The camera – stationary throughout – looks from above at an oblique angle at a square outlined on the ground. There are four figures, dressed in long cloaks and cowls, so that it is impossible to tell whether they are male or female. The colours of these costumes are white, blue, red and yellow. Each figure has a fixed route described by the sequence of the corners of the square through which it must pass – A, B, C and D. As this often involves a diagonal crossing of the square – to get for example from A to C or from B to D – the moving figures should have to pass through the central point E. But that centre point E seems to contain a deadly danger: when the figures approach it, they hesitate in a moment of panic and then must circle round it, always in a clockwise direction.

The structure of the four figures' movement is like that of a canon or fugue – first one figure pursues its prescribed and eternally fixed path alone, then a second one joins it on its second circuit just after the first figure has reached the second point on its path, then, when both have completed theirs and started the third circuit of the first, the second of the second, a third figure enters, then a fourth, then the numbers are reduced to three, two, one; and then the process starts again. When all four figures are moving at the same time, the congestion around the central point becomes acute, as they move around it in their clockwise circle.

The entire fuguelike movement is shown twice. Each figure's moves are accompanied by its own percussion instrument, Javanese gong, African woodblock, African talking drum and a wastebasket. So that the addition and subtraction of each figure alters the rhythmical accompaniment to the action.

In the original typescript – merely titled *Quad* – these two movements comprised the entire work. In performance, however, a second part – *Quadrat II* – was added. The producer at Stuttgart, Reinhart Müller-Freienfels, has told me the story of the genesis of *Quadrat II*. The recording, the first television piece by Beckett to use colour, had been completed; and in the evening Müller-Freienfels played the tape back to Beckett on his video-machine at home. Beckett liked the finished performance and Müller-Freienfels mentioned that it had also looked very good on the additional black-and-white monitor (that has to be present in any television studio so that the director can judge whether the picture is compatible for those viewers who don't have colour sets). Beckett was intrigued by this observation and suggested that they go back the next day to make a recording in black-and-white of only one complete circuit, but much slower and this time without the percussion accompaniment, the only sound being the shuffling of the four figures' feet. When this had been recorded and Beckett viewed it, he said: 'Good – this is a hundred thousand years later'! And so with the addition of the black-and-white section *Quad* became *Quadrat I & II*.

The impact of this wordless piece is tremendous. It is both wildly funny and deeply frightening. Are these figures in a Dantesque hell, doomed to repeat their prescribed circuit to all eternity? Or is the image that of all human destiny, where, seen from an objective vantage point outside ourselves, each of us has his preordained path on his journey through life and is thus destined to collide with all those whose preordained paths he is preordained to cross at preordained moments? And does the centre that must be avoided signify the impossibility of genuine contact between the endlessly journeying figures? These are some of the questions the image raises without, of course, answering them or even opening the way towards a valid answer. (There is a parallel here with *How It Is* and its complex image of endless traumatic encounters – but now it has been compressed into a single visual metaphor . . .).

Beckett's second piece produced at Stuttgart, in 1982, also dispenses with the spoken word altogether.

'Nacht und Träume' is the title of a late Schubert song, based on a short poem of eight lines by the Austrian poet Heinrich Josef von Collin (1771–1811):

> Heil'ge Nacht, du sinkest nieder
> Nieder wallen auch die Träume
> Wie Dein Dunkel durch die Räume
> Durch der Menschen stille, stille Brust.
>
> Die belauschen sie mit Lust
> Rufen, wenn der Tag erwacht:
> Kehre wieder, heil'ge Nacht
> Holde Träume, kehret wieder.
>
> (Holy night, you do descend
> And dreams descend as well,
> Like the darkness throughout Space,
> Into men's (human beings') silent, silent breast.
>
> They listen to them with pleasure
> And cry out, when day awakens:
> Come again, you holy night,
> Lovely dreams, oh come again).[11]

Beckett's televisual image is that of an old man sitting in a dark, empty room lit only by evening light from a window set high in the back wall.

He is the archetypal Beckettian character, old and grey, bent over a table. The last seven bars of the song are heard, without words, melody, 'Softly hummed, male voice'.[12]

These are the bars corresponding to the last two lines of the text: 'Kehre wieder, heil'ge Nacht/Holde Träume, kehret wieder' ('Come again, you holy night,/Lovely dreams, oh come again'). As the light fades on the image of the dreamer, the last three bars are heard again, this time with the words 'Holde Träume, kehret wieder' ('Lovely dreams, oh come again') clearly audible.

The old man reappears and now we can see his dream. In the upper right hand quarter of the screen there appears the 'dreamt self' of the dreamer in the identical position. A hand, marked in the script as a left hand, (L), then gently touches the dreamt self's head from above; it withdraws. A right hand appears with a 'cup of water' and conveys it gently to the dreamt self's lips; he drinks from it; the hand disappears. After a pause the right hand reappears with a cloth and gently wipes the dreamt self's brow. The dreamt self raises its head to gaze up at an invisible face. The dreamt self 'raises his right hand . . . and holds it raised palm upwards'. The right hand of the unseen person appears again and rests on the dreamt self's hand; the dreamt self raises its left hand and rests it on the joined hands. And then an unseen person's left hand reappears and rests gently on the 'dreamt self's' head.

The song is heard again and now the image that had been in the right hand corner, rather like a thought balloon in a cartoon, moves into the centre and occupies the entire screen; the entire sequence of actions is repeated in close-up and more slowly; after which the camera moves back to its initial position and first the dream, then the image of the dreamer too fades.

The structure of this piece closely corresponds to that of *Ghost Trio* and . . . *but the clouds* . . . except that here Beckett has succeeded in eliminating the spoken 'argument'. He still starts by instructing the viewer, as it were, in what to look for, but now he does it by simply showing the elements of the image first as an insert with the dreamer visible, and then moving into the dream in close-up. Again what results is an extremely powerful (if, in this case, for my taste, somewhat too sentimental) image. *Quadrat I & II* and *Nacht und Träume* then are neither ballet, nor mime play, they seem to me to represent a wholly new genre: they are poems without words, visual poetry.

V

Here, then, Beckett has reached the point zero of language, the compression of the maximum of experience into the most telling and graphic metaphor which could then be incarnated, made visible and audible, in the most concise and concrete form of a living, moving image.

A piece like *Quad* seems to me to be the culmination of that kind of endeavour. Here the metaphor, the poetic image, has been freed from the word altogether. It is not drama any more, it is poetry, wordless poetry. Nor is it strictly speaking cinema: it lacks the epic quality, the storytelling element of cinema; it is most akin to some types of contemporary perfomance art, where also, often, two distinct phases are distinguishable: first the ritual of building the image, secondly the display of the image. In some sense this is a kind of painting, the creation of an 'emblem' to be deciphered by the viewer, except that the image moves and has sound.

Ultimately this new genre seems to me to abstract *one* element from traditional drama, the concretised metaphor where the story of a play suddenly coagulates in one unforgettable poetic image: Lear, naked, raging against the storm; the Pope being dressed in *The Life of Galileo*; Hedda Gabler burning the manuscript; the red carpet being unrolled for Agammemnon; Oedipus blinded. . . . In the plays of Beckett, Ionesco and Genet the emphasis shifted very decisively towards this kind of poetic metaphor, while a narrative, storytelling element still remained to sustain it. Yet, clearly, the Theatre of the Absurd increasingly tended towards this kind of imagistic presentation of visual poetic metaphors.

Actors who have been directed by Beckett tend to describe his constant insistence on the correct visual image. In evoking the exact angle at which the head is to be lowered, a hand raised, Beckett, in Billie Whitelaw's words uses the actor's body to create a painting. His directing is a form of painting.

In Beckett's new televisual poetry, as, indeed in stage plays like *Not I*, *That Time*, *Footfalls*, *Rockaby*, *Ohio Impromptu*, *Catastrophe*, *What Where*, the ultimate limit of that tendency towards the creation of the most precise poetic metaphor has been reached. The metaphoric, poetical image is here isolated and presented in its purest state. And the *television* images have the additional advantage that they are fixed, and fixed by the poet himself, so that they attain a state of permanence denied to texts for live production. Here the poet's own imagination has been directly translated into concrete form and preserved for posterity.

From the very beginning Beckett's verse has been highly imagistic. And since the close of the period of the great internal monologues (from *Molloy* to *Texts for Nothing*) even in his narrative prose the internal stream of thought has more and more turned into a striving to fix visual images in words. Since his active entry into film and television this striving for the exact image sometimes expresses itself by the use of technical terms from these media: '. . . Umbrellas round a grave. Seen from above . . .';[13] '. . . The hands. Seen from above . . .';[14] '. . . Close-up then . . .';[15] '. . . Close-up of a dial . . .'.[16]

In these late pieces the internal monologue, which in his earlier narrative prose, tended to be an endless stream of words racing through the writer's mind rather like the logorrhoea that overwhelms the Mouth in *Not I*, has turned into a slow, deliberate attempt to create a visual image with words, often despairing about the subject's ability to achieve the construction of such an image, which, in the first place, will be 'ill seen' and then, having been imperfectly visualised, will be 'ill said', because words must, of necessity fail in producing a perfect reproduction of the visual image.

The late short stage plays – *Rockaby*, *Catastrophe*, *Ohio, Impromptu*, *What Where* – are essentially such images, realised in concrete form in the theatre, but necessarily fleeting, impermanent and always, once the script is generally available, liable to be subverted in their realisation by directors out of sympathy with the author's intentions.

Beckett's late television pieces are thus of considerable importance: for here the author's vision is permanently fixed and thus provides posterity with a glimpse of a great poet's world as he actually saw it with the eyes of his imagination.

Notes

1. 'German Letter of 1937', in Samuel Beckett, *Disjecta: Miscellaneous Writings and a Dramatic Fragment*, ed. Ruby Cohn (London: John Calder, 1983) pp. 53–4. [Translation: pp. 172–3].
2. Ibid., pp. 53–4.
3. Niklaus Gessner, *Die Unzulänglichkeit der Sprache* (Zürich: Juris, 1957).
4. *Film*, in Samuel Beckett, *Collected Shorter Plays* (London: Faber & Faber, 1984) p. 163.
5. Ibid., p. 169.
6. First broadcast on BBC 2 on 4 July 1966; producer: Michael Bakewell; director: Alan Gibson; Joe: Jack McGowran; Woman's voice: Sian Phillips.
7. *Ghost Trio*, in Samuel Beckett, *Collected Shorter Plays*, p. 248.
8. Ibid., p. 249.
9. Ibid., pp. 253–4.

10. It is published as *Quad* in Samuel Beckett, *Collected Shorter Plays*, pp. 289–94.
11. This, at least, is the text of Schubert's song. In Collin's collected poems the text is slightly different. I presume Schubert changed the words, which are even triter in the original version, himself.
12. *Nacht und Träume*, in Samuel Beckett, *Collected Shorter Plays*, p. 305.
13. *A Piece of Monologue*, in Samuel Beckett, *Collected Shorter Plays*, p. 268.
14. Samuel Beckett, *Ill Seen Ill Said* (London: John Calder, 1982) p. 31.
15. Ibid., p. 19.
16. Ibid., p. 45.

4

The Self Contained: Beckett's Fiction in the 1960s

Rubin Rabinovitz

Early in his career Samuel Beckett began to explore the possibilities for a new type of fiction that would focus on the inner lives of his characters.[1] In such fiction, the need to depict events in the material world would be reduced or even eliminated. This new approach, important in many of Beckett's earlier novels, became dominant in the fiction he completed in the 1960s.

Even at first glance it is apparent that most of the works of this period – *All Strange Away*, *Imagination Dead Imagine*, *The Lost Ones*, *Ping*, *Lessness* and the later 'Fizzles' – contain puzzling stylistic innovations.[2] The situation is something like that in non-Euclidean geometry and abstract painting: without an understanding of the new rules it is difficult to appreciate the advantages of the new form.

In conventional novel writing, characters and settings are modelled on people and places in the outer world. Beckett reverses this principle: his characters reflect aspects of inner reality and they inhabit a world that is at a distance from its material counterpart. Primarily concerned with issues that pertain to the inner realm – existence, selfhood and the processes of the mind – Beckett mainly relies on those fictional methods that are suitable for exploring it.

A sense of the magnitude of this change is conveyed in 'Enough', a story that was written in the same period as the more innovative fiction. 'Enough' retains many links with Beckett's older works, such as an external setting, a description of a journey, an orderly sense of chronology and an identifiable narrative voice. But there are also self-reflexive elements in 'Enough' that signal impending changes. In the following excerpt, the imminent abandonment of the journey theme and weakening of the narrative voice are hinted at: 'In the beginning he always spoke walking. So it seems to me

50

now. Then sometimes walking and sometimes still. In the end still only. And the voice getting fainter all the time' (140–1). A central event in 'Enough' is the parting of two companions, but the story can also be thought of as marking Beckett's departure from an earlier fictional style.[3]

In *Molloy*, *Malone Dies* and the other works written after World War II, Beckett's heroes leave a place of refuge and undertake a difficult journey. The narrator of *All Strange Away* decides he will not return to this theme: 'Crawl out of the frowsy deathbed and drag it to a place to die in. Out of the door and down the road in the old hat and coat like after the war, no, not that again (117). Different types of locomotion are considered: 'walking, kneeling, crawling' (117). But it turns out that a journey is out of the question: the central figures in *All Strange Away* are trapped in containers that restrict their movements.

There is a similar sense of transition in the short pieces called 'Fizzles'. Those completed in the late 1950s and early 1960s employ a relatively conventional style, contain echoes of earlier works and often include references to a journey. But the 'Fizzles' that were written after 1968 – 'Closed Space', 'Still', and 'For to End Yet Again' – utilise a compressed style and introduce relatively immobile figures.

In many of Beckett's earlier novels, the descent into the inner world is marked by a character's diminishing ability to make progress in the outer. Murphy ties himself into a chair; Watt is confined in an asylum; Moran goes from an autocycle to a bicycle; Molloy starts with a bicycle and ends with crutches; Malone is stuck in bed; Mahood lives in a jar. The transition is towards a type of physical immobility that leads to freedom of movement in the inner world.

Accompanying this transition is a related pattern. In early works like *Murphy* most of the action takes place in the outside world and most of its ideas seem to be concentrated on the surface of the novel, the level of dominant literal meanings. Readers who wish to learn about the characters' inner lives must penetrate to the novel's deeper levels; this may involve tasks such as tracing allusions or noting instances of narrative unreliability.[4] Beckett focuses more on the inner world in his later works, and it becomes the dominant setting in *The Unnamable* and *How It Is*. In these novels, the main setting is the world 'below', and the world 'above' is only glimpsed occasionally.

By the 1960s, references to the outside world become even rarer in Beckett's fiction. The expansive accounts of travels in strange lands give way to succinct descriptions of figures circling about in abstract settings. One of the few traces of life on earth in 'Closed Space' comes in a description of figures walking on dead leaves; the leaves, says the narrator, are a 'reminder of beldam nature' (200).[5] Nature is more remote in *The Lost Ones*, which has a similar setting. Here the figures are enclosed in a large cylinder; when they walk on its floor (now made of a rubbery material) they 'brush together with a rustle of dry leaves' (159).

Some of those who are trapped in the cylinder believe there is a way out, 'a secret passage branching from one of the tunnels and leading in the words of the poet to nature's sanctuaries' (163). The poet Beckett is alluding to is probably Alfred de Vigny, who in 'La Maison du Berger' describes forests and fields that are 'sanctuaries' from the misery of city life.[6]

There is a second allusion that is relevant here. The title of the French version of *The Lost Ones*, *Le dépeupleur*, is based on a line in Lamartine's 'L'Isolement'.[7] The futile searches in *The Lost Ones* ('lost bodies . . . each searching for its lost one') recall both Vigny's search for the idealised Eva and Lamartine's sense of isolation after the death of Mme Charles.

Lamartine, like Vigny, figured prominently in the French Romantic movement. In both poems the writers look to nature for relief from their unhappiness, and both are disappointed. Though Vigny sees nature as a refuge, he also speaks of its cruelty and indifference to human concerns; and Lamartine discovers that the death of the woman he loves has obliterated the beauty of nature. The figures in Beckett's works, however, have been cut off from the outside world for so long they are ready to return to nature. In *The Lost Ones*, nature is mainly invoked in order to emphasise the loss of external scenery as the figures walk in endless circles inside their walled enclosure.

Even this small amount of freedom is denied some of Beckett's other figures: they reside in tight containers that permit little movement. The sense of oppressive confinement is enforced by a terse style, as in the opening of *Ping*: 'All known all white bare white body fixed one yard legs joined like sewn. Light heat white floor one square yard never seen. White walls one yard by two white ceiling one square yard never seen' (149). The central figure is not a person but a 'body'. The setting in *Ping* is unearthly; the chronology is atemporal; the prose is spare. There is little dependence on conventional novelistic devices – characterisation, plot, motivation, action. It almost seems that the work has been so thoroughly drained of content that what remains is devoid of meaning.

But this notion cannot be maintained: the governing principle in *Ping* is not meaninglessness, but compression. Only that which is expendable has been deleted. If what remains now occupies a smaller space, it has also increased in significance: the volume and density are inversely related.

Expectations based on traditional fictional conventions are of little use in interpreting *Ping*. What, for example, is one to make of legs 'joined like sewn'? Clearly, the surface level of the work has given way to a figurative level dealing with the idea of a painful loss of mobility.

The being in *Ping* and the central figures in other works of this period are unlike ordinary fictional characters: the differences are so marked that Beckett seldom refers to them as people.[8] Instead they are called 'bodies' or given names that describe their predominant activities – 'climbers', 'searchers', 'the sedentary', 'the vanquished'. On occasion terms like 'man' or 'wife' are used, but this is mainly to emphasise the masculine or feminine attributes of the figures.

The figures are further dehumanised when the narrator of *The Lost Ones* refers to a body as 'it' (160, 173). Elsewhere he describes the 'dead' heads of the bodies (167). Like the word 'body', the phrase 'hell air' (181) in 'For to End Yet Again' suggests that the figures are shades in some kind of underworld setting. This also seems to be the case in *The Lost Ones*, where Beckett refers to 'sulphur' (169) and 'pandemonium' (166), and notes the similarities between the inhabitants of the cylinder and Belacqua, a shade in Dante's *Purgatorio*.[9]

But there are problems with this interpretation, because Beckett elsewhere indicates that the figures are alive. According to the narrator of *The Lost Ones*, 'flesh and bone subsist' within the cylinder (160). A comment in *Imagination Dead Imagine* indicates that the figures there are breathing: 'Hold a mirror to their lips, it mists' (147). This passage – reminiscent of Lear's speech after the death of Cordelia – is hardly one that Beckett would use about shades.[10] Such apparent contradictions indicate that narrow interpretations of these works cannot be sustained: the figures must be seen as complex metaphorical entities.

Beckett's unpublished early works contain descriptions of

similarly complex figures who inhabit underworld settings. These figures initially seem like the spirits of the dead, but they can also represent the souls of the unborn; they resemble inhabitants of the outside world, but at the same time also depict inner entities. When Belacqua, the hero of 'Dream of Fair to Middling Women', retreats into the inner realm he calls the 'Limbo' or the 'wombtomb', he sees such figures:

> The lids of the hard aching mind close, there is suddenly gloom in the mind; not sleep, not yet, nor dream, with its sweats and terrors, but a waking ultra-cerebral obscurity, thronged with grey angels; there is nothing of him left but the umbra of grave and womb where it is fitting that the spirits of his dead and unborn should come abroad.[11]

This wombtomb is more than Beckett's reworking of a Dantean setting. It is a place where one may glimpse the deeper workings of intellectual and creative processes, where discarded identities reside and unborn selves await their turn. The narrator of 'Dream', speaking of such an entity, refers to 'its hunger, darkness and silence'.[12] In this novel, as in *The Lost Ones*, 'it' refers to an aspect of the self. This level of selfhood runs deeper than one's sense of sexual identity; hence Beckett uses the neuter form of the pronoun to describe it.

Another description of Belacqua's 'wombtomb' is given in the unpublished story 'Echo's Bones'. Here it is an infernal region with 'shafts and manholes back into the muck'[13] – an image that anticipates the 'niches' and 'tunnels' (160 and ff.) of *The Lost Ones*. When Belacqua enters the 'wombtomb' he wonders whether 'his imagination had perished'.[14] This introduces a theme that is central in the later works: the phrase 'imagination dead imagine' is repeated in *All Strange Away* and in *Imagination Dead Imagine*.[15]

Ostensibly, 'imagination dead imagine' is an admission of defeat, the confession of a loss of artistic power. But at the same time it can be taken as a behest to go on creating even in the face of overwhelming difficulties.[16] The passage also alludes to the underworld setting: if the imagination has died, the next step is to invoke its shade and see what dead imaginings it can conjure up.[17] This type of activity is suggested in *All Strange Away*: although its first two words are 'Imagination dead' (117), the narrator speaks about a process he calls 'dead imagining' (122).

A related idea surfaces at the opening of *Imagination Dead Imagine*: the narrator agrees that the imagination is dead; possibilities for settings in the external world are blanked out; finally, all that remains is a 'rotunda' (145). But with the reference to the rotunda, the narrator has introduced the inner setting that will dominate the rest of the work.

In *All Strange Away* the fantasising process persists even after a death notice, for the imagination has been posted: if the imagination is dead, fancy becomes the 'only hope' (118 *et passim*). The narrator later declares that fancy is dead, but even so keeps insisting that an authorial entity 'imagine' or 'fancy' some descriptive detail.

Beckett's references to fancy and imagination recall Coleridge's use of these terms in the *Biographia Literaria*. Coleridge sees the imagination as the 'soul' of poetic genius; he associates it with the greatest poetry – the work of Milton, for example. Fancy is the source of a less powerful type of mental activity; Coleridge defines it as 'a mode of memory emancipated from the order of time and space'.[18] Given that Beckett is working to liberate his art from the strictures of time and space, fancy – the category that Coleridge belittles – becomes the 'only hope' for Beckett's figures. Yet even so, hope is an inflated currency on the Beckettian exchange, and in *All Strange Away* its ultimate value is revealed when fancy is declared dead.

Fancy and hope are often linked in *All Strange Away*, as when the narrator describes some of the phrases Emma murmurs: 'Fancy is her only hope, or, She's not here, or, Fancy dead . . .' (121). The references to fancy, hope and death in this context suggest that Beckett may be alluding to Tennyson's poem, 'Tears Idle Tears', which ends:

> Dear as remember'd kisses after death,
> And sweet as those by hopeless fancy feign'd
> On lips that are for others; deep as love,
> Deep as first love, and wild with all regret;
> O Death in Life, the days that are no more.[19]

Remembered kisses, hopeless fancy, death in life: these are all relevant to themes in *All Strange Away*.

The idea that fancy and imagination remain viable even after they are defunct can be interpreted in still another way, as an allusion to a famous epistemological problem. If we form a picture of our cognitive apparatus expiring, we soon discover that there is something working behind the scenes to generate this image. No matter how intent we may be on killing the imaginative faculty, a perverse remnant refuses to die.

This situation is like one Descartes describes at the beginning of the *Meditations*. He tries to imagine that everything he perceives is illusory, 'that there was nothing in all the world, that there was no heaven, no earth, that there were no minds, nor any bodies'. But the image of a cognitive entity cannot be annihilated, and Descartes retains a powerful sense of himself as 'a thing that thinks'. He does not ask whether this development has made his experiment a failure; indeed, the persistence of the cognitive self becomes the foundation of his argument proving the existence of God and of the world.[20]

Imagination Dead Imagine opens with a narrative voice engaged in a similar attempt at abolishing the world:

> No trace anywhere of life, you say, pah, no difficulty there, imagination not dead yet, yes, dead, good, imagination dead imagine. Islands, waters, azure, verdure, one glimpse and vanished, endlessly, omit. Till all white in the whiteness the rotunda. No way in, go in, measure (145).

Since Beckett is an artist, his version of the Cartesian exercise emphasises imagination rather than thought. But Beckett may also be adding an ironic note here. For all of Descartes' concern with logical processes, his arguments are finally based on an act of the imagination: as he says, if 'none of the things which I imagine are true, nevertheless this power of imagining does not cease to be really in use, and it forms part of my thought'.[21]

Beckett's skepticism about the outer reality leaves him closer to the idealism of Berkeley and Schopenhauer than to Cartesian dualism. Descartes, denying the existence of the world, can hardly wait to resurrect it. In Beckett's works the idea that the material world is illusory persists as his narrators remain immersed in a realm of introspective contemplation, their awareness of outer reality fading.

The rotunda in *Imagination Dead Imagine* can be seen as a setting in this realm, and its whiteness as the residual blankness left over after an attempt to obliterate the world. One's impulse is to gather specific information about the structures in the inner settings – to determine, in Beckett's metaphor, their dimensions. But such efforts are finally futile; by attributing stability to images of the inner world we tend to deny their underlying impermanence.

The shifting, contradictory reality of the inner world is again emphasised in paradoxical statements like 'imagination dead imagine' and 'no way in, go in'. Such paradoxes recall another problem in epistemology: whether the mind is capable of playing the role of investigating subject and investigated object simultaneously. Beckett sides with those philosophers who say it cannot. There is no set of logical statements that is capable of defining the mind: reason and language are constituent parts of the entity they intend to encompass.[22]

Beckett therefore uses figurative language to describe the inner world; without attempting to define it, he tries to depict aspects of its reality. Implicit in the fiction of this period is the idea that literal representations of an object's appearance in the outer world will overwhelm one's sense of its intrinsic qualities.

For this reason, Beckett's characters are transformed into homunculi, figures who clearly cannot be confused with inhabitants of the outer world. Often these figures are naked: clothing has associations with mundane preoccupations. The figures are contained as in a womb or a tomb. These restrictive enclosures, with their prenatal and postmortem connotations, evoke a sense of the chronological limits on life as well as the physical limitations that accompany existence on a mental plane.

Once the reminders of the material world have been removed, Beckett is left with little more than a figure in a setting, as in *All Strange Away*: 'A place, that again. . . . A place, then someone in it, that again' (117). The place that is depicted is a boxlike container that will later be transformed into a rotunda. In other works of this period the containers may be of different shapes and sizes, but the central metaphor of a being inside an enclosure remains the same.[23]

'For to End Yet Again' opens with a description of a person rapt in thought. The surroundings fade, and with them the person's sense of physical selfhood. At this point only the image of the box – clearly a locus in the inner world[24] – remains:

For to end yet again skull alone in a dark place pent bowed on a board to begin. Long thus to begin till the place fades followed by

the board long after. For to end yet again skull alone in the dark
the void no neck no face just the box last place of all in the dark the
void (179).

After this description a figure called 'the expelled' appears. This
pattern resembles one that Beckett uses in *All Strange Away* and in
Imagination Dead Imagine. There is first an effort to abolish the
awareness of the outer world; next an inner locale is established;
then figures appear. In the words that come after these – *The Lost
Ones*, *Ping*, 'Closed Space', and *Lessness* – the first step is taken for
granted, and readers are immediately introduced to the inner
setting.

Beckett continually emphasises the distinction between the
characteristics of these inner regions and those of locales in the outer
world.[25] Thus the light in the inner world is unlike ordinary light. In
a number of works the narrator observes that there is no visible
source of light, and the objects depicted are usually self-illuminated
(this of course is a good description of the appearance of imagined
entities). In some instances Beckett also reveals that these inner
objects are invisible to the eye fixed on the outer world, the 'eye of
flesh'.[26] The differences between Beckett's inner and outer settings
are again emphasised in the measurements of the figures and
containers in these works. Draeger, in *All Strange Away*, is larger
than life;[27] in 'Closed Space' the bodies 'appear six times smaller
than life' (199). The measurements in *All Strange Away* are revised
when the narrator says, 'suddenly clear these dimensions faulty'
(124).[28] The labelling of the corners of the box – 'Call floor angles
deasil a, b, c, and d' (118) – recall the idealised shapes of Euclidean
geometry.

The measurements and geometric details are part of an attempt to
provide these amorphous locales with a sense of solidity. But what
seems like verisimilitude finally signals a lack of it: these inner places
cannot possess the fixity of settings in the material world. The
dimensions are of imaginary structures, and the taking of
measurements is a process that will shortly be terminated: 'in the
end that is when all done with dead imagining and measures taken
. . .' (*All Strange Away*, 122).

Beckett hints at the immateriality of these settings in other ways.
The rotunda in *Imagination Dead Imagine* is called 'the little fabric'
(145), which recalls the insubstantial edifices in *The Tempest* ('the
baseless fabric of this vision/The cloud-capped towers, the gorgeous

palaces . . .') and the building of Pandemonium in *Paradise Lost* ('Anon out of the earth a Fabric huge/Rose like an Exhalation').[29] Narrative details are deleted when they seem superfluous: 'No candle, no matches, no need, never were' (*All Strange Away*, 123).

This emphasis on an evanescent, mutable reality permits Beckett to develop a number of metaphorical possibilities for the image of the contained self. On one level, it refers to various mythic or literary representations of the afterlife. The enclosures can be seen as aspects of hell or purgatory, and the figures as shades. Beckett alludes to the underworld settings of both Dante and Milton – the use of more than one source is part of the scheme for diminishing the fixity of the settings.

The contained self can also be associated with images of birth and death – a foetus in a caul, a corpse in a sepulchre, a brain decaying in a skull – and with the birth and death of portions of the self.[30] The skull is at times equated with a metaphorical place, the region one enters at the beginning of an introspective quest. The figures inside this place can represent thoughts, impulses, memories, fantasies; longed-for objects and longing subjects; searchers for lost portions of the self and the sought-after lost ones. Often, descriptions of these figures contain hints about the feelings evoked by the inner quest: curiosity, fear, loneliness, claustrophobia, nostalgia, a yearning for the outer world. When this occurs, the enclosure can also suggest a shell around repressed feelings, the self-contained facade we affect to conceal inner turmoil.

In other contexts the image of the contained figures can become an emblem for humanity trapped on an inhospitable planet or for a race of beings isolated in the universe and surrounded by vast regions of nothingness. It can represent minds enclosed in bodies or allude to the way humans are confined to familiar intellectual environs, unable to penetrate into the mysterious regions beyond. In *The Lost Ones*, the image even takes on social connotations when Beckett wittingly satirises the ethical pretensions of those who find it profitable to uphold the law.

On another level, the metaphor of the contained figure refers to a self-reflexive element in Beckett's fiction. Often his narrators speak in the imperative as they ask for descriptive details; and the entities that supply them represent aspects of both the author and his audience. In this way the container is at once the work the writer imagines and the one the reader reconstructs.

The figure in the container can also be seen as a metaphor for the

subject matter of the work constrained by its own formal system.[31]
A portrait in a frame; a feeling put into words: the more tractable the
enclosed things becomes, the more it tends to misrepresent its
prototype. So we try new forms, frames, terms; but a sense of the
inadequacies of the delimiting systems persists.

In *All Strange Away* the container keeps shrinking as the work
progresses: if expanding on a subject dilutes its essential qualities,
perhaps distillation is the answer. Anything that seems unnecessary is removed; the form becomes tighter; the work keeps
contracting. 'All strange away' (121), says the narrator, and another
extraneous detail is jettisoned.[32]

What is at first so striking about the works of this period is how
much has been removed: the house of fiction, it seems, has been
razed. But if so, a new structure has been built in its place: simple in
shape, economically constructed and – given its modest dimensions
– very spacious on the interior.[33]

Notes

1. For example, Belacqua, the hero of Beckett's first (unpublished) novel,
   'Dream of Fair to Middling Women' (1932), urges readers to liberate
   themselves from the need to bind 'the object to its representation'
   ('Dream of Fair to Middling Women', typescript in the collection of the
   Baker Library, Dartmouth College, p. 142). Hereafter cited as 'Dream'.
   See also Belacqua's description of the book he plans to write in 'Dream',
   p. 123; and Beckett's letter to Axel Kaun dated 9 July 1937, reprinted in
   Samuel Beckett, *Disjecta: Miscellaneous Writings and a Dramatic Fragment*,
   ed. Ruby Cohn (London: John Calder, 1983) pp. 51–4; translation,
   pp. 170–3.
2. There are problems in establishing dates of completion for some of the
   works of this period: Beckett worked on them intermittently, those
   originally written in French were translated at different times, and
   many were not published in the order they were completed. Mr Beckett
   has informed me that he can no longer remember exactly when these
   pieces were composed. Below the works are listed in the order I believe
   they were written; all but 'All Strange Away' and 'Still' were written
   originally in French. This list is based on information from the following
   works: Ruby Cohn, *Back to Beckett* (Princeton University Press, 1973);
   James Knowlson and John Pilling, *Frescoes of the Skull: the Later Prose and
   Drama of Samuel Beckett* (London: John Calder, 1979); and Richard
   Admussen, *The Samuel Beckett Manuscripts: a Study* (Boston: G. K. Hall,
   1979). According to Christina Rosset of Grove Press, the ordering of the
   pieces in the Grove Press edition of *Fizzles* (New York, 1976) was done
   according to Beckett's instructions. In the Calder edition, *For to End Yet*

Again and Other Fizzles (London: John Calder, 1976), and also in the Minuit edition, *Pour finir encore et autres foirades* (Paris: Editions de Minuit, 1976), the order is slightly different (see below).

Early 'Fizzles': 'He is Barehead', 'Horn Came Always', 'Afar a Bird', 'I Gave Up Before Birth', 'Old Earth' (numbered Fizzles 1, 2, 3, 4 and 6 in the Grove Press edition; given by title in the Calder edition); late 1950s or early 1960s.

All Strange Away, 1963–4.

Imagination Dead Imagine, 1965.

'Enough', 1965.

The Lost Ones. Begun after the completion of 'Enough'. Abandoned in 1966 and completed in 1971.

Ping, 1966.

'Closed Space' ('Fizzle 5' in the Grove edition of *Fizzles*; the seventh item in the Minuit and Calder editions); begun in 1968.

Lessness, 1969 or earlier.

'Still' ('Fizzle 7' in the Grove edition of *Fizzles*; the second item in the Calder edition; the eighth in the Minuit edition); 1973.

'For to End Yet Again' ('Fizzle 8' in the Grove edition of *Fizzles*; the first item in the Calder and Minuit editions); 1975 or earlier.

These texts are all included in Samuel Beckett, *Collected Shorter Prose 1945–1980* (London: John Calder, 1984). All quotations are from this edition; page numbers are given in the text.

3. As John Pilling says of 'Enough', the 'banishment of one self by another' raises the possibility that Beckett has decided to 'write in an absolutely new way' (*Frescoes of the Skull*, p. 153).

4. This argument is set forth in detail in Chapters Eight and Nine of my study, *The Development of Samuel Beckett's Fiction* (Champaign: University of Illinois Press, 1984).

5. There is some confusion about the title of this piece, which is called 'Fizzle 5' in the Grove edition of *Fizzles*, and 'Se voir' in the Minuit edition. In the two Calder editions (*For to End Yet Again* and *Collected Shorter Prose*) it is given the title 'Closed Space' in the text and 'Closed place' (or 'Closed Place') in the table of contents. The passage cited also recalls a passage where dead voices and leaves are compared in *Waiting for Godot* (London: Faber & Faber, 1956) p. 62; and comparisons by Homer and Dante of the dead and leaves, *Iliad*, VI.146–7 and *Inferno*, III.112–17.

6. In Beckett's original French version, the passage is 'comme dit le poète aux asiles de la nature' (*Le dépeupleur* (Paris: Editions de Minuit, 1970) p. 17). Line 26 of Vigny's poem reads 'Les grands bois et les champs sont de vastes asiles' (Alfred de Vigny, *Poésies complètes* (Paris: Editions Garniers Frères) p. 143). I am grateful to my colleagues, Professor Andrée Kail and Julia Frey, for locating the source of this allusion.

7. The line in 'L'Isolement' (stanza 7) is: 'Un seul être vous manque, et tout est dépeuplé'. (A. de Lamartine, *Premières et nouvelles méditations poétiques* (Paris: Pagnerre, Furne, Lecou, 1855), p. 7). This allusion was noted by Brian Finney in *Since How It Is* (London: Covent Garden Press, 1972) p. 11.

8. In *The Lost Ones* there is a reference to 'this little people' (162), but it is clear that 'people' is being used here in its collective sense, to mean a nation.

9. In *The Lost Ones* Beckett also describes figures 'sitting . . . in the attitude which wrung from Dante one of his rare wan smiles' (161). Dante smiles when he encounters Belacqua (*Purgatorio* 4, 1. 122); Belacqua is of course a very familiar figure in Beckett's fiction.

10. See *King Lear*, V.iii.262–4: 'Lend me a looking glass. / If that her breath will mist or stain the stone, / Why then she lives'. Beckett uses a similar image as an emblem of death in 'Da Tagte Es': 'the glass unmisted above your eyes' (*Collected Poems in English and French* (London: John Calder, 1977) p. 27). Laura Barge has also observed that the condition on the immobile figures in these works is not death in the ordinary sense; see '"Coloured Images" in the "Black Dark": Samuel Beckett's Later Fiction', *PMLA*, 92 (Mar. 1977) 278.

11. 'Dream', p. 39.

12. 'Dream', p. 35. The narrator of *Watt* also avoids the third-person masculine pronoun when speaking of the self: 'As for himself, though he could no longer call it a man . . . yet he could not imagine what else to call it, if not a man' (Samuel Beckett, *Watt* (London: Calder & Boyars, 1970) p. 80).

13. Samuel Beckett, 'Echo's Bones', typescript in the collection of the Baker Library, Dartmouth College, p. 1. 'Echo's Bones', written in the early 1930s, was to have been the concluding episode in *More Pricks Than Kicks* (Chatto & Windus, 1934); however, Beckett's editors at Chatto & Windus decided it should be dropped. See Deirdre Bair, *Samuel Beckett: a Biography* (London: Jonathan Cape, 1978) p. 162.

14. Ibid., p. 162.

15. *Collected Shorter Prose*, pp. 117, 120, 121, 145, *et passim*. There is a related passage in 'Closed Space': after the narrator withholds a descriptive comment he says, 'Did it need to be known it would be. No interest. Not for imagining' (199).

16. Thus 'imagination dead imagine' resembles the impasse ('I can't go on, I'll go on') at the end of Beckett's trilogy. John J. Mood discusses the ways this passage can be interpreted in ' "Silence Within": a Study of the *Residua* of Samuel Beckett', *Studies in Short Fiction*, 7 (Summer 1970) 390.

17. In a number of Beckett's works 'dead' refers to a condition of being alive – if barely, miserably; hence a dead imagination could still be capable of functioning. Thus Malone says, 'what matter whether I was born or not, have lived or not, am dead or merely dying, I shall go on doing as I have always done . . .' (*Malone Dies*, in Samuel Beckett, *Molloy/Malone Dies/The Unnamable* (London: Calder & Boyars, 1959) p. 226).

18. Samuel Taylor Coleridge, *Biographia Literaria*, ed. George Watson (London: J. M. Dent, 1956): imagination as the soul of poetic genius, ch. 14 (p. 174): imagination rather than fancy is associated with the poetry of Milton, chs 4, 12 (pp. 50–1, 252); fancy and fanciful poetry, ch. 4 (pp. 50–1); fancy defined, ch. 13 (p. 167). Peter Murphy's review

of *All Strange Away* (contains an interesting discussion of the question of Coleridge's influence on Beckett; see the *Journal of Beckett Studies*, 5 (Autumn 1979) 109–10. Another possible source for Beckett (and perhaps also for Coleridge) is Hume, who argues that even when we 'reject all the trivial suggestions of the fancy, and adhere to the understanding, that is to the general and more establish'd properties of the imagination', our perception of the world is deficient (David Hume, *A Treatise of Human Nature*, ed. L. A. Selby-Bigge (Oxford: Clarendon Press, 1967), book I, part iv, sect. 7, p. 267).

19. Alfred Lord Tennyson, *Selected Poetry*, ed. Douglas Bush (New York: Modern Library, 1951) p. 143. Another possible source is this passage from the fifth stanza of Thomas Gray's 'Ode on a Distant Prospect of Eton College': 'Gay Hope is theirs, by Fancy fed, / Less pleasing when possessed; . . .' (*Eighteenth Century Poetry and Prose*, ed. Louis Bredvold *et al.* (New York: Ronald Press, 1956) p. 591.

20. See René Descartes, 'Meditation I' and 'Meditation II', in *The Philosophical Works of Descartes*, trs E. S. Haldane and G. R. T. Ross (Cambridge University Press, 1972) I, 148–50. Susan Brienza has argued that the opening of *Imagination Dead Imagine* is based on Henri Bergson's rejection of the Cartesian approach in *Creative Evolution*. See Susan Brienza, ' "Imagination Dead Imagine": the Microcosm of the Mind', *Journal of Beckett Studies*, 8 (Autumn 1982) 67–8.

21. René Descartes, 'Meditation II', p. 153. The references to the imagination are not a translator's interpolation: the Latin original reads: 'nulla prorsus res imaginata vera sit, vis tamen ipsa imaginandi revera existit, & cogitationis maea pertem facit', *Oeuvres de Descartes* (Paris: Léopold Cerf, 1904) VII, 29.

22. In *The Development of Samuel Beckett's Fiction* (Champaign: University of Illinois Press, 1984) pp. 127–32 *et passim*, I argue that Beckett is sympathetic to Schopenhauer's view that mind cannot act simultaneously as perceiver and perceived, and that he distrusts the claims of those (like Descartes) who believe that the mind can be understood by using rational methods.

23. Beckett introduced an early version of the container image in 'Echo's Bones', where Belacqua attempts 'to conceive of his exuviae as preserved in an urn or other receptacle' ('Echo's Bones', p. 1). This image anticipates Mahood's urn in *The Unnamable*. Philip Solomon has noted the similarities between Mahood's urn and the containers in the later work; see 'Purgatory Unpurged: Time, Space, and Language in "Lessness" ', *Journal of Beckett Studies*, 6 (Autumn 1980) 68. Ruby Cohn points out that the urns in *Play* were boxes in an early version of the work; see *Back to Beckett*, p. 251.

24. In a review Beckett speaks of 'man alone thinking (thinking.) in his box' ('MacGreevy on Yeats', in Samuel Beckett, *Disjecta: Miscellaneous Writings and a Dramatic Fragment*, ed. Ruby Cohn (London: John Calder, 1983) p. 97). Brian Finney was the first to link the last image with Beckett's fiction of the 1960s (see *Since How It Is: a Study of Samuel Beckett's Later Fiction* (London: Covent Garden Press, 1972) p. 18).

25. Thus, depicting a character from the outer world, the narrator of 'Horn Came Always' says: 'It is in outer space, not to be confused with the other, that such images develop' (194).

26. See for example, 'light. . . . No visible source . . .', *All Strange Away* (117); 'The light that makes all so white no visible source . . .', *Imagination Dead Imagine* (145); 'The light. . . . Its omnipresence as though every separate square centimetre were agleam . . .', *The Lost Ones* (159); 'Thus then the skull makes to glimmer again . . .', 'For to End Yet Again' (179); 'invisible to any other eye . . . the expelled', 'For to End Yet Again' (179); 'indistinguishable to the eye of flesh . . .', *The Lost Ones* (167); 'invisible to the eye of flesh', *The Lost Ones* (171). Eric Levy makes a similar point in *Beckett and the Voice of Species* (New York: Barnes and Noble, 1980) pp. 98–9.

27. Draeger's height can be derived from the dimensions of the box that encloses him; and the narrator says of Emma that 'she still might be mathematically speaking more than seven foot long', *All Strange Away* (124).

28. Enoch Brater notes inconsistencies in the dimensions given in *The Lost Ones*; see 'Mis-takes, Mathematical and Otherwise, in *The Lost Ones*', *Modern Fiction Studies*, 29 (Spring 1983) 93 and ff. Inconsistencies of this kind can be seen as another tool for undermining the fixity of the inner settings.

29. William Shakespeare, *The Tempest*, IV.i.151; John Milton, *Paradise Lost*, I, 710–11. See also 'the sighting of the little fabric' (146).

30. H. Porter Abbott makes a similar point in *The Fiction of Samuel Beckett: Form and Effect* (Berkeley: University of California Press, 1973) p. 147.

31. As Raymond Federman says in 'The Impossibility of Saying the Same Old Thing the Same Old Way: Samuel Beckett's Fiction Since *Comment c'est*', *L'Esprit Créateur*, 11 (Autumn 1971) 35, the rotunda in *Imagination Dead Imagine* represents both 'vital space in its most reduced and confined dimensions' and 'the most condensed form of fiction'.

32. Beckett may have in mind the etymology of the word 'strange': it is derived from the Old French 'étrange' and ultimately from the Latin 'extraneus'.

33. I am grateful to the University of Colorado Council on Research and Creative Work for the support that enabled me to complete this essay.

5

Still to *Worstward Ho:* Beckett's Prose Fiction Since *The Lost Ones*

Brian Finney

Since the publication of *How It Is* Beckett has cultivated the art of minimalism. The dismissive epithets he applied to his prose fiction of the 1960s – 'residua', 'têtes mortes', 'fizzles' – have encouraged readers and critics of his later prose works to see them as minor works, all that is left of his repeated attempts to write novel-length works of fiction. In fact, however, the prose of the late 1960s and early 1970s differs significantly from that of the late 1970s and early 1980s. Between 1980 and 1983 Beckett published three substantial works of prose fiction – *Company, Ill Seen Ill Said* and *Worstward Ho* – each the length of a conventional novella, but so condensed that it takes as long to read them as it does a short novel. Each of these works shows a new confidence in the form and language it employs. These are not abandoned longer works, nor works-in-progress. They are *sui-generis*. In them Beckett has created a new subgenre to suit his imaginative needs. In the process of doing so he has pushed back the frontiers of postmodernist fiction in a highly original manner.

But this originality is accompanied by a complexity of image and language which makes all these works difficult to read, at times positively forbidding, especially to anyone unacquainted with Beckett's long search for an artistic means of portraying the nihilistic predicament of modern man. Chaos calls for chaotic modes of representation. Art calls for form. Beckett squarely faces the paradoxical nature of these conflicting needs in his art. In each of his fictions he tries to find a form to accommodate the formless and to find a mode of language with which to communicate the incommunicable. Necessarily this perverse yet logical quest leads him to a gradual abandonment of plot, character and continuity in favour of structures that celebrate the disintegration of conventional narrative features and of language that destroys everyday syntax and robs words of their familiar connotations. The result is a series of texts which make demands of the reader far in excess of most postmodernist avant-garde fiction. The effort required is not always in my opinion justified, especially where the texts are fragmentary or are genuine works-in-progress, such as, for example, 'One Evening'. But in the case of the three major pieces published between 1980 and 1983 the difficulty initially encountered on reading them is more than repaid by the stark and memorable images and by the haunting and highly original language that Beckett has created. Yet he takes most of the 1970s to reach the first of his major breakthroughs in this art of failure.

Although *For to End Yet Again* was not completed until 1975, it is related closely to 'Abandonné', written in 1971,[1] and reads more like a postscript to Beckett's fiction of the 1960s than as a prelude to the direction his writing has taken since the early 1970s. Its image of the figure expelled from its ruins facing a grey landscape is similar to that in *Lessness*. Here is yet another image of the Beckettian apocalypse. In this instance Beckett makes explicit the source and location of the image – inside the skull. Like a dying fire it flickers to life to throw up the image of the figure toppling over into the grey dust, eyes still open, breath still coming and going but indistinguishable from the dust. In *The Lost Ones* figures were shown progressing from vain movement to stasis. In *Lessness* the walls surrounding the static figure collapsed into the dust. Now the figure itself joins the dust. But the grey landscape is still enlivened by the white figures of two dwarfs carrying a litter between them in a random set of directions. 'It is the dung litter of laughable memory' (180), Beckett explains ironically.[2] Memory, then, remains bright (if so quixotic and distant as to be hard to discern) even while the body is disintegrating. Beckett has constructed here an image in which there are multiple receding images. There is that of the aimlessly wandering dwarfs; that of the figure; that of the skull; and that of the narrator.

The narrative voice in this text has some similarity to the voice in *Imagination Dead Imagine*. It adopts the same pseudo-impersonal, observational stance (in the present tense), as if the speaker were trying to bow out of his own performance. And this pseudo-objectivity is repeatedly breaking down. Even the title starts off with a word ('For') which suggests that the narrator is resuming an earlier discourse, and which has the slightest suggestion of the poetic about it. That poetic, archaic echo recurs in the first sentence with the appearance of 'pent' (meaning 'confined') and the alliteration in 'place pent' and 'board to begin'. Again and again the distanced voice of the narrator is undercut by these reminders of the emotive element in life and language, what Beckett calls 'remains of the days of the light' (179). Sometimes they take the form of a lengthy phrase – 'Sand pale as dust ah but dust indeed deep to engulf the haughtiest monuments' (179), or 'nor for God nor for his enemies' (180). Mostly they surface as brief word clusters – 'woe the little', 'carriage immemorial', 'cyclopean dome', 'yearns', 'sepulchral skull'. It is the presence of this emotional element which simultaneously imbues the piece with its haunting power and ensures its failure to arrive at that apocalyptic state to which the imagination aspires 'yet again'.

Still, 'Sounds' and 'Still 3' belong together. Written in English in 1972–3, these three texts are the product of much rewriting and revision, a process we have learned to expect in later Beckett. *Still* underwent four, and 'Sounds' no less than six revisions. *Still* represents Beckett's response to a request by the Italian publisher, Luigi Majno, for him to furnish a text which Stanley William Hayter could illustrate.[3] The first manuscript version of *Still* was twelve pages long and subsequently reduced to its published length of two pages. 'Sounds', which started off as one page of manuscript and rose to three pages, was refined back to one page. 'Still 3' also began its life in much longer form and had whole paragraphs deleted from it.[4] Condensation and refinement, then, lie behind all three texts.

Beckett is still searching in his imagination for 'the unthinkable end' he posited without great conviction in the final paragraph he added to *The Lost Ones* in 1970.[5] All three texts aspire to an unattainable state of stillness and soundlessness. The mesmeric repetition of 'quite still' throughout *Still* (it occurs fifteen times) is belied by the reminder that 'actually close inspection not still at all but trembling all over' (183). Overtaken by nightfall the figure relapses from visible movement to the appearance of stasis, eyes closed, head resting on hand, seated in a south-facing chair. But breathing still causes infinitesimal movements.

Meantime the figure is free to 'try listening to the sounds' (185). These also are unavoidable. In contrast to *Still*, 'Sounds' represents a determined effort to '[dream] away' (155)[6] all sounds, even the sound of the figure's own breathing. His movement from the room to the tree and back clearly represents an imagined silent re-enactment of an event in the past. (This is probably why Beckett chose to conflate the paragraph describing this movement with those before and after it in the penultimate version). This act of memory splits the self in two and causes it acute discomfort ('worse than none the self's when the whole body moves from its place . . . leaving the main unmoved' (155). In 'Still 3' memory throws up before the same dreamer's eyes a procession of figures from the past in search of the face that perhaps matches the sound he was listening for in the two previous pieces.

Despite their frequent revision these three linked texts read like transitional works. Because *Still* in particular employs an almost lyrical style, repeating key phrases and making frequent use of alliteration and assonance with mesmeric effect, John Pilling has claimed that it is 'as subtle and compelling in its language as any of Beckett's most recent prose'.[7] Similarly, Judith Dearlove praises 'Sounds' and 'Still 3' as 'increasingly tranquil depictions of reconciliation'.[8] With hindsight these texts appear as transitional pieces, experiments with a new tone, attempts to disrupt syntax without creating the aridity of *Ping* or the repetitiveness of *Lessness*. In 'Sounds' and 'Still 3' Beckett has chosen to foreground the problematical nature of his attempt to break new ground with phrases like 'try' ('try dreamt away' (156, 157), which reads, if more fully punctuated, 'try "dreamt away"'); and 'say' ('say back try saying back' (157)). It is surely indicative of their transitional nature that he withheld these latter two texts from publication until some five years after they were written.

In the three *Still* texts there is a faint trace of autobiographical material, memories from his past – of a tree for which he had some special affinity, for instance, or of faces from his childhood memory. In his short text, *As the Story Was Told*, written in English and first published in 1973 in a memorial volume to his friend Günter Eich,[9] Beckett once again draws on one of the most powerful images from childhood – his father's summer house with its childlike dimensions and its wicker chair facing the sunset as in *Still*. As James Hansford has suggested, this text is concerned with 'the relationship between story-telling and truth-seeking', a problem central to auto-biography.[10] The use of 'I' is rare enough in Beckett to draw attention to this more personal element in *As the Story Was Told*. Yet the division of the 'I' into both passive listener and far-from-omniscient narrator undercuts the deceptive simplicity of the use of that pronoun. Neither 'I' is in control of his life or of the story that is made out of that life. What the 'I' is told by its alter ego is a story of meaningless cruelty inflicted on a man who was required to confess something – but what neither he nor the 'I' knew.

Hansford is surely right to remind us that Beckett was asked to contribute this piece to a memorial volume for his German friend, the poet and playwright, Günter Eich, and that Eich, like the 'poor man' in the text, died by unnatural means, having committed suicide in 1973 at the age of 66. But the sheet of writing offered to the narrator is surely not, as Hansford argues, the finished story that Beckett offered the publisher of the memorial volume. It is more reminiscent of the news that reached Beckett of his friend's trials and eventual suicide. In conflating the two 'I's in the final sentence, Beckett implicitly identifies with his fellow artist. They are both tortured by their vocation into attempting to express artistically and meaningfully the meaninglessness of their existence. Ultimately, as Hansford argues, the story is that of its own story-teller, Beckett, for whom 'writing is its own occasion'.[11] Biography and autobiography have been conflated into another of Beckett's parables about the torture of man's life and of the inability of the writer to tell his own painful story aright.

Autobiography is a confessional mode and all confessants seek absolution. Yet confessants, as Roman Catholics know, are compelled to repeat the act of confession until the last hour of their lives, because absolution only applies to the past, and because life necessarily leads men and women into error. In *Company*, his most ambitious text since *How It Is*, Beckett explores this paradox at the heart of the autobiographical act.[12] *Company* was written in English between March 1977 and September 1979, translated into French and the English text then revised in the light of the French text.[13] Published in 1980, it consists of fifty-eight paragraphs of which fifteen are autobiographical vignettes (many of which feature in Deirdre Bair's biography of Beckett).[14] The fifteen autobiographical paragraphs divide into seven of childhood, two of early adulthood and six of old age.[15] Many of these fragments of memory are either tinged with pain or illuminated in a delusive halo of artificial light. His first memory is of his mother's unaccountable anger at his asking whether the sky is not more distant than it seems (she apparently prefers the delusion of proximity). Other negative memories include his suicidal leaps from the top of the fir tree in his garden at home into the branches below which break his fall (his mother saying, 'He has been a very naughty boy' (28)); or his act of intended kindness to a hedgehog, leading to its death. Inevitably, the voice of memory tells him, 'you . . . return to the woes of your kind' (83). Some of the most nostalgic memories of happiness are lit by a distorting light like that of the '[s]unless cloudless brightness' (32) which betrays its unreality by remaining unchanged when he falls asleep. Or there is the key scene in the summer where as a child he sees the landscape outside 'through a rose-red pane' (54), just as later at nineteen he sees his sweetheart through the distorting blue glass of the same summer house. Even more disturbing is his memory of seeing her at his own head level through the window when he was sitting down. Could she be on her knees outside? he wonders. Memory is clearly not to be trusted. And yet Beckett cannot rid himself of his memory of this early love affair. It occurs in *That Time* and in *A Piece of Monologue* as well as in *Company*.

This dichotomy between one's fascination with the fragmentary narratives that memory recounts and the untrustworthy nature of the stories one tells oneself about one's past self is mirrored in the structure Beckett adopts for *Company*. The fifteen autobiographical paragraphs are told to a passive recipient by a voice addressing him as 'you'. The voice is timeless: 'All at once over and in train and to come' (46). The recipient of these stories is referred to in the third person throughout the remaining thirty-three paragraphs. The use of the pronoun 'he' necessitates a third presence, that of a narrator with insight into the inner thoughts and feelings of the hearer, 'that cankerous other' (9). The largest part of *Company* is a series of complex reflections on the interaction that takes place between these three necessary configurations of the self implicit in any attempt at autobiography. Autobiography is the written life of the self. But who is the self who is writing the life of the self? He claims to be the same self, yet assumes the rights of a narrator. And a narrator is one who tells stories, creates fictions.

So *Company* accordingly opens with the command, 'Imagine' (7). That requires a voice to utter the command and an auditor to whom it is addressed (not to mention the implicit presence of the narrator). You and he. Yet most autobiographies conflate these two into that convenient fiction, 'I'. 'Could he speak to and of whom the voice speaks there would be a first' (9). For Beckett identification with one's discontinuous past is an impossibility within the fictive narrative of autobiography. Typically he illustrates this by the use of irony: 'To have the hearer have a past and acknowledge it. You were born on an Easter Friday after long labour. Yes I remember' (46–7). Quite apart from the fact that the date of Beckett's birth certificate differs from this account,[16] the absurdity of remembering one's own birth highlights the fictionality of the autobiographical 'I'. Only when life ends and with it the compulsion to tell stories about oneself can one recognise the 'unthinkable last of all. Unnamable. Last person. I' (32).

But why the urge to write autobiography? The self is 'Devising it all for company' (84). There is something essentially self-delusive about the autobiographical act. A search for identity, an attempt at self-validation, the whole enterprise is fraught with the distorting influence of the ego and its needs. For a start there is the complicity between the speaking and listening selves without which the voice would prove no company for the one on his back in the dark: 'a certain activity of mind however slight is a necessary complement of company' (11). The act of narrating one's own story is also necessarily one of self-aggrandisement. The hero of the autobiographical narrative is what Freud, speaking of the hero of fiction, called 'His Majesty the Ego'.[17] This fictional hero can become unpleasantly demanding. As Beckett puts it: 'Need for company not continuous. Moments when his own unrelieved a relief' (41–2). Those images of the autobiographer's essential vanity – the voice of memory and the adult to whom it addresses itself – are ultimately 'figments to temper his nothingness' (64). There is always the danger of their usurping their creator: 'Regret . . . at having brought them about and problem how dispel them' (42).

The many paragraphs of commentary and reflection introduce the reader to the numerous pitfalls present in all attempts to write autobiography. Beckett adopts a bewildering variety of tones and devices to make his point. In the midst of the voice telling one of its stories from the past ('You lie in the dark with closed eyes and see the scene') Beckett will slip in a quick rider ('As you could not at the time' (52)) before proceeding to describe the scene. Autobiographical memory necessarily involves retrospective interpretation, which alters the immediacy of experience with the knowledge of hindsight, in what Georg Gusdorf has called 'the original sin of autobiography'.[18] Frequently Beckett resorts to humorous word-play, thereby drawing attention to the verbal inventiveness inherent in the art of autobiography. Having decided for the sake of company to make the narrator crawl, he then pauses mischievously to pose the conundrum: 'Can the crawling creator crawling in the same create dark as his creature create while crawling?' (73). He tries naming his hearer M and the narrator W (its mirror image) only to conclude: 'Even M must go. So W reminds

Figment' (63). All these split selves are figments of the imagination just as autobiography itself is shown to be an act of imagination.

Beckett offers further evidence of the fictionality of his autobiographical endeavour in the form of frequent quotations from his own and other writers' work. Living most of his life in France, Beckett has long since absorbed the post-Saussurean assaults on the autonomy of the author and the Structuralists' emphasis on the dependence of any one text on other texts for its composition and comprehensibility. Autobiography, that seemingly most personal of genres, is – paradoxically – especially reliant on intertextuality, on the fact that the author is himself the product of all the other texts with which he has come into contact. Both John Pilling and Eric Levy have listed a large number of the allusions Beckett makes in *Company* to his own earlier prose works in particular.[19] Pilling also notes the extent to which Beckett alludes to Shakespeare's plays, Dante's *Purgatorio*, Milton's *Paradise Lost*, Aristotle and the New Testament's account of Christ's crucifixion and death. In addition, *Company* contains an ironic reference to Proverbs 13.12: 'Hope deferred maketh the heart sick'. In *Company* Beckett's narrator claims that both hope deferred and a sick heart are better company than none, only immediately to undermine this stance with 'up to a point', and 'Till it [the heart] starts to break' (34). He disagrees with his source and then disagrees with his disagreement – a very postmodernist form of intertextuality.

Just as autobiography reconstitutes fictions from the past, so his life retraces the footsteps of his father 'from nought anew' (19). 'Birth was the death of him', as Beckett puts it in *A Piece of Monologue*.[20] There is a circularity about life, as Beckett sees it, that is reflected in the circularity of his autobiographical text. There is the circularity of the walk his father, then he and his father, and then he alone took, a walk which slows down but continues in his head, where it reverses its course in the retrospection of memory: 'The unerring feet fast. You look behind you as you could not then and see their trail. A great swerve. Withershins' (52). If life is a circular journey from east to west and from light to dark, then memory retraces that journey withershins – in a counterclockwise direction. Near the end of *Company* the old man lies staring at the clockwise movements of the second hand on his watch. But it reminds him too powerfully of his own predicament to go on with the computations of the various possible permutations of hand and shadow. The tendency of the narrator to resort to numerical games is indicative of the slow failure himself of his creature as so far created. W? But W too is creature. of his powers of artistic invention. 'What kind of imagination is this so reason-ridden?' he asks (45). Even the autobiographical review of his past life turns from a journey to a computation of how many steps he has added up in his lifetime. 'How often round the earth already' (19).

Autobiography, then, is another act of the imagination, an act that entails inventing a whole series of *personae* for company on the long journey to death. However, one is always ultimately alone, 'alone' being the word with which the text ends. The autobiographical quest is a purgatorial search (hence the reference to 'the old lutist', Belacqua, 'waiting to be purged' (85)) for silence and release from the voice of memory. Yet the imagination which is responsible for the memorial act is an indispensable resource in Beckett's later prose, as he implies in his short *témoignage*, or testimonial, *La Falaise*, published in 1975 for a Bram van Velde exhibition.[21] Observed phenomena are unstable in themselves and offer nothing meaningful to the observer, he shows in *La Falaise*, unless transformed by the imagination, the same imagination that conjures up those untrustworthy scenes from the past which in *Company* hold the narrator in their illusory grip.

Beckett's next major work of prose fiction, *Ill Seen Ill Said*, was written in French and published in Paris in 1981 as *Mal vu mal dit*. The English version first appeared in *The New Yorker* on 5 October 1981.[22] *One Evening*, written in French in about 1979 as 'Un soir', was first published in English in the *Journal of Beckett Studies* in the autumn of 1980.[23] It reads as an early working towards the longer text – what an auction catalogue described as 'the opening page of what the author called "current work in French"'.[24] *One Evening* describes the same woman protagonist met in *Ill Seen Ill Said*, though in a landscape setting that is in an earlier and more verdant state than the ravaged scene in the longer text. It is raining, but whether in the morning or the evening the narrator cannot decide – 'It happened so long ago' (209). Are we back in the minefield of memory? or of fictive memory? There is no telling. But the controlling presence of a narrator warning himself, 'Not too fast' (209), or reassuring himself, 'All that seems to hang together (210), anticipates the far more obtrusive presence of 'the eye of flesh' and of 'the other' (17) in *Ill Seen Ill Said*.

Ill Seen Ill Said is a fictive construct about the process of constructing fiction, a work of imagination in which imagination is shown to be constantly at work. This quality of self-referentiality makes of it a quintessentially postmodernist text. The narrative is fragmented and disrupted by the controlling presence of the imagination, the gropings of which gradually subsume the ostensible story 'to devour all' (59). Beckett as always is pushing forward the frontiers of the genre he is using. It has become almost a commonplace in postwar avant-garde fiction for the writer to abandon the Joycean model of the disappearing narrator in favour of one who repeatedly intrudes to remind the reader of the fictional nature of the entire enterprise. For the narrator's concern with his craft to usurp his concern with the story, however, is to carry this trend to its logical, absurd conclusion. And it has its dangers. The reader's patience in this text is tried to the utmost. No sooner is interest in a situation aroused than it is dissipated by the narrator's whimsical changes in the scenario. Now you see it, now you don't. Beckett sets out to flout a normal reader's generic expectations. Yet if one accepts the premise that the story is arbitrary, changeable at will and untrustworthy, it is possible to read this text as the adventures of the imagination in the world of fiction.

From the first of its sixty-one paragraphs onward, the narrative voice addresses itself. 'On', it constantly urges itself, 'Quick then', or 'Careful', or 'Gently gently', as if it were a beast of burden that required expert handling. Towards the close of the work it is equally anxious to bring itself to a halt, with commands like 'Less', 'Enough', and 'No more'. The imagination here has a semi-autonomous existence over 'the eye' with which it sees; 'its drivelling scribe' (51), the writer, has only partial control. The text develops into a dialogue between the narrator and his imagination, one which repeatedly fails him when he calls on it, but persists when he would be done. Added to this is the complication of 'the eye of flesh', the observer of the real, whatever that is. In this text the real, an observable external object, for instance, is for ever proving less than objective, for ever moving when it should be still. There is no knowing whether the object or the observer is responsible for this further cause of confusion: 'How motionless it droops. Till under the relentless eye it shivers' (29).

What about the ostensible subject matter of the narrative? The first few paragraphs open confidently enough, constructing an image of the old woman in her house, her appearance and movements, the area around the house – its zone of stones and encircling grassland with the twelve figures constituting the horizon. This could be another variant of *The Lost Ones* with its rigid demarcation between areas and its predetermined rules for movement within and between each area. But the imagination's own needs invariably take precedence over the internal demands for narrative consistency. So the number of figures, for instance, is selected arbitrarily ('How many? A figure come what may' (10)), and the figure is only introduced at all to 'furnish the horizon' (10). Similarly, the narrator finds early on that the area under grass does not suit his needs as well as a moor. But having posited pasture, the narrator feels that it is 'too late' (11) to change his mind. Yet he changes his mind more and more as the text proceeds.

A certain degree of mad consistency prevails, nevertheless. 'If only', he laments of the female protagonist, 'she could be pure figment. Unalloyed. . . . In the madhouse of the skull and nowhere else' (20). Inventive imagination is still reliant on images originally observed in the flesh. Hence its lack of automony. The image of the woman and her surroundings comes and goes bewilderingly until, midway through, the narrator tries to dismiss his attempt to recall her original model in the flesh: 'Not possible any longer except as figment. Not endurable. Nothing for it but to close the eye for good and see her. Her and rest' (30). But the confusion persists, confusion between 'real' and 'how say its contrary?', 'once so twain' (40). At the same time the constant intervals between sighting the woman and her surroundings affects the observing eye. Responsible for the change is false memory: 'Remembrance. When all worse there than first ill seen' (52–3). Even first sight is distorting, and each subsequent viewing renders the original image less recognisable: 'Well on the way to inexistence' (54). Anxious to be rid once and for all of this troubling image (possibly, bearing in mind her endless pacing to and fro, based on his mother, who habitually spent her nights pacing the house in her insomniac state), the narrator at first doubts his ability finally to wipe his mind clean of any trace of it: 'And what if the eye could not? No more tear itself away from the remains of trace. Of what was never. Quick say it suddenly can and farewell say say farewell' (58–9). But in the final paragraph he discovers (once again) the irresistible, self-defeating urge to return in his imagination to these images he would simultaneously be rid of: 'No. One moment more. One last. Grace to breathe that void. Know happiness' (59). Illusion is addictive. The entire process of artistic production is circular – from observation through memory to imagination, which can only function by working on the observed material it is seeking to replace. And life, like art, is equally circular. Happiness is a delusion not easily surrendered in favour of the stark confrontation of the void of human existence.

In June of 1981 Beckett sent Joseph Browne a one-page untitled prose text for inclusion in a special Beckett number of *College Literature*.[25] In this brief parable of the pointlessness of human life Beckett constructs a model which combines vacuous rules for proceeding along two winding paths crossing one another up and down a hill with brief moments of choice at the extremities. The text is divided into two sections, the first headed by the symbol for 'indefinite number' (8) the second for infinity (∞), both configuring the shape of the two paths seen from different perspectives. The second section plays variations on the first, for instance substituting 'Bedrock underfoot' for 'Loose sand underfoot'. This in turn leads to the substitution of 'a' in place of 'no' in 'So no sign of remains no [a] sign that none before'. The new certainty of the second version in turn gives a different meaning to the unfinished sentence used for both sections: 'No one ever before so –'. Not even an identical sentence can be trusted to remain stable. Clever as it is, this piece is hardly representative of Beckett at his best.

Beckett's most recent prose work, *Worstward Ho*, takes up the artistic struggle where *Ill Seen Ill Said* left off.[26] 'On. Say on', the narrator begins, echoing the phrase with which the narrator of *Ill Seen Ill Said* goaded himself forward. The scene is 'All of old. Nothing else ever'. But he can at least 'Try again. Fail again. Fail better' (7). Even these short quotations indicate a new brevity, a frontal assault on the traditional language of prose. Convinced (as he once said to the critic Lawrence Harvey) that 'the slightest eloquence becomes unbearable' because it 'is so far from experience', Beckett has in this work pursued what he has called the 'syntax of weakness' to extraordinary new lengths.[27] Believing on the one hand that 'being *has* a form' and on the other that 'words are a form of complacency',[28] Beckett sets out to destroy normal syntax and narrative continuity in the hope of creating a new language out of which the form of being at last can be constructed. If he fails finally to achieve the wider objective he has nonetheless managed to fashion a startlingly new form of language out of the old.

Where *Ill Seen Ill Said* is about the workings of the imagination, *Worstward Ho* is about the inadequacy and treachery of language. The problem with words is that they carry with them so many emotive and – in Beckett's eyes – illusory associations that they betray the user into reverting to the deceptions his narrators are so desperately seeking to leave behind. As his narrator says of words: 'How almost they still ring. . . . How all but uninane' (33). His ultimate aim is to express being without words. The blank spaces between each paragraph offer a constant reminder of this paradoxical goal. Words only serve to dim the images he is laboriously constructing, or rather deconstructing. 'Till blank again. No words again. . . . Then all undimmed. . . . That words had dimmed' (39). The trouble is that without words there is no form: 'What when words gone? None for what then. . . . For what when nohow on. Somehow nohow on' (28). Faced with the paradoxical nature of his artistic endeavour, the narrator can only pursue his assault on language in the hope of finally achieving a literature of the unword. This attack on the verbal weapons with which he is conducting the attack results in some extraordinary word clusters.

One paragraph, for instance, ends with this seemingly incoherent 'sentence': 'Unlessenable least best worse' (32). Yet a careful reading of the paragraph renders this perfectly comprehensible. Beckett's aim from the start of the piece has been, as he humorously puts it, to go 'From bad to worsen' (23). In other words he is constantly trying to worsen his images in an effort to properly represent the nullity of human existence. So he begins by positing (imagining) a number of images – a woman's body stood upright from the prone position in which he had left it in *Company*; an old man and a child walking hand in hand (a situation reminiscent of *Enough*); a head or skull such as was encountered in *For to End Yet Again*; the void in which they appear; and the dim light which gives them all being. *Worstward Ho* traces the persistent reduction of these images as the text proceeds, condensing the woman to a headless, trunkless bowed back; splitting the pair apart and leaving them 'ever kneeling . . . on unseen knees' (44); and turning the head into a one-eyed stare. In the penultimate paragraph these images are further reduced to 'Three pins. One pinhole' (46). So to revert to the seemingly meaningless sentence, 'Unlessenable least best worse', these three pins and one pinhole represent the unlessenable (no further reducible) least beyond which words fail him. They are therefore the 'best worse' he can manage. That is how the text ends: 'Best worse no farther. . . . Nowhow worse. . . . Nohow on' (47). That is what enables him to end, the fact that he 'Said nowhow on' (47).

Charles Kingsley's *Westward Ho!* (1855), the book which the title of this text most probably parodies,[29] is a story of romance and adventure set in Elizabethan times in which the plot increases in complexity as the narrative develops. *Worstward Ho* operates in the reverse direction, for ever simplifying the story until virtually nothing of it survives. In the course of reducing the plot to three pins and a pinhole, Beckett has set out to employ words to defeat themselves, to acknowledge their incapacity and therefore to suggest by way of their negation the presence of being, a being the form of which can only be configured by the destruction of conventional concepts of form. Beckett has never come closer to his artistic goal than in this extraordinarily original assault on the foundations of verbal communication. And most surprising of all is the eerie beauty of the antilanguage he feels compelled to resort to: 'Vasts apart. At bounds of boundless void. Whence no farther' (47). But as all language is misleading, it is only too likely that in the near future another Beckett text will appear to take his reductive quest yet farther in his lifelong attempt to 'Fail better' (7).

Notes

1. See James Knowlson and John Pilling, *Frescoes of the Skull: the Later Prose and Drama of Samuel Beckett* (London: John Calder, 1979) p. 184. Hereafter cited as *Frescoes*.
2. Unless otherwise stated, all page references are to Samuel Beckett, *Collected Shorter Prose 1945–1980* (London: John Calder, 1984).
3. See Ann Cremin, 'Friend Game', *ARTNEWS*, 84 (May 1985) 87–8.
4. See Richard L. Admussen, 'Samuel Beckett's Unpublished Writing', *Journal of Beckett Studies*, 1 (Winter 1976) 73–4.
5. See *The Lost Ones*, in Samuel Beckett, *Collected Shorter Prose 1945–1980* pp. 177–8. For information about the added paragraph, see *Frescoes*, p. 157.
6. All quotations from 'Sounds' and 'Still 3' are from the appendix to John Pilling's 'The Significance of Beckett's *Still*', *Essays in Criticism*, 28 (Apr. 1978) 155–7. Page numbers are given in the text.
7. *Frescoes*, p. 177.
8. Judith E. Dearlove, *Accommodating the Chaos: Samuel Beckett's Nonrelational Art* (Durham, N.C.: Duke University Press, 1982) p. 150.
9. See *Frescoes*, p. 181.
10. James Hansford, 'Seeing and Saying in "As the Story Was Told"', *Journal of Beckett Studies*, 8 (Autumn 1982) 75.
11. Ibid., 93.
12. All quotations are from Samuel Beckett, *Company* (London: John Calder, 1980); page numbers are given in the text.
13. See Breon Mitchell, 'A Beckett Bibliography: New Works 1976–1982', *Modern Fiction Studies*, 29 (Spring 1983) 142–3.

14. See Deirdre Bair, *Samuel Beckett: a Biography* (London: Jonathan Cape, 1978) pp. 15, 23–4, for example.

15. For a more detailed breakdown of the order in which these paragraphs occur, see Linda Ben-Zvi, 'Fritz Mauthner for "Company"', *Journal of Beckett Studies*, 9 (1984), 76.

16. Bair, pp. 3–4.

17. 'Creative Writers and Day-Dreaming', in *The Standard Edition of the Complete Psychological Works of Sigmund Freud*, tr. James Strachey and Anna Freud (London: Hogarth Press, 1959) IX, 150.

18. Georg Gusdorf, 'Conditions and Limits of Autobiography', in *Autobiography: Essays Theoretical and Critical*, ed. James Olney (Princeton University Press, 1980), p. 41.

19. John Pilling, 'Review Article: "Company" by Samuel Beckett', *Journal of Beckett Studies*, 7 (Spring 1982); and Eric Levy, '"Company": the Mirror of Beckettian Mimesis', *Journal of Beckett Studies*, 8 (Autumn 1982) 95–104.

20. Samuel Beckett, *Collected Shorter Plays* (London: Faber & Faber, 1984) p. 265.

21. Published (without title) in *Celui qui ne peut se servir de mots*, (Montpellier: Fata Morgana, 1975) p. 17.

22. *Mal vu mal dit* (Paris: Minuit, 1981); *The New Yorker* (5 October 1981) 48–58. All quotations from *Ill Seen Ill Said* are from the Calder edition (London, 1982); page numbers are given in the text.

23. 'Un soir', *Minuit* (Paris), 37 (January 1980), [2]–3; Beckett's English translation first appeared in the *Journal of Beckett Studies*, 6 (Autumn 1980), [7]–8. All quotations from *One Evening* are from Samuel Beckett, *Collected Shorter Prose 1945–1980* (London: John Calder, 1984); page numbers are given in the text.

24. *Artists for Amnesty* [catalogue], (Dublin: Amnesty International, 1982).

25. Samuel Beckett, 'Crisscross to Infinity', [unauthorised title], *College Literature*, 8 (Autumn 1981) 310. All quotations are from this text.

26. Samuel Beckett, *Worstward Ho* (London: John Calder, 1983). All quotations are from this edition; page numbers are given in the text.

27. Lawrence Harvey, *Samuel Beckett, Poet and Critic* (Princeton University Press, 1970), p. 249.

28. Ibid., pp. 249, 250.

29. John Webster and Thomas Dekker's play, *Westward Hoe* (1607), seems a less probable source.

6

Beckett's Fundamental Theatre: the Plays from *Not I* to *What Where*

Charles R. Lyons

On the surface, each of the plays from *Not I* to *Ohio Impromptu* appears to be no more than an enigmatic narrative forced into a theatrical context. The audience confronts an ageing figure who does nothing except speak or listen to a repetitive and obliquely phrased story, and with the exception of brief stage directions, the narrative constitutes the whole text. The performance of these plays, therefore, seems to provide an arbitrary theatrical frame for the kind of discourse that is free to function in the corresponding prose works simply as a text to be read.[1] While narration has been an important component of drama since Aeschylus, in this sequence of plays Beckett seems to push the relationship between enactment and narration out of balance. Are these works inherently dramatic, or are they essentially works of prose fiction enclosed in a theatrical conceit?

The experience of reading or seeing Beckett's dramatic works performed in chronological sequence reveals the progressive economy of his writing.[2] In the later plays Beckett's process of reduction removes the context for the narrative and presents merely the figure and the text. We imagine that the discourse the figure speaks is his own story, or if we hear a detached (recorded) voice speaking the text, we assume the voice is the character's. In *Krapp's Last Tape* the playwright situates the phenomena of character, voice and recorded narrative in a bare but complete scenic context. While Beckett offers no explanation for Winnie's confinement in the mound of sand in *Happy Days*, his physical representation of the earth and sun gives a degree of plausibility to her impulse to return to the comforting behavioural patterns and the words of a time she identifies as 'then'. In the plays from *Not I* onwards, Beckett

80

exhibits character, voice and narrative discourse as pure phenomena with almost no other physical context than that provided by the presence of theatrical light. What remains, of course, is a paradigm that Beckett has exercised throughout his writing: an image of character whose consciousness processes a narrative. The following discussion clarifies why I use as emotionally uncoloured a verb as 'processes' rather than 'reviews', 'reconstructs', 'remembers', or, simply, 'tells'. Is what remains – the image of a figure processing a text – essentially dramatic?

Throughout his fiction and drama Beckett sets up paradigms that combine a character and a narrative. Despite apparent reference to the characters' past, the stories seem to function as imaginative structures that they use within the immediate present. In fact, the principal activity of many of Beckett's early dramatic and fictional figures is the writing, speaking, or imaginative invocation of a narrative as the principal activity that constitutes their present. In other words, the story is less important as the representation of a history than it is as a process that gives shape to the present. Of course, the narrative data of the story remains significant to the activity of telling it, and the act of reporting details about the past often appears to be an attempt to re-enact or to repossess an earlier moment.

In *Endgame* Hamm recites a narrative about a suppliant who, he asserts, came to him one Christmas Eve many years earlier. Shortly before he tells this extravagantly phrased story, he questions Clov about the servant's memories of his arrival at this household and about his memory of his father. In response to both questions, Clov reminds the older man that earlier Hamm told him that he was too young to remember either his arrival or his father. This brief exchange prompts us to speculate that the image of the petitioner in the narrative refers to Clov's father and that the starving child is Clov himself. While Beckett's text refuses to confirm or to deny the validity of our speculation, the play suggests the possibility that Hamm's story is an improvisation based upon the early history of his relationship with Clov in which he assumes the role of surrogate father. The relationship of character to narrative in this segment of *Endgame* exercises what are to become the sufficient components of Beckett's drama: a text that we assume to be a narrative of the past; a storyteller who recites the text regularly with some degree of obsession; and the use of telling or listening to the text as a strategy to sustain activity in the present. In addition, the following relationships between text and storytelling or principal obtain: the text seems to be memorised by the character who clarifies that fact either in his processes of self-correction or in the direct representation of the text as a story, repeated daily; the character does not reconstitute the past in memory through the act of reciting the narrative; the material he remembers is the text, not the events it represents; and the authenticity of the story, as history, is neither certain nor capable of being ascertained or disproved.

What do I mean when I suggest that the act of narration is more important than the status of the discourse as history? The nature of the story that Hamm tells allows him to improvise upon his perception of the relationship between himself and Clov. That is, within the activity of storytelling, he may play, conceptually and emotionally, upon the dynamics of a relationship by suggesting its likeness to that of son and surrogate father, indigent and benefactor. His didactic recitation of the story, supported by other references to the past, also characterises the pair as tutor and pupil. At this point in *Endgame*, the grounding of the relationship within a coherent history is less important than perceiving the coordinates of the relationship through the narrative, regardless of the accuracy or inaccuracy of the recitation as history. Beckett suggests that Hamm conceives his relationship with Clov within the ratios of master/ servant, father/son, tutor/student. The behaviour of the two figures suggests that their relationship manifests the consequences of habit, of both tasks and language reduced to routine. Hamm's use of the story invests that relationship with a potential history that may stand behind the residue that constitutes the present condition; and, as well, the story reveals Hamm perceiving or pretending to perceive that relationship as if it were the embodiment of a history, whether or not the story refers to actual events in time.

The early examples of storytelling in Beckett represent a character exercising the narrative act as a form of self-conceptualisation or self-invention. The transmission of autobiographical material into a narrative in which the image of the self functions not as *I* but as *he* or *she* accomplishes several objectives simultaneously: the act delineates the image of the self and gives it significance; the narrative confines a potentially transitive image of the self, fixing its presence within the limits of what the narrative can represent; and the function of telling the story, to oneself or to others, gives the speaker the temporary role of narrator, and the subjectivity of the character is appropriated by the identity of the narrator. The 'I' of the character becomes the objective figure of the story, and the 'I' of the storyteller functions as a substitute for that absent subject. Telling the story, in other words, allows the character to vacate his persona by allowing him to inhabit, temporarily, the role of the narrator and to distance his image of the self as the object described in the narrative.

Beckett's dramatic storytellers differ from the narrators of his fiction. The writer–protagonists of the trilogy produce daily pages, but each day's work is discrete and contributes to the text as a sequentially written whole. When Beckett's dramatic figures tell stories, the present recitation seems to be a variation of a discourse spoken periodically. The mind of the storyteller either focuses on the familiar text, working towards as accurate as possible a restatement of the words; or else, as in *Play*, *Footfalls*, *Not I* and *That Time*, the consciousness of the character succumbs to the text as though it were a record playing in the imagination. In either case, the behaviour of the speakers suggests that the narrative has a presence apart from the voice of the speaker; it seems to exist as a pre-existing object towards which the narrator moves as he attempts to speak the existing words in their correct order, or it functions as a presence that attempts to possess his mind, filling it with sound. While we assume that the narrative these characters speak is the product of their imagination or memory, the discourses have become independent artifacts distanced and, in a sense, alienated from the consciousness of the speaker/listener in frequent repetition. In *Ohio Impromptu* an old man sits listening to a man, dressed as his double, reading to him about an old man who sits listening to a man, dressed as his double. The narrative describes the final visit the reader of the narrative will make to the lonely, displaced old man. Here the narrative which, we assume, represents the character's experience, is removed from him by situating it in a physical text read to him by someone else whose presence mirrors his.

Because the recited discourses in Beckett's late stage plays overpower the dramatised action, they provoke us to re-examine the conventional relationship between narration and enactment in drama. Rather than functioning as a critical but discrete component of the dramatic structure, as do the messenger speeches of fifth century tragedy, the Ghost's report of the murder of Hamlet's father, or Fru Alving's revelation of the actual nature of Alving's character and the history of their marriage, these narratives subsume the structure; and there is no other text. The recitation of narrative, of course, constitutes a very important formal strategy in drama. Narration allows playwrights to reveal and examine events from the past in their relationship to the immediate moment dramatised. Oedipus confronts his image of the past as he speaks of the events of his previous life, and he receives the revised history of his birth in the narratives presented by the Theban and Corinthian shepherds; Hamlet learns of the assassination of his father from the narrative recitation of the Ghost; Oswald learns from Fru Alving's revision of his history that his inherited disease is the consequence of his father's dissolute life and her willingness to hide it. The physical space of the stage, representing the polis of Thebes, the political centre of Denmark and the Alving home, provides an arena in which the critical details of the past of that place may be revealed that determine its present corrupt condition. While plays such as *Oedipus Tyrannus*, *Hamlet* and *Ghosts* contain significant physical action, the events they dramatise represent a confrontation with the nature of the past as revealed in significant narratives. The dramatic structure of each of these tragedies frames the passages of narrative recitation and provides both the physical and psychological situation in which the presentation of narrative recitation appears plausible. In the plays from *Not I* to *Ohio Impromptu*, as I have mentioned, there is no physical scene that houses the narrative other than the physical presence of the actor, with the exception of the silent auditor in *Not I*, the rocking chair in *Rockaby*, or in *Ohio Impromptu*, the actor, his double and the table at which they sit. The body of the actor, or that part of the actor that is illuminated, provides both the physical and psychological space in which the narrative may play.

Not I retains the narration of the past, but the performance reduces the presence of a character to an illuminated mouth that speaks the almost incomprehensible series of words that forms the narrative. We assume that the body implied by the metonymic mouth is the figure of a character who repeats this story to herself. The story, told in the third person, describes an old woman who hears a kind of buzzing in her head and comes to realise that what she hears is herself. The performance of *Not I*, therefore, implies that the consciousness of the dramatic figure who speaks this text does not herself apprehend the text as memory, or even as story, but only as sound. We speculate that the narrative has attenuated in countless repetitions to become merely a sequence of sounds that are repeated for the satisfaction of the speaking rather than for the significance of the content. Beckett removes the presence of the narrative, as autobiographical story, from the consciousness of this implied character, and places the conventional relationship between speaker and recitation in an imaginative past. That is, we imagine that the speaker, represented by Mouth, formed the story at an earlier moment as a self-conscious description of her lonely existence, but that she now holds no emotional connection to that image of her history. Beckett represents the implied dramatic figure at a minimal level of conscious awareness, and her story is not told but, rather, is spoken as an obsessive gesture of the unconscious. What remains here is the representation of the debris of character and the trace of narrative. In performance we focus upon the visual image of the Mouth and the presence of the auditor, who responds arbitrarily to the words the mouth speaks, and we struggle with the narrative, which is almost incomprehensible because of the speed and volume at which it is spoken. However, the discourse is sufficiently repetitive that eventually we perceive a series of details. In light of this narrative data, collected gradually during the twenty-minute performance, we endow the almost static visual image with narrative significance; that is, we perceive the Mouth as a sign of a complete character – not merely as a striking theatrical metaphor. We assume that the 'character' speaking is identical to the 'she' of the discourse, that this character cannot bear to identify herself as 'I', that this 'I' has originated the discourse in an antithetical act of self-conceptualisation and self-denial, and that an obsessive repetition of the narrative has deadened its significance to her as story. The narrative itself tells us how to perceive the shocking image of the isolated Mouth.

It would be possible to argue that the words recited in these plays do not form communicative discourses – conventional narrations – but, rather, operate principally as aural texture. That is, it would be possible to read these late texts as the score for the sound track of performance events. While the recitations clearly do establish a mood by incantation like a passage of music that exercises an occasional realistic sound, or employs conventionalised emotional references like Wagnerian *leitmotifs*, to perceive the late plays principally as dramatised poetical metaphors, embellished by words that function as sound rather than sense, diminishes the subtle skill with which Beckett establishes a potential image of extended time within a highly condensed and economic theatrical representation.

In *A Piece of Monologue*, for example, Beckett presents a boldly simple and static spatial image: a dimly-lit figure of an old man, with white hair, white gown and white socks, standing by a standard oil lamp, the foot of a white bed barely visible. The actor who plays this old man speaks an extended, repetitive recitation. The discourse describes a nightly routine in which he follows a strictly defined procedure: he lights the lamp, moves towards the window to gaze out at the darkness, moves back towards the wall of the room and gazes at its surface. The wall has been discoloured by photographs once pinned there which, apparently long before this moment, he ripped off and tore into pieces. The figure does not act out this procedure, and he now describes the routine as an activity of the past. The speaking has replaced the doing; but, while the performance does not represent this compulsively repetitious physical action directly, the description of it establishes an image of years of restless movement whose palliative function has attenuated into the equally obsessive but more restricted activity of speech. The audience perceives that the speaker has arrived at this moment, near the end of his life, after years of painfully rehearsing the loss and renunciation of those 'loved ones' he cannot bear to identify as such. The nightly ritual he describes embodies this confrontation with loss and renunciation. The procedure itself evokes certain images from a more distant past – the past of family relationships of mother and father and the later past of the death and burial of these figures. The narrative also refers to that earlier time, extended over several years, in which he destroyed the family photographs. The implied physical routine and the discourse that has replaced it appear to be an attempt to exorcise his memory of key figures from the past. Despite his effort to distance himself from these images, reflected in the effort to keep from referring to the figures of mother and father as loved ones, the scenes of their funerals maintain a kind of cinematic clarity in his narrative text:

Grey light. Rain pelting. Umbrellas round a grave. Seen from above. Streaming black canopies. Black ditch beneath. Rain bubbling in the black mud. Empty for the moment. That place beneath. Which . . . he all but said which loved one? (268).

Almost at the end of the text, the speaker affirms that he has spent his life focused on the images of lost loved ones:

> Stands there staring beyond at that black veil lips quivering to half-heard words. Treating of other matters. Trying to treat of other matters. Till half hears there are no other matters. Never were other matters. Never two matters. Never but the one matter. The dead and gone. The dying and the going (269).

The phrase 'lips quivering to half-heard words', suggests that this repeated discourse had, even by the time described in this particular telling, attenuated almost to pure sound. The notion, 'Treating of other matters', implies a tension between the physical activity of the nightly routine and the content of the words spoken; the activity constitutes an effort, analogous to the ripping of the photographs, to deny the familial images, and the speaking emphasises the psychological centrality of the death of those figures, the fact that these deaths provide the single matter with which his consciousness deals. The narrative, therefore, represents an extended conflict in the mind of the speaker whose life has been divided between his movement towards those lost loved ones and his effort to free himself from the memory of them and the memory of their absence.

The recitation of the narratives in these plays reveals both the characters' need to speak the text and their desire to be free of that obsession. In *Rockaby* Beckett establishes a character whose story suggests that she is in the process of renouncing the kind of thinking that envisions the self as a character within a narrative. In the final section of the narrative that accompanies the visual image of the woman rocking in the chair, the voice speaks of the woman's decision to leave the upstairs room and terminate her quest for the evidence of another creature at the bank of windows facing her windows; her decision to function as another creature for herself (and, by implication, to function as another creature for herself by reciting her narrative); and, finally, her decision to abandon the creation of that narrative:

> so in the end
> close of a long day
> went down
> let down the blind and down
> right down

into the old rocker
and rocked
rocked
saying to herself
no
done with that
. . . (281–2).

This final section of the narration reports the character's decision not only to abandon her search for another creature like herself, but also to relinquish her effort to function as another for herself, to give up the process of formulating a conception of the self as the principal figure of the narrative. She is 'done' with 'saying to herself'. That decision does not take place in the immediate dramatic present, but is itself part of the narrative that revolves in the woman's mind; yet the moment represents, at least, the decision to abandon the repetition of the narrative. While the recitation that is dramatised may, indeed, suggest a continuation of that kind of conceptualisation, the present version may also be a successful attempt to come to the final speaking of the text that ends the text.

Earlier I referred to the fact that the narrative process, housed in the represented consciousness of a character, forms a physical and psychological space in which the drama of these plays may take place. To be more accurate, the substance of the narrative the character speaks or hears gives us, as spectators, material that we use in constructing an image of the consciousness of the figure on the stage. What the spectator sees, for example, in *Rockaby*, is not the presence of a character who enacts the behaviour of an extended experience, but a figure who manifests the signs of that experience. The theatrical presence of the character and the text that revolves in her head stimulate the spectator to establish a conceptual structure in which to place the details that are slowly revealed in the narrative. This active engagement allows the spectator to see the figure on the stage as a dramatic character, as the manifestation of an extended movement through a series of behavioural stages in her renunciation of the attempt to discover another creature like herself. The slowness of the tempo in which V speaks, the woman's decreasing engagement with the voice, the recognition that the narrative process itself is the substitution of the self for the other – all these elements are part of a dramatic movement that has occurred before the beginning of the performance. The narrative releases these details, and the spectator uses the information progressively throughout the performance as he or she invests the visual image of the woman with significance. That is, the spectator works from a provocative visual image to a speculative image of the preceding action through the agency of the spoken narrative. That gradual reconstruction of a sense of the character in time prepares the spectator to perceive the final moment as the possible last speaking.

It is important to repeat that the actual speaking of the narrative in these plays does not represent the consciousness of a character actively engaged in the past. Beckett locates that connection in the past; the speaking of the text produces a palliative activity; the words fill the mind as sound. The audience, however, should not themselves relate to the text as sound only; the function of witnessing the figure includes perceiving the relationship between the character and the text and extrapolating some kind of imagined coherence from the fragmented and partial narrative. However, Beckett stimulates us to perform that kind of reconstruction in order to clarify the fact that the coherence we extrapolate is itself hypothetical.

Consequently, as the character recites the narrative to sustain his or her experience in the present, the spectator constructs an image of the character in time as a fulfilment of his function as spectator. The spectator's task of locating the visible dramatic figure within the coordinates of the recited narrative has as its objective, not the clarification but the process. Some readers may feel that my description of the means by which we, as spectators, use the details of the narration to invest Beckett's late dramatic figures with a 'character' and a 'history' is an attempt to read into these plays and their performance a mimetic function that is simply not there. I do not, of course, equate my analysis of the processes of relating figure and narrative with the question of how many children had Lady Macbeth; Beckett's strategy of providing clues for the audience to extrapolate a dramatic situation and action provokes the spectator to make connections that are tentative, equivocal, uncertain. That is, Beckett demands that we, as spectators, use narrative, as the characters use narrative, to create a hypothetical structure that sustains our sense of the present. As members of the audience we should recognise, as the voice in *The Unnamable* claims, that these equivocal narrative structures and images of character are nothing more – and yet nothing less – than rhetoric:

And all these questions I ask myself. It is not in a spirit of curiosity. I cannot be silent. About myself I need know nothing. Here all is clear. No, all is not clear. But the discourse must go on. So one invents obscurities. Rhetoric.[3]

The engagement of the audience in the speculative process of establishing a narrative context and an image of character and, at the same time, recognising the hypothetical nature of these constructs, transforms the static scene of plays such as *A Piece of Monologue* and *Rockaby* into dynamic theatrical experiences. At the beginning of this essay, I asked the question: 'Are these works inherently dramatic, or are they essentially works of prose fiction enclosed in a theatrical conceit?' I trust that the discussion that fills the intervening pages documents my judgement of the implicit theatricality of Beckett's use of narrative discourse in these provocative and challenging plays.

Catastrophe marks a transition from Beckett's experimentation with dramatic narration, although his next dramatic work, *What Where*, uses dialogue in the form of questions and answers to reveal data about a possible series of events in past time. In *Catastrophe* four figures interact. An aged man stands on a pedestal, ostensibly a character within a play. The attention of a director, his assistant, and an unseen lighting technician focus on a specific moment in a forthcoming production. A (the assistant) has dressed the standing figure, identified in the text as P (for Protagonist), in a black dressing gown that hangs to his ankles. His hands are in his pockets, and his face is obscured by a broad-brimmed black hat. D (the director) demands that A remove the dressing gown to reveal the ash-coloured night attire underneath; that she discard the hat in order to show the cranium and tufts of remaining hair; and that she open the top buttons of the shirt and roll up his trouser legs to reveal more flesh. He also commands that, for performance, all the old actor's exposed flesh should be whitened. He agrees to experiment with joining the Protagonist's hands, and after a period of trial and error, he decides that they are to be held together at breast level. The director rejects the assistant's suggestion that the figure be gagged: 'For God's sake! This craze for explicitation! Every i dotted to death! Little gag! For God's sake!' (299). Here Beckett exercises an ironic reference to his own practice of eliminating the visual context that makes the character's behaviour – silence, in this case – plausible. With the assistant as intermediary, the director rehearses a lighting sequence that includes fading out the general light, lighting the figure of P alone, fading out the light on the body, and, finally, illuminating P's head during a long pause. The director also responds negatively to her suggestion that P raise his head to reveal his face to the audience: '. . . Where do you think we are? In Patagonia? Raise his head? For God's sake!' (300).

When the figure and the lighting are modified to the director's satisfaction, he declares: 'Good. There's our catastrophe' (300), and he demands one more rehearsal of the dramatic moment. During this final repetition D claims that the Protagonist will have the audience on their feet, and 'a [d]istant storm of applause' (301) is heard. At this point the figure raises his head and fixes it upon the actual audience, and the distant applause 'falters, dies' (301). After an extension of this moment, the play ends.

The term 'catastrophe' has come to signify a structural part of tragedy, that dramatised moment in which the hero suffers the ultimate reversal. The literal meaning of the Greek noun, a turning up and down, held a more encompassing and less technical significance in the language of the tragic poets; for example, in *Eumenides*, the Chorus uses the term to describe the potential overthrow of values that would be the consequence of Orestes' vindication.[4] In *Oedipus at Colonus* Sophocles' aged hero uses the noun to refer to death. The catastrophe of Oedipus' prayer encompasses the sense of a conclusive episode that would embody the death of the hero.[5] Beckett's writing consistently represents self-conscious movements towards death – processes of dying, not death. The term 'catastrophe', which includes the idea of a dramatic segment, movement, or process working towards the death or destruction of the principal character, is obviously one that would intrigue Samuel Beckett. The play *Catastrophe* presents its catastrophe as the final moment of the play-within-a-play that constitutes the representation of a representation, as *Endgame* may be one of a series of enactments of a game of ending rather than the enactment of an ending. *Catastrophe*, however, seems to dramatise a unique moment when the Protagonist unexpectedly breaks out of the bounds of his rehearsed behaviour and confronts the hypothetical audience with his gaze. This moment, in which the playwright represents an actor working through the persona of the character to confront the audience as audience, relates to that moment in *Endgame*, when Clov, peering through his glass, reports to Hamm, with amused irony, that he perceives the audience as 'a multitude . . . in transports . . . of joy'.[6] Winnie, in *Happy Days*, may use the presence of the audience, with less specificity, when she focuses upon the presence of an external eye: 'Someone is looking at me still. (*Pause.*) Caring for me still. (*Pause.*) That is what I find so wonderful.'[7]

In each of these instances Beckett's character uses the presence of the external perceiver to imagine and to characterise himself or herself as an object – the focus of the perception of that hypothetical external witness. Throughout Beckett's dramatic writing, the possibility of a public witness allows the character to conceptualise himself; that conceptualisation allows him to sustain a sense of experience, to be a presence for himself. The conceptualisation also traps him, confines him in a hypothetical image of the trap from which he wishes to be free. Each of Beckett's principal figures manifests those antithetical demands.

Beckett identifies the visible characters by their official function within the rehearsal context: the Director (D), his female assistant (A), the Protagonist (P). While Luke, the lighting assistant, who never appears on stage, is the only character who has an actual name, that name relates to his theatrical function because it derives from the Greek word for whiteness or light, which in turn has its source in the root verb 'to see'. This Luke provides the light that illuminates P, focuses on his face, and allows the moment of catastrophe to be witnessed. The spotlight, which manifests the will of D, seeks out the character, just as the shifting light in *Play* stimulates the voices of the three figures who speak only when the light shines on them demanding speech. Luke's light expands the gaze of the audience to encompass the figure of P. That perception frees him to return the stare and, by that act, to assert himself.

P provides the primary focus of the attention of the other characters and the audience; it is, after all, his physical image the action concerns. His identification as Protagonist, however, apparently derives from his function within the fictional play being prepared, just as the titles 'director' and 'assistant' refer to that project. Beckett plays with that name ironically because – while 'protagonist' has come to be synonymous with hero – our use of the term derives from Aristotle's statement concerning Aeschylus' addition of the second actor: 'Aeschylus first raised the company of actors from one to two and diminished the choral odes and gave the dialogue the leading role . . .'.[8] The presence of a second actor makes dialogue possible, and dialogue becomes the principal part of the tragedy. By derivation, the term 'protagonist', designating the chief participant in the dialogue, refers to the leading personage or actor. In the plays immediately preceding *Catastrophe*, Beckett reverses Aeschylus' process, so that narration replaced dialogue, and the interaction is not between the language generated by two dramatic figures, but between the consciousness of the single character and the words that revolve in his or her consciousness. The use of the term 'protagonist', therefore, functions ironically, because there can be no principal actor, no protagonist, if there is no secondary one. Beckett's Protagonist, of course, is mute; and he is both the innocent and pathetic victim of the dialogue spoken by the director and assistant. As actor, he submits passively to the manipulation of his body, the modifications in dress and stance that develop from the dialogue between the Director and his female assistant. He does, of course, assert his subjectivity as he confronts the audience with the stare that silences the applause.

Beckett's use of the noun 'catastrophe' for the title of the play refers, obviously, to the director's identification of the moment from the play-within-a-play that is rehearsed. Catastrophe can also refer to a process of subjugation, as in Herodotus I.6.92, or to a sudden overthrow of authority as in the citation from Aeschylus mentioned above. As the decisions of the director impose themselves upon the character of the Protagonist, that fictive actor is dominated; the power of the authoritarian director implements *his* catastrophe is that sense. As the protagonist lifts his head to confront the audience, in opposition to the aesthetic judgement of the director, this rebellion constitutes the *director's* catastrophe in the sense of a sudden reversal of power.

The play-within-a-play in *Catastrophe* has, of course, no existence apart from the metonymic fragment we witness being rehearsed. The appearance of the old man on the pedestal and the specific moment rehearsed suggest that, if we were to observe that nonexistent play, it would be very much like the pieces that precede *Catastrophe*, the sequence of plays in which an ageing figure speaks or hears an extended and repetitive narrative. While we know that this protagonist remains silent, the preceding plays also include silent figures whose voices sound only on tape. *Catastrophe* presents a theatrical figure similar to the single figures of these plays, but here Beckett widens the frame to include the theatrical structure that surrounds the actor, revealing the aesthetic process of dramatic representation and the interaction amongst director, actor and those implementing the director's aesthetic judgements. *Catastrophe* eliminates the narrative that would place the figure psychologically, as W is positioned in time by the text she hears, for example, and dramatises instead the process of building the physical image of such a character within a theatre. Within the fictional drama being rehearsed, this character, like all the protagonists in Beckett's drama, is at that final painful stage of life, caught in a movement towards the resolution death brings. But, typically with Beckett, the character is in the process of rehearsing that moment, repeating, re-enacting, or describing the process of dying, not enacting the moment of death. In that sense, *Catastrophe* is clearly related to those works that precede it immediately, but is, simultaneously, both more cryptic and more expansive. The playwright returns to the representation of dialogue and situates it once again within the Hegelian paradigm of master and servant; but he focuses the attention of that language on the silent figure of the old man. In the plays of narrative recitation, the process of speaking or hearing the narrative constitutes the character's experience. Here, the dialogue amongst director, assistant and technician provides the experience of the protagonist; and the assistant's suggestion that the protagonist could raise his head and confront the audience gives the actor/character a model for the singular act he performs. In the economy of Beckett's late drama, the events of the time leading up to the moment of catastrophe remain unseen and unvoiced. Within his arena of jurisdiction, D exercises political power absolutely until the old actor defies and silences the unseen audience. Beckett's play is dedicated to the Czech playwright, Vaclav Havel, and while the text embodies motives of dominance and servitude consistent with Beckett's typical representation of relationship, the political implications of this work may hold more direct and specific reference.

Beckett's most recent play, *What Where*, integrates narration and dialogue. Beckett locates the narrative voice in a small megaphone at head level, downstage left. The playing area, a rectangle with an entrance upstage centre and at either side, provides the space for the human actors. The source of the voice is the 'player', Bam. This voice begins the action with the following assertion:

> We are the last five.
> In the present as were we still (310).

The other players are Bem, Bim and Bom. Ostensibly, the voice of

Bam establishes a situation in which the four players re-enact a series of dialogues in the rectangle, each episode relating to a season: spring, summer, autumn and winter. The voice of Bam controls the light that illuminates the playing area and directs the re-enactment of the dialogues, aborting the re-enactment if it does not satisfy him or, ostensibly, if the words or actions are not correct. The presence of the narration, with illustrative re-enactment that may or may not satisfy the narrator, suggests that the action is a representation of a series of earlier events; however, the conflation of past and present in the voice's statement, 'We are the last five. / In the present as were we still', obscures a clear division between then and now, event and re-enactment.

Each dialogue represents an interrogation by Bam: in the spring segment Bam questions Bom about Bom's interrogation with 'him'. Bom asserts that this unseen character refused to 'say it'; in the second section of this episode, Bim enters and Bam directs him to take Bom away and 'give him the works until he confesses . . . [t]hat he said it to him' (313). In the summer segment, Bam interrogates Bim about his interrogation (perhaps of the first unseen figure, perhaps of Bom). Here the question concerns the confession of 'where', and when Bem enters, Bam instructs him to take Bim away 'and give him the works until he confesses . . . [t]hat he said where to him' (315). In the briefer autumn segment, Bam interrogates Bem about his own interrogation and the unachieved confession of 'where'. Bem asks 'Is that all?' (315) and the dialogue moves toward closure. In the very brief winter segment, Bam's voice accompanies the presence of Bam in the rectangle and asserts that

> I am alone.
> In the present as were I still.
> It is winter.
> Without journey.
> Time passes.
> That is all.
> Make sense who may.
> I switch off (316).

The enacted or re-enacted sequence of episodes concerns interrogations that take place offstage. It could be that the interrogation is limited to the trio, Bom-Bem-Bim, or it could be that there is a 'fifth' character since Bam refers to the five. He could, of course, be referring to five by counting the figure of Bam, himself, and the narrative voice as two. *What Where* appears to be a highly self-conscious dramatic invention that parodies the very processes I have been discussing: the spectator's extrapolation of images of character, situation and time from the limited and equivocal data the playwright provides. The 'itness', 'whatness' and 'whereness' of these figures, who are almost interchangeable, does not exist; the form of dramatic action is precisely that, a form, that sustains the dramatic event and has reference to nothing external to the performance. Here the spectator's efforts to invest the action and dialogue with significance is confounded parodistically. Each of the plays I have discussed confounds that effort, but the playwright's clarification of the impossibility of making those connections necessitates stimulating the spectator to posit their hypothetical existence.

Notes

1. The narratives of *Pour finir encore* (Paris: Minuit, 1976) and *Worstward Ho* (London: John Calder, 1983), for example, do not need the physical presence of an actor/character to contain them or to position them in relationship to the reader.
2. The plays discussed in this essay were written, first performed and first published as follows:
   Not I. Written originally in English, 1972. First performed at Lincoln Center, New York, Forum Theater, September 1972. First published in London: Faber & Faber, 1972.
   That Time. Written originally in English, 1974–5. First performed at Royal Court Theatre, London, on 20 May 1976. First published in New York: Grove Press, 1976.
   Footfalls. Written originally in English, 1975. First performed at Royal Court Theatre, 20 May 1976. First published in New York: Grove Press, 1976.
   A Piece of Monologue. Written in English for actor David Warrilow and performed by him in New York in 1980. First published in *Kenyon Review*, NS1, No. 3 (Summer 1979) 1–4.
   Rockaby. Written originally in English, 1980. First performed in Buffalo, New York in 1980. First published in New York: Grove Press, 1981.
   Ohio Impromptu. Written originally in English, 1980. First performed at Ohio State University, 9 May 1981. First published in New York: Grove Press, 1981.
   Catastrophe. Written originally in French, 1982. First performed at Avignon Festival, 1982. Dedicated to Vaclav Havel. First published in *The New Yorker* (10 Jan. 1983) 26–7.

What Where. Written originally in English. First performed in New York, Harold Clurman Theatre, 15 June 1983. First published in *Evergreen Review*, 98 (1984) 47–51.

These texts are all included in Samuel Beckett, *Collected Shorter Plays* (London: Faber & Faber, 1984). All quotations are from this edition; page numbers are given in the text.

3. Samuel Beckett, *Molloy/Malone Dies/The Unnamable* (London: Calder & Boyars, 1959) p. 296.
4. See Aeschylus, *Eumenides*, 490–3.
5. See Sophocles, *Oedipus at Colonus*, 103–4.
6. Samuel Beckett, *Endgame* (London: Faber & Faber, 1958) p. 25.
7. Samuel Beckett, *Happy Days* (London: Faber & Faber, 1963) p. 37.
8. Aristotle, *Poetics* (49a, 15–30; tr. Gerald K. Else). See also Else's *Aristotle's Poetics: the Argument* (Cambridge, Mass.: Harvard University Press, 1963) p. 164.

7

Human Reality and Dramatic Method: *Catastrophe, Not I* and the Unpublished Plays

Dougald McMillan

In *Catastrophe* the Director finishes arranging a mute male Protagonist on a pedestal for a tableau, turns to his Assistant and says, 'There's our catastrophe. In the bag.'[1] The Director is using the word 'catastrophe' partly in the everyday sense of 'disaster' to refer to the figure before him. He is saying that they have successfully captured an image of the universal human condition. It is 'our catastrophe' in the sense that it is common to us all. But he is also using the word in its more technical, theatrical sense, derived from its Greek roots, *kata* (down), *strophien* (turn), to allude to the scene of classical tragegy depicting the downward turn of the protagonist's fortunes. When he speaks of 'our catastrophe', he is distinguishing between, on the one hand, the tableau which he, his Assistant and the lighting technician have arranged, and the plotted structure of theatrical tradition on the other. He is asserting that the static stage image of the single mute figure, with trouser legs turned up to expose his flesh, is sufficient dramatic presentation. There will be no catastrophe in the etymological sense. Their performance will not contain a plot accounting for a turn in the protagonist's fortunes and leading to an inevitable final scene depicting them. In effect the Director is asserting that his tableau *supplants* the classical theatrical tradition.

The conflict between the two kinds of catastrophe – the universal human predicament presented in mime and the artificial plots and verbal explanation of conventional drama presenting an individual destiny – has occupied Beckett since the start of his career as a playwright, and has become the subject of much of his drama. From his first unfinished play to his most recent works, Beckett has continued to associate words and imposed theatrical contrivance with the presentation of individual personal psychology.

No other problem concerns Beckett more in his unpublished drama than the differing methods required to represent the universal and the individual aspect of human reality. On the one hand the permanent, causeless and unchanging universal condition of mere existence is best represented by summary static images. On the other hand individual reality and consciousness seem to require the narrative plot and verbal explanation which Beckett distrusted in other writers. As he stressed in his 1931 Trinity College, Dublin lectures on Gide, Balzac and Racine, the problems of rendering what he called 'human reality' were so great that they of necessity resulted in the artist's imposition of inadequate roles on his subjects[2] – a process depicted throughout his drama as tyrannical, brutal, futile and interminable.

Beckett's struggle to find an acceptable dramatic method to render both the universal and the individual aspect of 'human reality' is most evident in the unpublished and abandoned works which anticipated *Endgame, Krapp's Last Tape* and *Not I*.

His first *serious* attempt at playwriting was to have been a work of individual psychology.[3] Beginning in 1936 he made extensive biographical notes for a long realistic psychological study of Dr Johnson in love.[4] The play was to have been entitled 'Human Wishes', leaving the audience to supply the more metaphysical commentary of Dr Johnson's own title, 'The Vanity of Human Wishes'. In it he wanted to explain 'what has never been explained, i.e. his grotesque attitude toward his life and Mrs Thrale'.[5] But the more universal question raised by Dr Johnson himself of the general possibility of human happiness was also in the foreground. The play was thus a personal psychological response to the universal human condition. Johnson was, Beckett told his friend Thomas McGreevy, 'spiritually self-conscious, was a tragic figure, i.e. worth putting down as part of the whole of which oneself is part . . . '.[6]

Beckett abandoned 'Human Wishes' after writing only a twelve-page opening exposition scene. That scene, however, is an integral work which Beckett has allowed to be published and performed.[7] It is the first of Beckett's 'dramaticules', demonstrating the impossibility of realistic psychological drama for him. In it the three women of Dr Johnson's household at Bolt Court discuss whether any member of the household can be said to be happy. Attention is focused on Johnson's apothecary, Levett, who in moments of inebriation exhibits some signs of happiness. Already in his first attempt at drama, Beckett juxtaposes mimed action to the failure of conventional dialogue and characterisation. Levett is presented in pantomime independently of the intentionally artificial dialogue of the exposition scene. He staggers across the stage without even acknowledging the presence of the three women. His only sound is a hiccup. The women break character to comment: 'Now this is where a writer for the stage would have us speak . . . explain Levett. . . . To the public. . . . The ignorant public. . . . To the gallery. . . . To the pit. . . . To the boxes.' But they cannot: 'Words fail us.'[8] Where words fail and an explanation for the audience is not available, there remains the visible presence of the inebriated Levett as a lamentable commentary on the possibility of human happiness.

The delay between Beckett's attempt at a play of psychological explanation and his second play suggests the extent of his dissatisfaction with existing dramatic methods. Beckett's first completed, but unpublished play, 'Eleuthéria', was not written until 1947, just prior to *Waiting for Godot*.[9] Like 'Human Wishes', it questions the ability of drama to explain personality. It is an exhaustive catalogue of parody scenes centred on the struggle of the young protagonist, Victor Krap, to elude the other characters who demand that he assume a recognisable role in their play and that he reveal his motives for leaving the family context. Victor succeeds, however, in winning the 'freedom' of the play's Greek title. He expels the other characters who intrude into his room and extricates himself from the machinations and devices of a plot reminiscent of Ibsen. He demands and achieves for himself the right to 'be nothing'. In the end he does not fill any of the conventional dramatic roles, offer any explanation for his conduct, or participate in a contrived solution to his unsatisfactory predicament.

At the conclusion of the 'tour de horizon' of dramatic methods and devices, when all the intrusive action and dialogue of previous drama have been cleared away from the scene and the bourgeois Krap family drawing room from which they came literally swept into the pit, there is a poignant mime. On several previous occasions Victor has approached the footlights as if to reveal himself in a soliloquy, but each is given up with a gesture of futility, presenting in physical action alone the inadequacy of words and theatrical conventions. The play concludes, however, with silent action indicating from Victor's point of view the conflict between his reality and the demands of art. He again approaches the audience, looks pointedly at each section of the auditorium, then 'turns his thin back towards humanity'. The words of conventional dramatic constructions, even voluntary soliloquy, have failed. In their place is the visual stage image of humanity as embodied in Victor, who has recoiled from the world into his own reveries. Implied is an awareness of the universal malaise which precludes action and makes a more individual explanation or response irrelevant.

In two abandoned works which were both preliminary steps towards *Fin de partie* and *Krapp's Last Tape*, Beckett continued to examine the alternatives for presenting character.

In 'Mime du rêveur A', an abandoned four-page mime play composed about 1954,[10] Beckett presents a protagonist, 'A', who is clearly a prototype of both Hamm in *Endgame* and Krapp in *Krapp's Last Tape*. In A we can see the beginnings of the stylised Hamm making almost symbolic responses to the confines of his consciousness. He inspects the exterior from two circular windows, makes circuits about the stage, examines the wall of his room, seeks relief from existence via a painkiller and sleeps intermittently in his chair. We can also see in A the more realistic and individualised Krapp. He is an old man with poor sight holding objects close to his eyes. He is alone with his dreams. He digs for the mundane articles of his daily life stored in his pockets, keeps a ledger. And his major waking activity – apart from increasingly desperate attempts to ease his pain through drugs – is the same as Krapp's. He oscillates between contemplation of memories recorded in the realistic medium of an aged photograph and contemplation of himself in a small mirror.

Beckett left 'Mime du rêveur A' unfinished. But he invested certain elements of 'A' in the protagonist of another abandoned play, which he ultimately designated 'Avant Fin de Partie'.[11] As Beckett's algebraic designation 'X', as opposed to his usual 'A' for unnamed characters implies, the protagonist is an undetermined quantity. The question raised by X in his opening monologue about the veracity of his presentation and what it means to be a 'simple particular' – whether he is a representative of all humanity like 'billions' (or perhaps only 'thousands' or 'hundreds'), or is a unique individual 'alone of his species' – is also the question Beckett faced in determining how he would develop the protagonist taken over from 'Mime du rêveur A', who was both a potential Hamm and a potential Krapp.

Beckett answered the question by withholding the realistic exposition required for personal characterisation. In its place he wrote another parody of exposition like those in 'Human Wishes' and 'Eleuthéria', with blatant and arbitrary questions, predictably concerned with X's milieu, occupation and exact physical condition. The exposition is followed by a comic scene with his servant in disguise, playing the role of his mother. The scene fails in its announced purpose of elucidating his infirmity, but ironically does account for the circumstances of the mother's health. The fragment ends by again juxtaposing the parody of exposition with a reference to mime and universal subject matter. 'Avant Fin de Partie' closes with an allusion to the pantomime clowns Bim and Bom and the idea of thirst as metonymy for all human desire, the subject of *Act Without Words I* (also composed in this period before *Fin de Partie* and published with it).

In *Krapp's Last Tape* Beckett went on to develop the more individual and realistic aspects of his character A. And he developed further the method of portraying personal psychology through mime implied in 'Mime du rêveur A'. Although it is seldom described in such terms, *Krapp's Last Tape* is primarily a mime play performed to an accompanying monologue. The primacy of the mime element in Krapp has frequently gone unnoticed because Beckett did not provide in the original text of the play detailed directions for Krapp's response to the recordings of his own voice. In effect he left the central plot and action of the play – Krapp on stage in the present responding to his past – largely unwritten, to be supplied by directors and performers. It is not an exaggeration to say that only when he directed it in Berlin in 1969 did he complete the play. There, working with Martin Held as Krapp, he created a very detailed series of gestures and postures which depict Krapp in a complex and interrelated relationship to his memory of himself and of the women in his life. Krapp is seen in a pattern of repeated attitudes and gestures oscillating 'up and down and from side to side' to a climax of rejection of himself and others and subsiding to absolute stillness and 'dream-eaten' solitude.[12]

The special combination of mime and monologue arrived at in Krapp did finally provide Beckett with an acceptable method for depicting individual psychology. It was no longer a matter of mime *or* individual psychology, but of mime *as* individual psychology. And having found that he could depict character through a sustained mime action not totally dependent on the words of a text, Beckett seems to have relinquished some of his hostility to the old methods. He continued to parody plot in *Play* and exposition in *Come and Go*, but by the time he was working on the material which ultimately became *Not I*, he displayed a new willingness to present realistic background revealing of character.

The development of *Not I* parallels that of *Fin de partie* and *Krapp's Last Tape*. *Not I* also began as an aborted mime play and progressed through intermediary stages exploring characterisation before becoming a finished play. Two abandoned plays – 'J. M. Mime' and 'Kilcool', written nine years before *Not I* was begun[13] – show Beckett actively concerned with elements found later in *Not I*. Both mimes are contained in a notebook given by Beckett to Trinity College, Dublin, bearing the heading 'fragments of theatre'.[14]

The 'J. M.' of 'J. M. Mime' refers to the actor Jack MacGowran, whom Beckett envisioned in the role of aged male protagonist. The draft contains detailed notes and diagrams for a mime for a man and his mother, a half-page of dialogue between them, a three-page monologue by the son with formalised stage actions, and a few marginal notes on characterisation. The order of the segments of spoken text and mime suggests that Beckett had it in mind to write a play much like the one he produced later in *Footfalls* – a play progressively reducing theatrical elements from dialogue accompanied by the action of both characters, to monologue accompanied by mime action, to pure mime. Reduction to mime was from the outset inherent in the material from which *Not I* evolved. In one of the earliest notes Beckett considered how to 'reduce' the mime of exhausting possible paths about a quincunx by stipulating different opening trial paths.

The subject of 'J. M. Mime' is mime itself, or life as mime. The son and his mother wander through an undifferentiated landscape now devoid of the flowers it once had and dotted with fewer stones than before. Daily they carry out instructions in a book of maze puzzles for setting up figures with names like Double Diamond, Star, Every Maze and Loops. They 'jump about in the book and wander in space'.

While the mother lags behind offstage and must be urged to come on, the son selects the next maze, 'quink', interrupts his monologue to perform a kind of mime-within-a-mime as he marks each corner and the centre with a stone, and takes his place at the centre of the figure ready to perform the mime he has set up.

The unintegrated dialogue between the son and mother with which Beckett began the work bears no resemblance to *Not I* beyond reference to confusion and wandering. Many elements of the man's monologue, however, do recur in *Not I*. Though now aged, the speaker first casts himself as a son, remembers his boyhood, the fact that he was 'born strange', and says, 'I feel far more naked under my coat than when I was born.' The coalescence of age and infancy so prominent in *Not I* is further brought by the remark that he and his mother are so old now that they 'might be of the same generation'. Like Mouth, the speaker spends much of his time walking aimlessly and talking to himself.

A passage describing the son's talking presages Mouth's bifurcation into speaker and listener, her confusion at the sound of her voice, and the discomfort it causes her:

> When I say talking to myself I mean there are two of me, one talking, the other listening. Or not of course. Otherwise I couldn't. So not always clear what I'm saying. Moments of incomprehension. Then on. Leave it dark. Silence? (*Five seconds. Clasps hands to ears. Cringing. Five seconds. Anguished.*) No, no!

In the pattern of the son's speech there is the beginning of the pattern of starting, stopping briefly, then continuing on, which is even more evident later in the description of the mother and which is the overwhelming pattern of Mouth's whole experience. A marginal note calls for physical action to stress the pattern: 'Begin with nonunderstanding. Baffled expression throughout. Pauses now and then with deepening of same as though puzzling over what he has just said.'

In the son's description of his mother the basic shape of *Not I* is even more apparent. The pattern of her past life, present wandering, speech and thought is the same pattern of beginning, pausing briefly, and then continuing on to an imagined but unattained goal. As the monologue points out, she has been talking to herself for 'many many years', but had stopped and has now resumed speaking. In her present wanderings 'She lags behind looking for flowers. . . . She would give all she has for a daisy. She finds things. I wouldn't bother. She must think this is heading somewhere. Someplace with flowers and fruit and wells.' As she wanders she speaks in interrupted sentences – a phrase, 'then a silence', then another few words, 'then a silence again', then the completion of her sentence. As the son says, 'She's like that. You think she's finished, and she's not.'

In the son's description of his sister are the beginnings of Mouth's personal background: 'Presumably old virgin. Never met a man who liked her. Not a kiss all her days. . . . Mother never kissed us. Turned her head away and held us off when we tried. . . . Freak of nature . . . then changed. Sudden change.' In this passage is Beckett's earliest and most explicit attempt to provide a biographical background to explain character. The compulsion to speak, so pervasive in his work, has here for the first time a realistic origin.

Beckett abandoned 'J. M. Mime' without writing any further drafts, but he did not abandon the concepts contained in it. Parts of son, mother and sister are the basis of the characterisation of Mouth, providing her internal bifurcation, realistic biographical background, and perhaps most importantly, the basic shape of her experience. And the impulse towards reduction to more concentrated mime seen here was the essence of the composition of *Not I*.

Following 'J. M. Mime' in the Trinity College notebook is a ten-page 'fragment of theatre' which Beckett began in late August of 1963 and abandoned near the end of December. Entitled 'Kilcool', it contains notes and trial portions of a female monologue, and a list of themes to be incorporated in the monologue.

The opening directions of 'Kilcool' begin with the concept of a concentrated stage image of speech:

> Woman's face alone in constant light
> Nothing but fixed lit face and speech.

After trial passages developing his character, Beckett amplified these directions in a new start to include a surprisingly realistic description: 'Old woman's face. Grey hair drawn slightly back from forehead. Shrill voice, bad enunciation.'

Here the flow of speech, compulsive and interminable in 'J. M. Mime', has become tormented, and the speaker seeks escape in denial. But while Mouth's denial of self-recognition, 'no! . . . she!' (217 *et passim*) refers to herself as speaker, the denial of the speaker of 'Kilcool' emphasises that she is not the intended hearer.

I am not speaking to myself, more than that I cannot say, I am not speaking to myself, I have no need whatsoever of that. There's nothing I have to say, every word is mild torture. I would give all I have to stop, but I have nothing left, or there are no takers now to understand them, more than that I cannot say, I am not speaking to myself and would give all I have to stop this is not intended as information.

The notes for trial passages develop different stages in the life of the unnamed speaker (referred to here as 'Face' for convenience) – a loveless woman reminiscent of the mother and sister in 'J. M. Mime'. Both she and Mouth deliver monologues uninterrupted by other characters. In their monologues both refer very early to the loss of a father and then of a mother in quick succession. The feeling of being orphaned has remained with both. Face calls herself a 'widowed child'. Mouth remembers herself as a 'waif' (217). Each monologue includes an unanswered prayer for relief and a vivid fantasy of an anticipated moment of funereal stillness.

The arrangement of the material in the notebook makes the chronology of composition and the relationship of the various fragments difficult to establish with certainty, but the essentials of the process are evident. As the temporal progression of the successive trial passages indicates, Beckett was constructing a complete life story for his character. He was consciously providing for the character who would become Mouth the realistic psychological background which he so pointedly refused to provide for Levett, Victor Krap, X/Hamm and Krapp.

The first trial passage describes the train journey from Dublin 'through the tunnels through the Head' of a young orphaned girl to her 'widowed childless aunt' in Kilcool, as well as the aunt's reassurances that the girl will be happy with her. A subsequent passage depicts her as an adult who remembers being deserted by a lover who left without even listening to her protestations: 'Leave her like that in the state she was in. . . . To hear her out would be only to hear again what he had heard a thousand times already and to explain would be only to say again what he had said a thousand times already.' And a final trial section is of thoughts of her present condition as an old woman in her coffin awaiting burial.

Beckett's attitude towards the presentation of realistic personal psychological background in 'Kilcool' and *Not I* is most readily detectable in the way he incorporated the eight themes which he instructed himself to 'lay down before writing' in the two plays.

Themes
1. Light-dark leading to prayer for dark and tears. Three times: opening, midway, end.
2. Voice imitated.
3. Thoughts.
4. Love.
5. Age.
6. Never properly seen, heard.
7. Her body.
8. Burial.

In those items from the list which were retained in *Not I*, Mouth is in each case more particularly and realistically characterised than Face. Beckett retained only part of what was suggested in theme one. Both Face and Mouth pray as called for in the first item, but Face's prayer is to a vague 'Giver of light and taker of it away', while Mouth's cries for help are to a 'merciful' (217) Christian God.

In the treatment of theme three, Face's thoughts about the source of her torment, like her prayer to the 'Giver of light', remain general and are even expressed without first-person pronouns. 'The thoughts (*Pause.*) How is that – (*Pause.*) – one cannot see the . . . (*Pause.*) . . . cause – (*Pause.*). Lie there knowing all the facts and nothing more to do and never see the cause.' Mouth's 'first thought' (217), that she is being punished for her sins, is the product of her particular upbringing. Her religious background is explicitly offered by Mouth as a psychological explanation: 'brought up as she had been to believe . . . with the other waifs . . . in a merciful (*Brief laugh*) . . . God' (217).

The treatment of love in theme four is the one area where the characterisation of Mouth is apparently more generalised than that of Face. Face's lovelessness comes not only from loss of parents but also from abandonment by a lover, leading to her description of herself as a 'widowed child'. Mouth has known 'no love of any kind . . . spared that' (216, 218). But the more generalised depiction results in a more coherent psychological portrait. In place of the single traumatic experience is a general deprivation (like that of the sister in 'J. M. Mime') so great as to account for Mouth's peculiar behaviour.

Both Face and Mouth express awareness of their advanced age, as indicated in theme five. Face thinks of 'coming up to the end when they would carry her away'. Mouth thinks of 'coming up to seventy . . . wandering in a field . . . looking aimlessly for cowslips . . .' (216). Not only is Mouth's formulation more specific, it comes in the context of reference to an active life, and it occurs immediately following the account of her birth, which begins the play and obviously functions as realistic exposition.

Theme six – 'Never properly seen, heard' – is hardly present in 'Kilcool'. It is indicated only by Face's brief general reference to moments of happiness 'when I was unseen'. In *Not I* this aspect is a vivid part of life scenes in supermarkets and public lavatories as others 'stare at her . . . uncomprehending' (219) of her silence or flow of words. The theme culminates in Mouth's speculation that even her prayer to God is 'unheard . . . too faint' (222).

The themes which Beckett did not incorporate in *Not I* are even more interesting in relation to the presentation of Mouth than those he did incorporate. Most notably, *Not I* contains no burial as mentioned in theme eight. That theme found expression only in the final trial section of 'Kilcool'. There, almost as an afterthought, Beckett followed (as he had in 'Avant Fin de Partie') an impulse to resist naturalistic character portrayal. Face lies in her coffin 'coming up to the end alone quite still on her back her head on the pillow under the light'. The image provides a plausible (if unreal) physical situation to account for what is presented on stage. But Beckett was guided by more than this practical concern in this final depiction of Face. Generalised in death, enclosed in her coffin away from the particulars of daily activity, Face will not even have the memories of the life Beckett had been constructing for her. 'Memory gone . . . this too a help', she says. Had Beckett remained with this version of his protagonist, all the work of 'Kilcool' would have been eliminated. But in the end Beckett only temporarily rejected the background he had created for his character. Mouth does have a fantasy of returning to the 'early April morning' (216) when all is 'dead still . . . sweet-silent as the grave . . . face in the grass (218, 222); but in contrast to Face in her coffin, Mouth's fantsy is part of an active life and she remains in contact with the realistic context of the living earth.

One of the most significant changes between 'Kilcool' and *Not I* was the elimination of the two voices implied in theme two. Face has an alter ego which speaks to her in her 'normal' voice and is answered in a breathless 'assumed' voice. With one important exception, Mouth speaks with 'her voice alone'. In *Not I* there is no alter ego and no reported speech of others like that of the aunt and lover in 'Kilcool'. Only in the scene in court when Mouth is apparently on trial for accosting strangers with her flow of speech do we hear words other than Mouth's. They are carefully introduced by Beckett first as indirect address ('what had she to say for herself?' (221)) and then direct quotation ('stand up woman . . . speak up woman' (221)). These words which Mouth relates to her present condition, saying 'now this . . .' (221), are salient exceptions, concentrating attention on Mouth's own voice.

Just as the elimination of other voices concentrated attention on Mouth's own speech, the elimination of references to her body in dealing with theme seven concentrated the focus upon her mouth. Though 'Kilcool' was to have been a play for a 'face alone', that face is still very much in contact with the rest of her body. 'Mouth and body', she says. As she awaits burial in the final trial passage, she is almost preoccupied with her body. She things, 'in position . . . meaning of course no further positions', and enumerates other possible postures. Mouth, by contrast, experiences only the loss of her body. 'Whole body like gone . . . just the mouth' (222), she says. She does not know what position she is in, 'whether standing . . . or sitting . . . or kneeling . . . or lying' (217). When she thinks of her eyes she thinks of an unconscious 'reflex' and for her it is only 'presumably' that she blinks and forms tears. Her description of returning bodily sensation moves backward and inward to focus only on her organs of speech, 'the lips . . . the cheeks . . . the jaws . . . the tongue' (219).

In dealing with the first theme, 'dark and light', in *Not I*, Beckett does include prayer. And he does incorporate the structural pattern of pronounced mime action at the start, at the midway point, and at the end of the play with Mouth's laughs and screams associated with her plea to God for help. But he excluded rather than developed the emphasis on visual sensation called for in the first theme. In 'Kilcool' the sensory focus on light and dark is diluted by the audible elements of compulsory speech emphasised by interchange in 'assumed' and 'normal' voices, and the buzzing in the background. By contrast, *Not I* is pointedly not visual, 'not eye'. It focuses exclusively on auditory sensation. The beam in Mouth's head is a growing visual presence; however, it occurs each time as an afterthought, following her awareness of words, then buzzing, and is clearly only a secondary source of distress. The tactile

awareness which Mouth experiences is a major element of *Not I*, but
it is connected with the auditory element by being concentrated on
her speaking apparatus.

While the intensification of a single sensory focus was important,
the choice of auditory rather than visual sensation was an even
greater factor in the making of *Not I*. Its most important consequence
was to make the text itself into mime.

In *Not I* Beckett allows himself for the first time to present what the
inquisitors of his plays have demanded of their victims – a clearly
recognisable formulation of a life story. It is not enough to stop her
torment, but Mouth does reveal a complete life beginning with
birth, progressing chronologically through a series of life scenes to
old age and the awareness of coming up to the end of life. If the facts
of her life as a seventy-year-old neurotic suburban Dublin spinster
raised a Catholic orphan do not explain her predicament
metaphysically, they do offer a means of accounting for her
behaviour and responses. The words of her monologue explain
Mouth in a way that Beckett had self-consciously refused to explain
other characters.

And yet, as numerous critics have pointed out, Beckett has
consistently maintained that the text of *Not I* is not paramount and
that it is not essential for the audience to comprehend every word of
it. When director Alan Schneider asked about the realistic details of
Mouth's situation, Beckett replied: 'I no more know where she is or
why than she does.' He had provided 'the text and the stage
image. . . . The rest is Ibsen'.[15] Interpretation of the content of
Mouth's words is relegated to the secondary status of artificial
contrivance like the plots of Ibsen which he had ridiculed in
'Eleuthéria'. When actress Jessica Tandy was concerned that the
rapid pace of delivery stipulated by Beckett would make the
monologue unintelligible, he replied: 'I am not unduly concerned
with intelligibility. I hope the piece would work on the necessary
emotions of the audience rather appealing to their intellect.'[16] To
director Anthony Page and actress Billie Whitelaw he discounted
attention to the psychological detail contained in the text and
stressed its purely physical aspect by comparing the performance to
athletic feat.[17] As he told Charles Marowitz in 1962, mime was for
him a 'self-sufficient substitute for language'.[18]

At the very beginning of the play Mouth herself discounts the
importance of biographical detail. She is born in a 'godforsaken hole
. . . called . . . called . . .'. One might even expect her to supply the

name 'Kilcool'. But she continues: '. . . no matter' (216). Mouth has a background of which she is aware, but it is not paramount for her and need not be for the audience.

Because his play could function on the purely physical level of mime, and because Beckett did not have to rely solely upon the artifice of explanation to depict his character, he could admit realistic psychological background to his work. What was unreliable as a primary method was admissible as a secondary one.

Beckett's statement that the play should work on the necessary emotions of the audience is more than manner of expression. The detailed depiction of the act of speech itself is sufficient to present the essence of Mouth's personal psychology. What the only partially comprehended text may reveal of her past and the details of her present thoughts is not superfluous, but it is ancillary. Mouth's situation in the present is apparent in the mime action alone. The personal reality of Mouth's present existence is the sense of being reduced to a pair of blubbering lips compulsively uttering an interminable flow of only partly comprehensible words – interrupted briefly by two pairs of ironic laughs and two screams for help, followed by two silent pauses for a response – and then continuing on.

The experience of the audience as it responds to the unusual conditions of performance is like that of Mouth herself. The lit mouth within the larger context of a darkened proscenium stage requires a concentration of focus corresponding to Mouth's sense of the loss of her body. The amplification of the monologue by a hidden microphone transmits more of the extraneous and redundant sounds of speech than we are normally aware of. Like Mouth, the audience will have an intensified sense of every sound her voice makes.

The audience will share with Mouth the effort of 'straining to hear . . . piece it together' (220), except that Mouth has the awareness of the physical movements of her tongue and lips to help her comprehend. Some of that experience is, however, engendered in the audience. The mouth is too small and too fast for the audience to see all its movements. They will have to recreate the words of the text from visual and auditory cues. Even if they do not move their lips to try to form the words, they will experience subliminally the stimulus to do so. Their sensual awareness will be focused on the musculature of the vocal apparatus, just as Mouth's is.

How skilfully Beckett employs his own awareness of the physical presentation of speech can be seen in his choice of the opening and closing words of the text. In them Beckett provides on a smaller scale summary images like those which mark the beginning and ending of *Waiting for Godot* and *Endgame*. The speaker of *A Piece of Monologue* 'Waits for first word always the same. It gathers in his mouth. Parts lips and thrusts tongue forward. Birth' (268). 'Birth' was originally the first word of the text of *Not I*. In typescript 6 (now in the Reading University Samuel Beckett Archive), however, Beckett revised 'birth' to 'out'. Although the meaning of the word 'out' refers to birth and still expresses the idea of expulsion, depicted in the physical image of the tongue thrust out in pronouncing 'birth', the new physical image of 'out' emphasises the act of speech itself. The lips and jaws open to the maximum to produce the diphthong in the formation associated with cries of pain. The final word, 'Up', in 'Pick it up', expressing Mouth's resolve to go on, echoes the 'out' with which she began but in a slightly diminished form, the lips open but less wide in a single long vowel, and there is total closure on 'P' before the lips continue by opening again for inspiration to complete the image.

If Beckett was satisfied enough with the method of *Not I* to employ it again in *Footfalls*, where he again presented a character whose whole existence was reduced to a single obsessive action, he also acknowledged its limitations in *Catastrophe*.

Beckett's own successful development of wordless methods of presentation would seem to confirm the Director's implication in *Catastrophe* that his mimed presentation of the catastrophe of human existence is superior to the plots and catastrophes of previous drama. However, the spectacle arranged by the Director which appears so successful at first proves to be a theatrical fiasco. It is a form of imposed artifice. The protagonist may not keep his hands in his pockets or clench his fist in anger or hide his withered 'claws' (298), ravaged by disease. Instead he must join his crippled hands awkwardly at his breast for all to see. And he may not lift his head to show his face directly.

When the Protagonist causes the anticipated '*storm of applause*' to falter and die by raising his head to '*fix*' (301) the audience directly in defiance of the Director's earlier scornful prohibition, the Protagonist transforms a moment of popular approval for a passive spectacle into a moment of interactive understanding and compassion. In this gesture there is the implication that human reality can be freed from the tyranny of art to present itself more directly to an audience that will respond with silent awareness rather than a storm of facile approval. Beckett's ultimate comment on dramatic method as it appears in *Catastrophe* is thus of the need for a means of presentation even more direct and compassionate than he has already developed. Those means would be derived from greater attention to the reality of the human subjects portrayed rather than from the artist's aesthetic conceptions or the expectations of an audience.

Notes

1. *Catastrophe*, in Samuel Beckett, *Collected Shorter Plays* (London: Faber & Faber, 1984) p. 300. Unless otherwise noted, all subsequent quotations from Beckett's plays are from this edition; page numbers are given in the text.
2. This information comes from an interview conducted in 1982 with Dublin actress Ms. Rachel Burrows, a student enrolled in Beckett's course of lectures on French literature at Trinity College, Dublin in Michaelmas term, 1931. (The interview is to appear in the *Journal of Beckett Studies*, vol. 11). Ms. Burrows provided a copy of her notes on Beckett's lectures; a photocopy of the notes has been deposited in the Trinity College, Dublin Library.
3. Beckett's very first play, 'Le Kid', was a parody in French of Corneille's *Le Cid*, composed with exchange lecturer Georges Pelorson for the 1931 annual Trinity College, Dublin Modern Language Society evening of foreign drama. (See Deirdre Bair, *Samuel Beckett: a Biography* (London: Jonathan Cape, 1978) pp. 127–8). The text of this play has been lost.
4. Ruby Cohn discusses the notes and play fully in *Just Play: Beckett's Theater* (Princeton University Press) pp. 143 and ff.
5. Quoted in Bair, p. 254.
6. Quoted in Bair, p. 256.
7. Published as 'Human Wishes' in Samuel Beckett, *Disjecta: Miscellaneous Writings and a Dramatic Fragment*, ed. Ruby Cohn (London: John Calder, 1983) pp. 155–66. It was performed at Beckett's suggestion at the 1983 University of Texas Symposium, 'Translating Beckett'.
8. *Disjecta*, pp. 161–2.
9. All quotations are from the original typescript in French, held in the Baker Library, Dartmouth College. All translations are mine. For further information about the typescript, see Richard L. Admussen, *The Samuel Beckett Manuscripts: a Study* (Boston: G. K. Hall, 1978) pp. 106–7.
10. See Admussen, p. 110.
11. See Admussen, p. 109, where the play is said to be untitled. All quotations are from the copy held in the Trinity College, Dublin Library. All translations are mine.
12. The Suhrkamp trilingual edition of *Das Letzte Band* (Frankfurt, 1969)

contains the actions arrived at in rehearsals and significant textual alterations to accommodate the text to the mime. It is in that respect the only complete published text of the play as Beckett has conceived of it.

13. See Admussen, pp. 113–14.
14. Trinity College, Dublin MS 4664.
15. Quoted by Alan Schneider in 'Working with Beckett', in *Samuel Beckett and the Art of Rhetoric*, ed. Edouard Morot-Sir, Howard Harper and Dougald McMillan (Chapel Hill: University of North Carolina Press, 1976) p. 279.
16. Quoted in Bair, p. 625.
17. Interview with Billie Whitelaw, 1975.
18. Quoted by Charles Marowitz in 'A Walk Away from Beckett', *Encore*, 9 (Mar.–Apr. 1962), 44.

8

The Shape of Ideas: *That Time* and *Footfalls*

James Acheson

I

In 1956 Harold Hobson asked Beckett why, as a nonbeliever, he had included so many references in *Waiting for Godot* to the two thieves crucified with Christ. Beckett replied: ' "I am interested in the shape of ideas even if I do not believe in them. There is a wonderful sentence in Augustine. I wish I could remember the Latin. It is even finer in Latin than in English. 'Do not despair; one of the thieves was saved. Do not presume; one of the thieves was damned.' That sentence has a wonderful shape. It is the shape that matters" '.[1] *Godot* mirrors the antithetical shape of the sentence from Augustine in a number of ways. The play is in two acts, and presents two characters – Vladimir and Estragon – awaiting the arrival of the mysterious Godot. They are visited by two other characters: Pozzo, who is blessed with wealth, and Lucky, who is condemned to poverty. The English version of the play is subtitled 'a tragicomedy in two acts', and thereby invites us to ponder the tragedy of the characters' situation and the comedy of their response to it. By way of such dualities as these, Beckett raises the question of whether modern man should or should not believe in divine salvation, and with Godot's nonarrival, strongly hints that he should not.

Similarly, in his first radio play, *All That Fall*, Beckett makes use of Psalm 145.14 – 'The Lord upholdeth all that fall, and raiseth up all those that he bowed down' – both to give his play structure and to bring into question God's existence and benevolence. As the play's main character, Maddy Rooney, makes her way to the station to meet her husband, the possibility of falling is brought repeatedly to our attention. First she is overtaken by a certain Christy, who walks in front of his cart, rather than ride on top of it, because he is afraid he might fall; then by a Mr Tyler, who rides a bicycle, and asks if he might steady himself by putting one hand on her shoulder; and finally by a Mr Slocum, who in helping Maddy into his car, nearly causes her to fall to the ground. No one does fall, however, until the end of the play, when we are told that a little child has tumbled under the wheels of the train. The question this raises, of course, is how a benevolent God could have allowed such a thing to happen.

In *That Time* and *Footfalls* Beckett again employs his 'shape of ideas' approach, with the structure of each play arising, as in *All That Fall*, from his choice of title. Significantly, the title of *That Time* is ambiguous. As James Knowlson has observed, it should be read 'both as "that time" and as "that *Time*". Beckett had great difficulty in rendering this play into French for the recurring phrase "that time" clearly means at once "cette fois" (or "la fois où") and "ce Temps". His title *Cette fois* was, as he put it [in conversation with Knowlson], a "recognition of the impossibility of capturing both senses" '.[2]

Knowlson suggests that the 'ce Temps' ('that Time') sense of the title derives from a passage at the end of *Le Temps retrouvé*, a passage Beckett quotes at the start of his 1931 essay on Proust. ' "But were I granted time to accomplish my work", Proust's narrator writes, "I would not fail to stamp it with the seal of that Time, now so forcibly present to my mind, and in it I would describe men . . . as occupying in Time a much greater place than that so sparingly conceded to them in Space . . ." '.[3] Like the narrator's projected characters, those in Proust's novel are presented temporally rather than spatially, in recognition of the fact that people change with the passing of time. An individual is not the same person today as he was yesterday, and has not the same outlook. 'The aspirations of yesterday', comments Beckett, 'were valid for yesterday's ego, not for today's. . . . For subject B to be disappointed by the banality of an object chosen by subject A is as illogical as to expect one's hunger to be dissipated by the spectacle of Uncle eating his dinner.'[4] Each of Proust's characters is thus a succession of personalities, extended in time, rather than a single, essentially spatial personality. Similarly, in *That Time*, Listener attends to memories of the persons he once was: A in middle age, B in youth and C in old age.[5] That he is distanced from all three in time is evident from the fact that he refers to each as 'you' ('tu' in Beckett's French translation).[6] In the opening stage directions, he is said to have an '*Old white face*' and '*long flaring white hair as if seen from above outspread*': the sense we have is that he is on his deathbed, recalling key episodes from his past.[7]

Beckett's essay on Proust sheds light on the 'ce Temps' aspect of the title of *That Time*, but it does not explain why Beckett chose to call the translation *Cette fois*; why he is concerned in the play with only three of Listener's selves, when Proust's characters exhibit a larger number; or why, more generally, the play abounds in structural and thematic groupings of three. In his study of the play's manuscripts, S. E. Gontarski reveals that Beckett 'had from the first both a clear, if almost rigid, format for *That Time*, a triadic structure, like that of *How It Is*, and a thematic link for the three incidents: "3 fold text [the earliest holograph reads] in single voice coming from text (A). Light (B). Above (C). Recurrence of element time in all 3, e.g., "the time they . . .", "that time she", "one time – we . . ."'.[8] The final version of the play is in three parts, the first two ending with a brief silence where Listener appears to gather his thoughts, and the last with the final curtain. Each part consists of four groupings of three memories, which are presented to us by a single voice through three different loudspeakers:

1.	ACB	ACB	ACB	CAB	(First silence)
2.	CBA	CBA	CBA	BCA	(Second silence)
3.	BAC	BAC	BAC	BAC	(End of play).[9]

Where the dramatic shape of *Godot* and *All That Fall* was suggested to Beckett by St Augustine and the Bible, respectively, the shape of *That Time* derives partly from Proust and quite possibly from another source: Wordsworth's famous poem, 'Lines Written a Few Miles above Tintern Abbey'.[10] Like *That Time*, 'Tintern Abbey' embodies a number of structural triads and deals with three stages in an individual's life. Moreover, of the second stage in his own life, Wordsworth says in the poem:

> That time is past,
> And all its aching joys are now no more,
> And all its dizzy raptures. Not for this
> Faint I, nor mourn nor murmur: other gifts
> Have followed, for such loss, I would believe,
> Abundant recompence (11. 84–9).[11]

'That time' is past for Listener as well: each of the three stages of his life is now behind him and can only be recovered through memory. But whereas for Wordsworth there are 'other gifts' to compensate for what has been lost, for Listener there is nothing. Beckett adapts the shape of 'Tintern Abbey' to *That Time*, but not its optimistic view of God's presence in nature and benevolence to man, his play being not simply a dramatised version of Wordsworth's poem, but a post-Romantic variation on it instead.

In the first of 'Tintern Abbey's' four parts, Wordsworth describes the woodland scene he has revisited after the passage of five years. The scene has been present in his mind throughout that time, he says in the second part, and it has affected him in three ways. The memory of its beauty has, first of all, brought cheer to the life he has led 'in lonely rooms, and mid the din / Of towns and cities . . .' (ll. 26–7); secondly, it has given rise to feelings of 'unremembered pleasure' (l. 32) which might not otherwise have been evoked; thirdly, it has helped to lighten a heavy metaphysical burden: '. . . the burthen of the mystery, / . . . Of all this unintelligible world' (ll. 39–41).

In the third part of the poem, Wordsworth describes his response to nature at each of three stages in his life: childhood, youth and maturity. Though he dismisses his childhood response as naively sensual, it serves as an important contrast in the poem to his youthful view of nature, which he says was characterised by deep feeling:

> The sounding cataract
> Haunted me like a passion: the tall rock,
> The mountain, and the deep and gloomy wood,
> Their colours and their forms, were then to me
> An appetite: a feeling and a love,
> That had no need of a remoter charm,
> By thought supplied, or any interest
> Unborrowed from the eye.

(ll. 77–84)

Significantly, the emotion described here has reference to no one but the poet himself. The mature Wordsworth is more aware of his fellow man, and of the existence of human suffering:

> For I have learned
> To look on nature, not as in the hour
> Of thoughtless youth, but hearing oftentimes

The still, sad music of humanity,
Not harsh nor grating, though of ample power
To chasten and subdue.

(ll. 89–94)

His awareness of the suffering of others marks the first of three differences between his youthful view of nature and his mature view. The second difference is that in maturity Wordsworth has developed a sense of God's immanence in nature:

. . . a sense sublime
Of something far more deeply interfused,
Whose dwelling is the light of setting suns,
And the round ocean, and the living air,
And the blue sky, and in the mind of man,
A motion and a spirit, that impels
All thinking things, all objects of all thought,
And rolls through all things.

(ll. 96–103)

The third way in which Wordsworth's mature view of nature differs from his youthful response is that it is informed by a new moral sense. It follows from the poet's awareness of human suffering and of the presence of God in all things that he now finds in nature 'The anchor of my purest thoughts, the nurse, / The guide, the guardian of my heart, and soul / Of all my moral being'. (ll. 110–12)

In the last part of the poem, Wordsworth moves from the personal to the more general. He says that he sees in his sister Dorothy someone who has reached the stage of viewing nature as he himself did in his youth; he feels confident that she, too, will progress to the third, mature level. The three levels, Wordsworth emphasises, can be experienced by anyone with the right attitude to the natural world, for

. . . Nature never did betray
The heart that loved her; 'tis her privilege,
Through all the years of this our life, to lead
From joy to joy: for she can so inform
The mind that is within us, so impress

With quietness and beauty, and so feed
With lofty thoughts, that neither evil tongues,
Rash judgments, nor the sneers of selfish men,
Nor greetings where no kindness is, nor all
The dreary intercourse of daily life,
Shall e'er prevail against us, or disturb
Our chearful faith that all which we behold
Is full of blessings.

(ll. 123–35)

The last few lines are of particular interest, because whereas Wordsworth maintains a 'chearful faith' not only that God is present in nature, but that His presence means that the natural world is 'full of blessings', Beckett takes a much darker view of man's relationship to nature in *That Time*.

The play opens with the first of Listener's A memories – his memories of travelling from England to Ireland as a middle-aged man in order to visit the folly where he hid as a child. As in 'Tintern Abbey', what is involved here is a return not only to a place visited earlier, but to a scene featuring a ruin. Significantly, in neither the poem nor the play is the ruin described, for what is important in both cases is not the natural setting so much as the human response to it. Wordsworth is drawn back to the countryside by its beauty and by the fact that his memory of it has had in the interim three beneficial effects. A's reasons for wanting to go back to the folly are, by contrast, unclear. However, from the way he describes his return, there can be no doubt about his single-mindedness: 'straight off the ferry and up with the nightbag to the high street neither right nor left not a curse for the old scenes the old names straight up the rise . . . that time you went back that last time to look was the ruin still there where you hid as a child . . .' (228–9).

Wordsworth emphasises in 'Tintern Abbey' that his boyhood enjoyment of nature was straightforward and naive: in two lines he dismisses the 'coarser pleasures of my boyish days, / And their glad animal movements . . .' (74–5) as trivial in comparison with his later response to nature. Listener's childhood experience is more complex, for just as in the period between his two trips to Tintern Abbey, Wordsworth found that revisiting the scene in memory dispelled feelings of loneliness in towns and cities, so as a child Listener goes to the folly to escape his loneliness in the company of adults. Once there, he spends his time poring over picture-books and 'making up talk breaking up two or more talking to himself being together that way where none ever came' (233). Nature clearly has little to do with the child's solution to loneliness, apart from supplying him with a refuge from the adults who come 'out on the roads looking for you' (230), sometimes late at night. As a child Listener finds the pictures in his books more appealing than natural beauty, and derives consolation for his loneliness from imaginary conversations rather than from the memory of scenes he has viewed.

That he finds it difficult in middle age to form and maintain relationships with other people is implied near the start of the play when he tries to recall where he slept the night of his visit: '. . . where did you sleep no friend all the homes gone was it that kip on the front where you no she was with you then still with you then just the one night in any case off the ferry one morning and back on her the next . . .' (229). A finds on his return to Ireland that he has no friends he can stay with, all the houses having been torn down in the areas where they used to live; he spends only one night away from England because he is anxious to return to the unnamed woman who has been living with him there. The woman may be his mother, though *she* appears to have died earlier ('was your mother ah for God's sake . . . gone long ago' (229)). Alternatively, she may be his mistress, or even his sister, for a woman named 'Dolly' – named, perhaps, after Wordsworth's sister Dorothy – is mentioned in the A sections of early drafts of the play.[12] Whoever the woman is, she eventually dies or leaves him, and Listener spends the rest of his life as a solitary.

Having arrived in Ireland, A discovers that the trams that used to run to the folly are gone ('not a wire to be seen only the old rails all rust' (229)), and that the train no longer runs there either ('Doric terminus of the Great Southern and Eastern all closed down and the colonnade crumbling away' (231)). Clearly he has been away for a long time, and although he desperately wants to revisit the folly, it does not occur to him to walk there, as Wordsworth and Dorothy might have done.[13] Instead he sits down on someone's doorstep and begins talking to himself: '. . . there on the step in the pale sun you heard yourself at it again not a curse for the passers pausing to gape at the scandal huddled there in the sun . . . drooling away out loud eyes closed . . . forgetting it all' (233–4). The 'passers pausing to gape' put us in mind of the parable of the Good Samaritan, though in the play, no one stops to help.[14] Listener is reminiscent, too, of Wordsworth's old Cumberland beggar, particularly when he pictures himself 'tottering and muttering all over the parish' (231–2). In 'The Old Cumberland Beggar', Wordsworth shows how the beggar's misfortunes prompt members of the community to acts of charity that ensure his continued wellbeing. Wordsworth says in the poem that a 'benignant law of heaven'[15] is responsible for preserving the beggar, the implication being that the people who look after him are, in effect, agents of Providence. In *That Time*, by contrast, it is implied that God either does not exist, or if He does, is indifferent to the sufferings of His creatures.

A sits on the doorstep talking to himself rather than get up and ask someone whether, apart from tram or train, there is another way to get to the folly, for he has resolved at some earlier time not to utter 'another word to the living as long as [he] lived' (231). His trip to Ireland has been a failure: not only has he been unable to visit the ruin where he hid as a child, he has been denied the possibility of gaining a firmer grip on his identity by revisiting an important childhood scene. His sense of who he is and was slips away from him, and he finds himself 'making it all up on the doorstep as you went along making yourself all up again for the millionth time' (234). For Wordsworth, just remembering the scene surrounding Tintern Abbey is enough to lighten 'the burthen of the mystery, / . . . Of all this unintelligible world' (ll. 39–41). For A, by contrast, nothing short of a visit is necessary to help him fathom the mystery of his unintelligible identity. Frustrated by his inability to return to the ruin, he falls back on the expedient of manufacturing a fictional version of himself 'for the millionth time'.

The other benefits that accrue to Wordsworth from remembering the scene are also denied A. A's memory of Foley's folly has done nothing to dispel his loneliness or to help him form lasting relationships with other people. Nor has it evoked feelings of 'unremembered pleasure' associated, as in 'Tintern Abbey', with 'little, nameless, unremembered acts / Of kindness and of love' (ll. 32; 35–6). Such feelings arise not in A – Listener in middle age – but in B, Listener as a youth.

In the B memories, Listener pictures himself either standing, sitting or lying next to an unnamed girl, exchanging vows of love. Before them as they sit is a beautiful autumnal scene, consisting of a 'little wood and as far as eye could see the wheat turning yellow'

(228). The scene is the 'one thing could ever bring tears till they dried up altogether that thought when it came up among the others floated up that scene' (229), and Listener is careful to stress that it often 'floated up' involuntarily, displacing 'whatever thoughts you might be having whatever scenes' (230). Because the scene presents itself to his memory spontaneously, rather than by way of a conscious act of recollection, it may be said to be a source of 'unremembered pleasure' – though whether the pleasure arises from the scene's beauty or from the vows of love is not immediately clear. Late in the play, Listener confesses that both the girl and the vows are fictions, not memories, but says that they come so clearly to mind that he finds it 'hard to believe you even you made [them] up . . .' (234). The delight that accrues from the scene is thus 'unremembered' in the sense of being invented, as well as in the sense of being subsequently involuntary. When B admits that he viewed the beautiful autumnal scene and the two others by himself, it becomes clear that at least some of the pleasure he associates with youth arises from his enjoyment of nature.

His invented relationship with the unnamed girl is an odd one. Whether standing, sitting or lying, the two keep a deliberate distance between them, and are careful not to touch. While with her, B has

> no sight of the face or any other part never turned to her nor she to you always parallel like on an axle-tree never turned to each other just blurs on the fringes of the field no touching or anything of that nature always space between if only an inch no pawing in the manner of flesh and blood no better than shades . . . (231).

B and the girl are mere blurs on the fringes of each other's perceptual field, and by virtue of their commitment to a non-physical relationship, are no better than 'shades' – no better than the souls of the departed in Dante's *Divine Comedy*. They might be brother and sister, but for their vows of love; yet it is clear from their inattention to each other than B is unable to claim, as Wordsworth does of Dorothy, that he can see an earlier version of himself in the girl.

[A]lways parallel like on an axle-tree', they are joined by the bond of mortality – a bond implicit in the axle-tree image, which appears to derive from Eliot's 'Burnt Norton':

Garlic and sapphires in the mud
Clot the bedded axle-tree
The trilling wire in the blood
Sings below inveterate scars
Appeasing long forgotten wars.[16]

The 'trilling wire' of life sings in the blood of B and the unnamed girl as they stand together on a towpath in another of the memories; a dead rat floating past them from upstream is a reminder, however, that eventually they will die. We are not surprised when Listener admits that the story of his love for the girl is one he made up 'to keep the void out just another of those old tales to keep the void from pouring in on top of you the shroud' (230). Listener is much preoccupied with the inevitability of death, and finds his narrative a convenient means of keeping morbid thoughts at bay.

Two of the B memories are of Listener alone in the dark, 'harking to the owl' (230), then hooting to it, but failing to get it to hoot in return. These memories are again intimations of mortality, for they are clearly based on the famous passage in Book Five of *The Prelude* where Wordsworth tells of a boy who took pleasure in hooting at the owls at night, and who died before his time.[17] Beckett departs from Wordsworth in the second of the two memories when Listener recalls the time an owl flew 'to hoot at someone else or back with a shrew to its hollow tree' (234). Nevertheless, the shrew is another reminder of death, and B follows his mention of it with the comment that he gave up hooting at the owls, 'gave up for good and let it in . . . a great shroud billowing in all over you . . .' (234). Here he accepts his own mortality with an attitude of helpless resignation.

The B memories provide Listener with 'unremembered pleasure' in the form of both invented and involuntary pleasure, and because they are based partly on his enjoyment of natural beauty, they may be said to be consistent with Wordsworth's delight in nature in 'Tintern Abbey'. On the other hand, the autumnal scene B lingers on, with 'the wheat turning yellow' (228, 230), does nothing to lighten 'the burthen of the mystery/. . . Of all this unintelligible world' (ll 39–41), for it is a reminder of mortality (the wheat will soon be harvested, with winter to follow) rather than a source of comfort. Death for Listener is associated with 'the void'. He does not share Wordsworth's 'chearful faith that all which we behold/Is full of blessings' (ll. 134–5), blessings sufficient to allay his feelings of loneliness: these persist in spite of the beauty of the scenes he describes, and impel him, as in the A memories, to invent imaginary conversations in the absence of remembered real ones.

Listener's youthful view of nature resembles Wordsworth's in that it is emotional and essentially self-absorbed. But whereas in maturity Wordsworth exchanges self-absorption for a new awareness of the 'still, sad music of humanity' (l. 92), Listener remains preoccupied with himself both in middle age, when he tries to return to the folly, and in old age, as he approaches death. In maturity, Wordsworth develops a sense of God's omnipresence in nature, and comes to regard nature as 'The guide, the guardian of my heart, and soul/Of all my moral being' (ll. 111–12). By contrast, Listener makes no mention of God as he grows older, and in old age – as C – finds that nature is best avoided.

The C memories are all of city scenes in winter, and are almost all related to C's need to find shelter from the rain and cold. Evidently he has become a homeless old tramp – an even clearer counterpart to Wordsworth's old Cumberland beggar in old age than earlier. He has found that the Portrait Gallery, the Post Office and the Library are all suitable places to shelter, since admission to them is free, but he enters them with some trepidation, fearing that he may be asked to leave. Once indoors, he sits with his own 'arms round [him] whose else hugging [himself] for a bit of warmth' (229); for years he has been living entirely on his own. There are various hints that he is soon to die, one of the clearest being his experience of examining a portrait one day of 'some famous man or woman or even child . . . behind the glass where gradually as you peered trying to make it out gradually of all things a face appeared had you swivel on the slab to see who it was there at your elbow' (229). The face may be his own, which, reflected in the glass, has suddenly joined the faces of those long dead; or it may be the face of death itself, the same that threatens Krapp in *Krapp's Last Tape*.[18]

C says that he was never the same after this experience, adding however, 'but the same as what for God's sake did you ever say I to yourself in your life come on now (*Eyes close.*) . . . always having turning-points and never but the one the first and last that time curled up worm in slime when they lugged you out and wiped you off . . .' (230). James Knowlson has suggested that the image of the worm in slime is a reference to birth,[19] in which case it would seem that Listener has spent a lifetime grappling with the problem of defining his own identity. Another possibility, though, is that Beckett is raising the more general question of human identity by echoing Job 25.4–6: 'How . . . can man be justified with God? or how can he be clean that is born of a woman? Behold even to the moon, and it shineth not; yea, the stars are not pure in his sight. How much less man, that is a worm? and the son of man, which is a worm?' If Job is a source for the worm image, Beckett is probably implying that if there is a God, He takes such a dim view of man as to deny him satisfactory solutions to the problems of identity and death. Such a God would be the antithesis of the God of 'Tintern Abbey', who is all too willing to furnish man with a sense of His caring presence.

Where Wordsworth finds that in maturity, he is led to a sense of God's existence and immanence in nature, and from there to the conviction that nature may be regarded as a 'nurse', 'guide' and 'guardian of [his] heart' (ll. 110–11), Listener's experience is that every man must find his own way in life, independently of God and nature. In old age he approaches the problems of identity and death with three possible solutions of his own devising. The first of these is to behave as though he were a complete stranger to himself, 'trying how that would work for a change not knowing who you were from Adam no notion who it was saying what you were saying whose skull you were clapped up in whose moan had you the way you were . . .' (231). In this connection, he recalls once again the time he was 'alone with the portraits of the dead . . . not believing it could be you till they put you out in the rain at closing-time' (231). Pretending to be completely detached from himself keeps the questions of identity and death temporarily at bay, but when he finally accepts that the intimation of mortality experienced at the Portrait Gallery is of his own mortality, it becomes clear to Listener that his first solution will not do.

His second solution is to behave as though he has never existed, trying 'how it would work that way for a change never having been how never having been would work . . . tottering and muttering all over the parish till the words dried up and the head dried up and the legs dried up whosever they were or it gave up whoever it was' (231–2). This solution is no more satisfactory than the first, for Listener finds it impossible to deny the fact of his own existence when, whether or not he walks and speaks, he is all too obviously alive. Thus his third solution is to accept the fact that he exists and to assume that, despite his anxiety over the questions of death and identity, he is better off than other people. He enters the Post Office one winter's day, full of self-congratulation that 'bad and all as you were you were not as they till it dawned that for all the loathing you were getting you might as well not have been there at all the eyes passing over you and through you like so much thin air . . .' (234). What brings him up short is the realisation that other people are wholly indifferent to his presence and continuing existence.

Here his situation differs radically from Wordsworth's in 'Tintern Abbey', for whereas Listener must live with a haunting awareness of his own solitude, Wordsworth has a source of comfort in the company of his sister Dorothy.

> For thou art with me, here upon the banks
> Of this fair river; thou, my dearest Friend,
> My dear, dear Friend, and in thy voice I catch
> The language of my former heart, and read
> My former pleasures in the shooting lights
> Of thy wild eyes (ll. 116–20).

The phrase 'For thou art with me' is of course an echo of the twenty-third Psalm, and suggests that Dorothy is, in effect, an agent of Providence. For Dorothy supplies the poet not only with the reassurance that his experience of nature is shared by someone else, but with the further implicit assurance that God exists and provides the companionship of fellow man as a balm to the indifference or unpleasantness of strangers, and to our fear of the 'valley of the shadow of death'.

In contrast to Wordsworth, Listener must face death alone: there is nothing in 'Tintern Abbey' as chilling as his final intimation of mortality. This occurs one day when he enters the Public Library to shelter from the winter rain. He sits down and drifts off to sleep; when he opens his eyes, he sees 'from floor to ceiling nothing only dust and not a sound only what was it is said come and gone come and gone . . . come and gone in no time come and gone in no time' (235). As various critics have observed, this passage is an echo of Genesis 3.19 – '. . . dust thou art, and unto dust shalt thou return' – and conveys not only that Listener's life is nearly ended, but that life in general comes and goes 'in no time' relative to eternity.

Listener ends the play with an enigmatic smile. 'Is it', asks James Knowlson, '. . . a smile of satisfaction at the restoration of . . . old times? A smile of relief and contentment that at last the torment is nearly over? A wry reflection on the insignificance of the individual human existence in the context of infinity? Or a smile indicating that even capitulation to the void can still be endured with serene acceptance?'[20] Surely the smile is all these things and more. In the light, however, of Beckett's 'shape of ideas' approach to dramatic structure – his use of 'Tintern Abbey' as a point of departure for the structuring of *That Time* – it is certain that the smile does not arise from a Wordsworthian sense that God is good and can be relied upon to confer meaning and value on life. Beckett's post-Romantic variation on 'Tintern Abbey' promotes a much darker view altogether.

II

Beckett has said that his next play, *Footfalls*, arose from an image that came to mind of a figure pacing up and down, and it may be, as Deirdre Bair has suggested, that the figure was biographical in origin.[21] Bair points out that, like the play's main character May, Beckett's mother May Beckett was in the habit of pacing the house at night when she had difficulty sleeping; she had some of the carpets removed because, again like the character, it was important to her to hear the sound of her own footsteps. *Footfalls*, says Beckett's biographer, 'seems to be primarily one version of May Beckett's insomnia'.[22]

It would be a mistake, however, to identify May too closely with May Beckett. Beckett's mother married at thirty; *Footfalls'* May, in her forties, is a single woman who has remained at home to look after her invalid mother. Moreover, as Enoch Brater has observed, May seems to be based not only on May Beckett but also on Dickens' Miss Havisham and Shakespeare's Lady Macbeth.[23] Like Miss Havisham, who has not been out of the house since the day her fiancé jilted her, *Footfalls'* May has not been out of the house 'since girlhood' (241); like Lady Macbeth, she paces the floor at night, troubled by past events.

The play's title may also be partly literary and partly biographical in origin. Though it may derive from Beckett's memories of his mother's footfalls, another possibility is that it is taken from some famous lines in 'Burnt Norton', the first of Eliot's *Four Quartets*:

> What might have been is an abstraction
> Remaining a perpetual possibility
> Only in a world of speculation.
> . . .

> Footfalls echo in the memory
> Down the passage which we did not take
> Towards the door we never opened
> Into the rose-garden (ll. 6–14).[24]

Like *Four Quartets*, *Footfalls* is divided into four parts, though in accordance with Beckett's 'shape of ideas' approach to drama, neither the parts nor the whole endorses Eliot's Christian outlook. Beckett's use of 'Tintern Abbey' as a source for *That Time* invites point-by-point comparison between the play and the poem. By contrast, the four-part structure of *Footfalls* is merely a nod in the direction of Eliot: Beckett's interest in this play is in developing the dramatic potential of the lines quoted above, rather than in writing a variation on 'Burnt Norton' or on *Four Quartets* as a whole.

The first part introduces May, who is seen pacing back and forth across the stage – nine steps in each direction[25] – while holding a conversation with her mother. Her mother never appears in her own person; throughout, she is a disembodied voice from upstage, the voice of an old woman nearing death. From their conversation it emerges that May has arisen from bed to brood on the past. Her footfalls take her down passages of memory and imagination; as she walks, she reflects on 'how it was' (241) and, by extension, on '[w]hat might have been'. The fact that May has not ventured outside for many years means that she has denied herself the pleasure not only of any actual rose-garden, but of various figurative rose-gardens as well. Eliot's comment to an interviewer that 'Burnt Norton' was based partly on a passage at the beginning of *Alice in Wonderland*, where Alice is unable to get through a door into a flower garden,[26] suggests that May is preoccupied with what her childhood might have been like in different circumstances. Critics of Eliot agree, however, that the rose-garden in 'Burnt Norton' is open to a number of symbolic interpretations, and since the rose is a traditional symbol of romantic love, May is perhaps also dwelling on lost opportunities for romance.

The first part of the play draws us into a 'world of speculation' in the sense that it presents May speculating on what might have been; and in the sense, too, that it invites us to speculate on what is troubling her. Yet it is an essentially naturalistic world, a world of solid objects and familiar physical needs:

M[ay]: Would you like me to inject you again?

V[oice]: Yes, but it is too soon. . . .
M: Straighten your pillows? [*Pause.*] Change your drawsheet?
        [*Pause.*] Pass you the bedpan? [*Pause.*] The warming-pan?
        [*Pause.*] Dress your sores? [*Pause.*] Sponge you down?
        [*Pause.*] Moisten your poor lips? [*Pause.*] Pray with you?
        [*Pause.*] For you? [*Pause.*] Again. [*Pause.*]
V: Yes, but it is too soon (240).

Though she never appears on stage, May's mother is no less a flesh-and-blood character in the first part of the play than May herself: she is defined as such by the fact that she is an invalid who requires attention at fixed times.

As the first part of the play ends, the light dims; when the second part begins, the lighting is a 'little less' bright than before (240). This change of lighting is more important than it might at first seem, for it is Beckett's way of hinting that the second part of *Footfalls* presents us with a slightly different world from that of the first. As before, it is a 'world of speculation'; but now we are being asked to consider the possibility that May's mother has died and come back as a ghost to observe her daughter's continued pacing. 'I walk here now', says the mother. 'Rather I come and stand. [*Pause.*] At nightfall. [*Pause.*] [May] fancies she is alone' (241).[27]

May is silent throughout the second part of the play,[28] but opens the third, which is cast in an even dimmer light, as follows:

> Sequel. A little later, when she was quite forgotten, she began to –
> [*Pause.*] A little later, when as though she had never been, it had
> never been, she began to walk. [*Pause.*] At nightfall. [*Pause.*] Slip
> out at nightfall and into the little church by the north door, always
> locked at that hour, and walk, up and down, up and down, his
> poor arm. [*Pause.*] . . . No sound. [*Pause.*] None at least to be
> heard. [*Pause.*] . . . A tangle of tatters. [*Pause.*] Watch it pass –
> [*Pause.*] – watch her pass before the candelabrum . . . like moon
> through passing rack' (242).

The 'tangle of tatters' that makes its way through the locked door of the church and walks up and down the north transept – the part corresponding to one of Christ's arms on the Cross – is clearly a ghost, though whether it is May's ghost or her mother's is open to speculation. May's use of the word 'Sequel' at the start of the passage tells us only that the ghost begins to appear after her mother's death; Beckett has said, however, that the word is a pun on 'seek well'.[29] If it is her mother's ghost she is describing, it would seem that May pictures her as a restless spirit seeking to discover something that was hidden from her during her lifetime. Earlier in the play, her mother is anxious about May's obsessive nocturnal pacing and her longstanding refusal to go outdoors. The fact that the ghost appears in church suggests that it *is* the departed mother's, seeking a religious explanation for May's psychological malaise – an explanation, perhaps, as to how a benevolent God could have allowed May to suffer.

On the other hand, the ghost May describes may well be her own. Like May, it resembles Lady Macbeth in that it is given to pacing at night; it also resembles some of Pip's Gothic visions of Miss Havisham in *Great Expectations*.[30] If the ghost is May's, it could (as before) be seeking answers to questions about God's benevolence – about His part in her psychological problems, for example, and in the loss of her mother. Alternatively, the ghost may represent a wish fulfilment on May's part, since, unlike May, who has not left the house for years, it is clearly free to come and go as it pleases.

During rehearsals of the German premiere of *Footfalls*, Beckett revealed that May is to be understood in relation to a case history Jung described in a lecture he (Beckett) attended in 1935.[31] Jung spoke of 'a little girl of ten who had some most amazing mythological dreams. Her father consulted me about these dreams. I could not tell him what I thought because they contained an uncanny prognosis. The little girl died a year later of an infectious disease. She had never been born entirely'.[32] Earlier in the lecture, Jung made the point that young children have an awareness of mythological elements in their minds that suggests to them the idea of a former existence. This must be cast off as they grow older, for if it is not, they will experience a yearning to return to their former state – that is, a yearning to die. In Jung's view, the ghosts that appear in dreams or fantasies are mythological images.[33] Thus, if the ghost May fantasises about is her own, and if it indeed represents a wish fulfilment, it would appear that what May desires is her own death.

It would also seem that she is trying to compensate for 'never [having] been born entirely' by giving birth to an alternative version of herself in the story she tells near the end of the play. This concerns a young woman named Amy (an anagram of 'May') and her mother, Mrs Winter, whose name is suggestive of approaching death. May

records a conversation in which Amy insists that she was not
present earlier at Vespers, and her mother insists that she was. 'Mrs
W: But I heard you respond. [*Pause.*] I heard you say Amen. [*Pause.*]
How could you have responded if you were not there? . . . The love
of God, and the fellowship of the Holy Ghost, be with us all, now,
and for evermore. Amen. [*Pause.*] I heard you distinctly' (243). Since
May has told us earlier that the ghost appears 'at certain seasons of
the year, during Vespers' (242), the implication is that it is the
ghost's voice Mrs Winter hears.

Significantly, May's story not only gives birth to a character like
herself, but, through its inclusion of the words of the Vespers
blessing, raises once again the question of the love of God. Eliot
speaks of 'Footfalls echo[ing] in the memory / Down the passage
that we did not take'; May explores a passage that she did not take in
her story of Amy, whose absence from Church suggests that she is
doubtful about God's existence. May's offer to pray with her mother
in the first part of the play suggests that she (May) is a Christian – a
Christian who has spent her life venturing down passages within
herself in search of a religious experience she has never had. For if
the rose-garden is, as Derek Traversi has argued, a symbol of the
vision of the Divine Reality deriving from Eliot's interest in Dante,[34]
it would appear that May has been trying to achieve the mystic's
inner experience of God. In contrast, however, to Eliot's rose-
garden and Dante's Paradise, which are both flooded with light, the
world of *Footfalls* is a twilight world, and its fourth part, the final
tableau, is even more dimly lit than the three parts preceding it.
Since May's onstage pacing corresponds to her explorations within,
the dimming of the lights suggests that her quest for spiritual light
has been in vain.

More generally, the final tableau casts doubt on God's existence
and benevolence to man. If there is a God, Beckett seems to be
asking, why has he denied May the inner light she has sought? Why
does He allow the protracted suffering of individuals like May's
invalid mother and the people like May who look after them? Why
was it necessary for His only begotten Son to die a lingering death on
the Cross? As in other plays which embody his 'shape of ideas'
approach, Beckett hints at two cynical possibilities: either there is no
God, in which case disappointment and suffering are simply
inescapable facts of life; or God exists and is inexplicably cruel to His
creatures.[35]

Notes

1. Harold Hobson, 'Samuel Beckett: Dramatist of the Year', *International Theatre Annual*, No. 1 (London: John Calder, 1956) 153.
2. James Knowlson and John Pilling, *Frescoes of the Skull: the Later Prose and Drama of Samuel Beckett* (London: John Calder, 1979) p. 213. Hereafter cited as *Frescoes*.
3. 'Proust', in Samuel Beckett, *Proust/Three Dialogues with Georges Duthuit* (London: John Calder, 1965) p. 12. Here Beckett is quoting from *A la recherche du temps perdu* (Paris: Gallimard, 1954) III, 1048.
4. 'Proust', pp. 13–14.
5. See Walter D. Asmus, 'Rehearsal Notes for the German Premiere of Beckett's *That Time* and *Footfalls* at the Schiller-Theater Werkstatt, Berlin (directed by Beckett)', tr. Helen Watanabe, *Journal of Beckett Studies*, 2 (Summer 1977) 92.
6. See Samuel Beckett, *Cette fois* (Paris: Minuit, 1978).
7. *That Time*, in Samuel Beckett, *Collected Shorter Plays* (London: Faber & Faber, 1984) p. 228. All quotations from *That Time* and *Footfalls* are from this edition; page numbers are given in the text. Our sense that Listener is on his deathbed is strengthened by an examination of the play's manuscripts. As James Knowlson points out (in *Frescoes*, p. 206), up to the fifth typescript, Listener is described as having his head framed by a pillow.
8. S. E. Gontarski, ' "Making Yourself All Up Again": the Composition of Samuel Beckett's *That Time*', *Modern Drama*, 23 (June 1980) 116. For a fuller discussion of the play's triads, see Antoni Libera, 'Structure and Pattern in *That Time*', tr. Aniela Korzeniowska, *Journal of Beckett Studies*, 6 (Autumn 1980) 81–9.
9. Gontarski discusses the evolution of this grouping in the article just cited. In *A Student's Guide to the Plays of Samuel Beckett* (London: Faber & Faber, 1978) p. 203, Beryl Fletcher *et al.* comment that in his grouping of the three memories, 'Beckett does not appear to have any particular kind of sequence (such as bell-ringing) in mind. His own comment to the authors was that the control is stylistic through the technique of association; he wished, he said, to make each passage verbally interesting and to provide it with some associative connection with the next'.
10. Beckett's interest in 'Tintern Abbey' is evident as early as *Watt*, written in the early forties. (See *Watt* (London: John Calder, 1970) p. 98, where Beckett speaks of 'little acts of kindness and of love', echoing ll. 35–6 of Wordsworth's poem). In *The Development of Samuel Beckett's Fiction* (Urbana and Chicago: University of Illinois Press, 1984) p. 221, Rubin Rabinovitz identifies some allusions to other Wordsworth poems in *Murphy*, Beckett's novel of the early thirties.
11. William Wordsworth, 'Lines Written a Few Miles above Tintern Abbey', in Wordsworth, William and Samuel Taylor Coleridge, *Lyrical Ballads* (London: Methuen, 1963) p. 116. All quotations from the poem are from this edition; line numbers are given in the text.
12. Gontarski, 114.

13. In *William Wordsworth: the Early Years, 1770–1803* (London: Oxford University Press, 1957), p. 402, Mary Moorman observes that on the tour which included Tintern Abbey in 1798, Wordsworth and Dorothy walked over fifty miles in three days.

14. See St Luke 10.30–7. Asmus, 93, says that at a rehearsal of the German premiere of *That Time*, Beckett cited the Bible as his source for the passage beginning 'the passers pausing to gape . . .'. He was unable to remember more exactly where it was from, but agreed with Klaus Herm, the actor playing Listener, that it could have been from St Luke.

15. 'The Old Cumberland Beggar', l. 160, in *Lyrical Ballads*, p. 210 (see note 11 for edition).

16. 'Burnt Norton', ll. 47–51, in T. S. Eliot, *Four Quartets* (London: Faber & Faber, 1959) p. 15. All quotations from 'Burnt Norton' are from this edition; line numbers are given in the text.

17. William Wordsworth, *The Prelude: a Parallel Text*, ed. J. C. Maxwell (Harmondsworth: Penguin, 1971) Book V, ll. 389–42 (1805 version); ll. 364–97 (1850 version) pp. 188–91. An earlier version of this passage appeared in the 1800 edition of *Lyrical Ballads*; this may be where Beckett first encountered it.

18. Jean Martin, the actor who played Krapp in a 1970 production of *Krapp's Last Tape* directed by Beckett, has said that 'Sam insisted very often on a presence in the darkness, a continual presence, of someone who attracts Krapp's attention, of someone who makes him turn his head to the left at certain moments, slowly. Once Sam went so far as to say – I am sure I remember this correctly: "it is death who is waiting for him there" '. (James Knowlson, 'An Interview with Jean Martin', in *Theatre Workbook 1: Samuel Beckett, Krapp's Last Tape* (London: Brutus Books, 1980) p. 82.

19. *Frescoes*, p. 213.

20. *Frescoes*, p. 210.

21. Deirdre Bair, *Samuel Beckett: a Biography* (London: Jonathan Cape, 1978) p. 10. See also Asmus, 83.

22. Bair, p. 636.

23. See Enoch Brater, 'Fragment and Beckett's Form in *That Time* and *Footfalls*', *Journal of Beckett Studies*, 2 (Summer 1977) 80.

24. Beckett's interest in Eliot dates back to at least 1934, the year he published 'Recent Irish Poetry', an essay in which he praises *The Waste Land*. See 'Recent Irish Poetry', reprinted in Samuel Beckett, *Disjecta: Miscellaneous Writings and a Dramatic Fragment*, ed. Ruby Cohn (London: John Calder, 1984) p. 70.

25. In *Frescoes*, p. 236, n. 42, James Knowlson observes that in '*Footfalls*, London, Faber & Faber, 1976, May paces seven steps across the stage, but this was corrected in the Royal Court performance to nine steps, to give greater width. In *Ends and Odds*, London, Faber & Faber, 1977, the text is amended to nine, although an error has crept in on p. 33, where the steps are mistakenly left as seven. In the French premiere of *Pas* . . . at the Théatre d'Orsay (11 Apr. 1978) nine steps were also adopted.'

26. See Helen Gardner, *The Composition of Four Quartets* (London: Faber & Faber, 1978) p. 39.

27. In *Frescoes*, p. 224, James Knowlson comments that the first scene in the play is 'clearly that of a "dying mother" and is referred to as such by Beckett in a manuscript note'.

28. In *A Student's Guide to the Plays of Samuel Beckett*, p. 209, Beryl Fletcher *et al.* comment that 'V's words are not heard by M, who in the Berlin production (which Beckett directed after the London one) muttered to herself to make the point clear to the spectator.'

29. See Asmus, 85.

30. Cf. Charles Dickens, *Great Expectations* (Harmondsworth: Penguin, 1968) pp. 93, 321, 325 and 413.

31. Asmus, 83. Bair, pp. 208–10, provides an account of Beckett's attendance at the lecture, which impressed him deeply.

32. C. G. Jung, 'The Tavistock Lectures', in *The Symbolic Life: Miscellaneous Writings*, tr. R.F.C. Hull (London: Routledge & Kegan Paul, 1977) Lecture 3, p. 96.

33. See 'On the Nature of the Psyche', in C. G. Jung, *The Structure and Dynamics of the Psyche* (London: Routledge & Kegan Paul, 1960) pp. 205–6.

34. See Derek Traversi, *T. S. Eliot: the Longer Poems* (London: Bodley Head, 1976) p. 99.

35. I should like to thank Professor Melvin J. Friedman of the University of Wisconsin-Milwaukee and Dr Howard McNaughton of the University of Canterbury for their thoughtful readings of a draft of this essay.

9

Texts for *Company*

Kateryna Arthur

The same old stories. . . . Yes, to the end, always muttering, to
lull me and keep me company.

(Texts for Nothing)[1]

He speaks of himself as of another. Himself he devises too for
company. Leave it at that. Confusion too is company up to a
point.

(Company)[2]

Beckett's novella *Company* exhibits more strikingly than any other of
his later works a double impulse – towards order and coherence on
the one hand and towards chaos and indeterminacy on the other.
Associated with these poles are other antithetical positions between
which the work moves. Whereas *Texts for Nothing*, written two and a
half decades earlier and exploring many of the same problems as
Company, could be said to have adopted confusion as its governing
principle, *Company* is governed by division and rupture.

Although doubleness and multiplicity have been features of
Beckett's work from the beginning, *Company* is unusual in the
explicitness with which the opposing or contradictory drives are
presented in its structure as well as in its themes. The suppression of
the subjective 'I' which is everywhere implied in *Company*, its
dispersal into the second- and third-person narratives, is the most
immediately visible structural evidence of the deeply and variously
divided nature of this work. The 'company' that the work speaks of
is the accumulation of self-generated constructions in the form of
inventions and memories which inhabit the world of the
imagination and which, for a writer, provide the material (the
Yeatsian 'rag and bone') for the world of his works. But what
companionship can these fragments offer and what relationship do
they bear to the writer? Is he their creator or do they create him?
These are some of the questions that *Company* asks. Avoiding simple

answers and single positions, *Company* takes up various attitudes provisionally and experimentally and, unlike many other of Beckett's works that explore problems of the speaking subject and of writing generally (notably *The Unnamable* and *Texts for Nothing*), *Company* does not generate a sense of despair or futility. Although it is schismatic to the point of schizophrenia, it is creatively and constructively so.

The term 'schizophrenia', used in a nonempirical way and without any clinical implications, is peculiarly appropriate for *Company*. It is adopted as the basis of a theory of analysis and interpretation by Gilles Deleuze and Felix Guattari in their book *Anti-Oedipus*.[3] Their theory, which I can only briefly outline here, provides a useful interpretative framework for the reading of *Company* and also, more generally, for reading Beckett. There is much in the Deleuze/Guattari approach that is in harmony with Beckett. While Beckett is quoted as having said 'I'm working with impotence, ignorance. I don't think impotence has been exploited in the past',[4] Deleuze and Guattari in a similar spirit claim: 'We are still too competent. We would like to speak in the name of absolute incompetence.'[5] The theorists and Beckett both align themselves against closure, smoothness of form and unification of meaning.

They give primacy to *process* rather than to completed events and they recognise process (in this context the process by which language yields interpretations) as chaotic and broken. 'For literature', write Deleuze and Guattari, 'is like schizophrenia; a process and not a goal, a production and not an expression', and they argue for an understanding of language as 'no longer defined by what it says, even less by what makes it a signifying thing, but by what causes it to move, to flow and to explode – desire.'[6] *Company*, a work which is driven by clusters of conflicting desires, is, in their terms, a schizophrenic text. It exemplifies and illuminates their theory.

The anti-Freudian approach that Deleuze and Guattari advocate has its roots in an anti-fascist vision. In proposing 'schizoanalysis' to replace Freudian analysis, they offer the freewheeling schizophrenic consciousness as a model for a politics and an interpretative approach that are goal-free and undirectional. As Michel Foucault explains in his preface to their book, Deleuze and Guattari's politics is

a radical politics of desire freed from all beliefs. Such a politics dissolves the mystifications of power through the kindling, on all levels, of anti-Oedipal forces . . . that escape coding, scramble the codes and flee in all directions: orphans (no daddy-mommy-me), atheists (no beliefs) and nomads (no habits, no territories).[7]

It is striking how well this description of schizoanalysis accommodates Beckett's writing practice in general and also how closely the metaphors used for the anti-Oedipal forces describe his typical characters.

Company, by virtue of its explicitly schismatic construction, is a special case of schizophrenic writing or of what might be called 'scripsophrenia'. It is unusual (though by no means unique in Beckett's oeuvre) in that it sets up a very orderly and well-defined structure from which to present a vision of unstructuredness and indeterminacy. The earlier work to which *Company* is related in many ways – *Texts for Nothing* – adopts a much looser structure. The comparison allows us to see how the incongruence between form and content in *Company* brings to the foreground its contradictory and fractured nature, so strengthening the barriers against interpretative procedures that might seek to unify or homogenise it.

At the centre of Deleuze and Guattari's theory is the idea that the will to unification or totalisation, whether in analysis or in writing, tends towards unproductive closure and needs to be resisted. Hence their concept of disruptive driving impulses called 'desiring machines' which work not by linear movement towards a known goal but in fits and starts, taking no predetermined course:

In describing machines everything functions at the same time, but amid hiatuses and ruptures, break-downs and failures, stallings and short-circuits, distances and fragmentations within a sum that never succeeds in bringing its various parts together so as to form a whole. That is because the breaks in the process are productive. . . . Desiring production is pure multiplicity, that is to say, an affirmation that is irreducible to any sort of unity.[8]

In their individual ways *Company* and *Texts for Nothing* both correspond closely to the terms of this description. Putting aside the question of affirmation for the moment, *Texts* appears to offer the closer correspondence. Here, for example, is a piece from Text XI:

[W]hen comes the hour of those who knew me, it's as though I were among them . . . watching me approach, then watching me recede, shaking my head and saying, Is it really he, can it possibly be he, then moving on in their company along a road that is not mine and with every step takes me further from that other not mine either, or remaining alone where I am, between two parting dreams . . . (110).

The inability clearly to define and locate the speaking subject, the fragmentation of self, the sense of separation from self and others and the general confusion about place and identity are all recognisably schizoid features of the narrative as are, in other parts of *Texts*, the sudden shifts in point of view, grammatical dislocations, disruptions of time and space. But, in a less overt way, *Company* is at least schizophrenic. Beginning with the clear statement, 'A voice comes to one in the dark' (7), the narrator explains and elaborates: 'That then is the proposition. To one on his back in the dark a voice tells of a past' (7–8). The narrator describes, with painstaking care, not only the relationship between the supine figure and the voice, but also the grammatical patterning of the work with its explicit prohibition of the first-person pronoun:

Use of the second person marks the voice. That of the third that cankerous other. Could he speak to and of whom the voice speaks there would be a first. But he cannot. He shall not. You cannot. You shall not. (9)

The precise scene-setting appears, at least superficially, to be the antithesis of the scene-dissolving that occurs in the extract from Text XI, but far from establishing certainty, it wittily generates confusion about the relationship of the 'you' and the 'he' to the reader, the narrator, the author and to the third (infinitely multipliable) possible 'other' to whom the narrative periodically alludes: 'May not there be another with him in the dark to and of whom the voice is speaking?' (9–10).

The narrative, with fluctuating degrees of irony and self-parody, generates indeterminacy at the same time as it appears to fix its fictional participants into a rigid frame, and while adopting the tones and postures of omniscience, it comically questions the convention of the omniscient narrator. Further, by carrying to extremes the judicious 'objectivity' of its reporting, it mocks the task that it is engaged in and, once again, questions the convention.

It can be argued, then, that *Company* is a more subversively schizophrenic text than *Texts for Nothing* or *The Unnamable*, which consistently admit to and dramatise their confusion, ignorance and failure. *Company*, by contrast, adopts voices and structures that suggest order and clarity without ever actually providing them. There are two main ways in which structural order and clarity of communication are undermined in *Company*. One is by direct and carefully reasoned questioning of its own logic, of the kind that occurs early in the work when doubt is cast on the number of listeners there might be:

> If the voice is not speaking to him it must be speaking to another. So with what reason remains he reasons. To another of that other. Or of him. Or of another still. To another of that other or of him or of another still. To one on his back in the dark in any case. Of one on his back in the dark whether the same or another (13–14).

The effect of this kind of 'reason-ridden' speculation is to draw attention to the general literary question of *whom* texts address. Readers as well as the multitudes of supine listeners conjured by the writing are drawn into the wide circle of speculation. In the process of being infinitely multiplied, the 'one on his back' loses any tenuous identity he may have been gathering. The reader is forbidden identification of any kind as the 'one' loses its unitariness and the single focus of traditional third-person narrative on a specific 'he' or 'she' is splintered. The effect of this is to keep the reader's attention wary and mobile, forcing it away from any central focus, enabling it to move freely from the worlds of the work to the worlds of reading and writing.

The second way in which the text subverts its own coherence is by the strategy of splitting the narrative into the apparently orderly arrangement of alternating segments of third-person commentary directed at the reader and second-person description directed at the listener (with some minor further shifts within these segments).

While this gives to *Company* a much more neatly symmetrical shape than that of *Texts*, which appear to have been organised more by chain of association and the panic of the moment than by a predetermined formula, the ultimate effect of the dividing of the narrative in this self-conscious way is to reveal the splits, chasms and lacunae that exist *everywhere* in narrative. Manipulation of point of view becomes a subject of the writing as well as being an element of its own practice. In *Texts* the voice is continuously compelling. However much it speaks of fractured identity and dissolution of purpose, the voice induces the reader to follow it along its tortuous ways. In *Company* the double narrative prevents that kind of following by forcing attention repeatedly upon the divisions themselves and so upon the process of narration, especially upon the arbitrariness of its organisation. The elaborate explanations of how the individuals and speech segments are organised lead the reader to ask why this should be so and thus to engage with the writing's strategies as much as with the voices and figures that it shapes – its company of figments. Because of the high degree of metafictional foregrounding of narrative processes this company is repeatedly dispersed and dissolved while it is being made: 'Need for company not continuous. . . . Regret then at having brought them about the problem how dispel them' (41–2).

The writing allows no resting place for the reader, not with the initially comfortable notion of company which is progressively eroded nor with the carefully prepared narrative structure which is itself a disorientating and alienating device. There are frequently moments in the third-person commentary when speculation leads the voice into the sphere of the second-person narrative or even towards the forbidden first as, for example, in this extract: 'To confess, Yes I remember. Perhaps even to have a voice. To murmur, Yes I remember. What an addition to company that would be! A voice in the first person singular' (20–1).

Here and elsewhere the writing constructs and simultaneously deconstructs the concept of company, developing it as a reassuring possibility with all its human connotations of community, communication and friendship, while also parodying it by presenting it as merely an aspect of narrative, a textual device or a conjuring trick invented by the writer–deviser who is himself 'devised': 'Devised deviser devising it all for company' (64). Beckett's elusive deviser is an example of Deleuze and Guattari's 'vagabond, nomad subject', and his oscillating narrative answers to their description of disjunctive writing that ceaselessly 'composes and decomposes the chains [of meaning] into signs that have nothing that impels them to become signifying'.[9]

However, not all of *Company* is as resistant to interpretation and reader identification. While the third-person commentary tends to be mobile and disruptive, the second-person narrative is frequently devoted to the telling of stories whose mode is autobiographical in spite of the second-person construction they adopt. Some of these stories are more movingly evocative of highly significant personal experiences in childhood and youth than anything else Beckett has written. How do these pieces of undisguised autobiography fit in with the metafictional scripsophrenia of the rest of the text? And how can Beckett justify including highly expressive stretches of romantic evocation in a work that elsewhere questions, as Beckett's work has consistently done over the years, the possibility of expression? The 'contradiction' can again be explained by invoking the Deleuze / Guattari model which, as the authors explain, allows us 'to think about fragments whose sole relationship is sheer difference'.[10] The memory fragments are each coherent, unified and highly expressive. But by virtue of their difference from the third-person sections they deepen the text's disjunctiveness and make their own metafictional contribution by throwing as much light on rhetorical processes as they do on remembered events. They also bring into focus the *act* of remembering with its internal rifts and fissures. *Company* is very much concerned with the puzzles and paradoxes inherent in the closely related processes of remembering, imagining and writing.

'The important thing for the remembering author is not what he experienced', writes Walter Benjamin, 'but the weaving of his memory.'[11] This tells us that the remembering writer is at least twice removed from the experiences he recalls – once by the act of recollection (which is an act of the imagination) and once again by the act of writing. Both acts demand that experiences are sifted and sorted in ways that require as much forgetting as they do remembering – 'Penelope work', as Benjamin calls it, of weaving and unravelling. A memory is never complete or finite. It is open to endless revision as Beckett well knows. *Company* demonstrates the extent to which remembering is not simply recuperative. It involves processes of cutting and editing. To remember is also to dismember. And so memory, in its contradictoriness, contributes to *Company's* dividedness, to its scripsophrenia. For to remember is both to come close to one's experience and to distance oneself from it sufficiently to observe it. It is simultaneously a journey back to lived events and an artificial construction of a new thing which itself alters the one who remembers. When Beckett offers variations on the formula, 'Deviser of the voice and of its hearer and of himself. Deviser of himself for company' (34), he is giving recognition to this paradox.

Beckett's choice of the second-person narrative for the memory segments throws into prominence the way in which a person is constructed by memory (and by the imagination more generally), made 'other' by it, and even, in the process of 'conjuring something out of nothing', *invented* by it: 'He speaks of himself as of another. He says, speaking of himself, he speaks of himself as of another' (34). And this other joins the ranks of all the fictional creations – in Beckett's case a long lineup, many of them alluded to in *Company* – of the imagination. Far from being simply a matter of recovering something lost, memory, understood in these terms, allows a dizzy glimpse into the abyss of infinite change and motion.

In *Company* Beckett is like Deleuze and Guattari in his ability to view endless change and difference 'without having recourse either to any sort of original totality (not even one that has been lost), or to a subsequent totality that may not yet have come about',[12] and to recognise this vision as being creative and liberating. *Company* demonstrates that writing is, as another writer has put it, *inaugural* – 'the writer is himself a new idiom, constructing itself'.[13] The work's highly schismatic nature with its multiple breaks and interruptions underlines for the reader the fact that all writing is like this, however much it might appear otherwise, and so it gives the reader a lesson in reading. All texts are what Roland Barthes calls 'broken texts', requiring plural readings or commentaries. 'The work of commentary', writes Barthes, 'once it is separated from any ideology of totality, consists precisely in *manhandling* the text, *interrupting* it.'[14] In *Company* Beckett has already done much of this work for the reader and made it all the more visible by doing it within a symmetrical structure. *Company* is a *reading* as much as a writing of the bits and pieces that can be gathered to shape identities, memories and dreams.

While in *Texts for Nothing* the gaps and chasms that the narrative faces moment by moment are presented, however comically, as disabling, *Company* exploits them, making them a part of its orderly structure and so bringing them under control. *Company* has a double vision of writing, of memory and of self. For all its recognition of writing as conjuring, of the world as phantasm and of the self as infinitely dispersed, *Company* affirms writing's power to create worlds that are substantial and significant and that can momentarily hold at bay the chaos of endless multiplicity while at the same time fully acknowedging it. Although the work ends with the observation that the listener is 'as you always were. Alone' (89), that aloneness, like the 'nothingness' that is also confronted, *is* to the same extent tempered by the narrative's 'fabling'. While this work can be described as schizophrenic because it generates contradictory visions, it is also schizoanalytic in that it allows the reader to see that all texts are caught in the same tangle of unresolvable contradiction and that this can be a source of power.

Notes

1. *Texts for Nothing*, in Samuel Beckett, *Collected Shorter Prose 1945–1980* (London: John Calder, 1984) p. 74. All quotations from *Texts for Nothing* are from this edition; page numbers are given in the text.
2. Samuel Beckett, *Company* (London: John Calder, 1980) p. 34. All quotations from *Company* are from this edition; page numbers are given in the text.
3. Gilles Deleuze and Felix Guattari, *Anti-Oedipus: Capitalism and Schizophrenia* (New York: Viking Press, 1977).
4. Quoted by Israel Shenker in 'An Interview with Beckett (1956)', reprinted in *Samuel Beckett: the Critical Heritage*, eds Lawrence Graver and Raymond Federman (London: Routledge & Kegan Paul, 1979) p. 148.
5. Deleuze and Guattari, p. 380.
6. Ibid., p. 133.
7. Ibid., p. xxi.
8. Ibid., p. 42.
9. See Deleuze and Guattari, pp. 64, 26, 39.
10. Ibid., p. 42.
11. Walter Benjamin, 'The Image of Proust', in *Illuminations* (London: Fontana, 1968) p. 204.
12. Deleuze and Guattari, p. 42.
13. Jacques Derrida, *Writing and Difference* (University of Chicago Press, 1978) p. 11.
14. Roland Barthes, *S/Z* (New York: Hill and Wang, 1974) p. 15.

10

Ill Seen Ill Said and the Sense of an Ending

Nicholas Zurbrugg

Ill Seen Ill Said is not so much a story, as a poetic evocation of those rituals by which the living and the dead within Beckett's fiction endlessly, and quite ineffectively, strive to attain a definitive 'sense of an ending'. Try as they may, they fail. Over and over again, both in this world and the next, Beckett's long-suffering protagonists reluctantly revive old sufferings, as they respond to the pangs of involuntary memory and unwanted self-awareness. For all their efforts, the dying narrator of *Ill Seen Ill Said* and the ghostly 'she', whom he can never quite forget, remain permanent victims of 'Remembrance! When all worse there than when first ill seen.'[1]

In this respect, 'he' and 'she' are quintessentially postmodern protagonists, if the postmodern period (or the years since the mid-1930s) be defined as an era in which writers radically reverse the prevailing optimism of the modernist epoch (or those years from the mid-1880s to the mid-1930s).[2] Whereas most of the major modernist writers – such as Marcel Proust and Paul Eluard – celebrate the advantages of intense memories and unexpected revelations, 'he' and 'she' deplore lucidity and do their damnedest to evade and avoid self-awareness. Far from sharing the modernist hero's 'need . . . to be faithful to his true sense of self', or 'the artist's goal, inner being',[3] and far from triumphantly transcribing intimations of 'inner being' like Proust or Eluard, 'he' and 'she' try to 'ill say' and 'ill see' their inner condition, in the hope that it will somehow or other go away.

Somewhat as Beckett's *Footfalls* focuses upon the strange realm of shades, and presents the phantasmal dialogue between the compulsively pacing May, and her mysteriously absent, and almost certainly departed Mother, *Ill Seen Ill Said* bewilderingly interweaves ghostly traces of the dying and the dead. It begins by describing the torments of 'she', a shadowy figure who is 'already dead' (41). 'She', the reader gathers, no longer suffers from 'the misfortune to be of this world' (8).[4] Unfortunately, rather than finding the grave a fine and private place, the dead 'she' suffers from 'helplessness . . . she cannot help', and, having notionally left life, still 'rails at the source of all life' (7). From its very first lines, then, *Ill Seen Ill Said* depicts perceptual torments over which death itself has no dominion.

Significantly, 'she' is also described as being 'erect and rigid' (7), and in her 'Memnon pose' (35); an allusion, clearly, to the statue of Memnon, which was said to sing for *joy* when first touched by sunlight, or 'the source of all life'. The same allusion is used on several occasions by Proust, whose narrators enthusiastically refer to the Memnon legend, both in order to express their exaltation before sunshine, and to celebrate the more literary pleasures of poetic inspiration. Marcel, the hero of Proust's *A la recherche du temps perdu*, repeatedly responds to the uplifting inspiration of sunlight, declaring: 'it only takes one ray of sunshine to engender and nurture happiness';[5] while the narrator of *Contre Sainte-Beuve* makes even more explicit reference to this legend. Bubbling over with quite unBeckettian *joie de vivre*, this Proustian persona proclaims:

> As the ray of morning sunshine fell upon me, I jumped to the foot of my bed, I improvised a thousand happy dances and . . . I burst into song, for the poet is like the statue of Memnon: it only takes one ray of early morning sunshine to make him burst into song.[6]

Nothing could be less like the experience of 'she'. Both an archetypally Beckettian figure and an archetypally anti-Memnon figure, 'she' celebrates neither the birth of a new day nor the birth of a new *anything*, but 'rails' at her susceptibility to unwelcome self-awareness. While instants of involuntary insight make the modernist hero's day, such stimulation only prolongs and intensifies the 'helplessness' of Beckett's hapless postmodern anti-heroes. At best, Beckettian beings yearn to experience oblivion and to witness their own ending. At worst, Beckett's protagonists, such as the mysterious figure in *Still* (who also resembles 'that old statue some old god twanged at sunrise and sunset'), anxiously await painful lapses into self-consciousness, as they sit, temporarily 'still', 'listening for a sound', or anticipating an image, a memory, or a 'something', which threatens their tranquillity.[7]

The curious sense of dread with which 'she' appears to anticipate visitations from her past, and which the dying 'he' seeks to neutralise by ending all experience of 'this world' (8), is best understood with reference to Beckett's poem 'something there'. Encapsulating the primary motif of most of Beckett's later writing, this poem's haunting evocation of the way in which an inanimate mind may find itself involuntarily and irrevocably restored to sentience cautiously recounts:

> something there
> where
> out there
> out where
> out there
> outside
> what
> the head what else
> something there somewhere outside
> the head

Upon identifying this 'something there' as a 'faint sound so brief', this talking or thinking head admits that its 'globe' – or *the* 'globe' – is 'not yet bare', as

> the eye
> opens wide
> wide
> till in the end
> nothing more
> shutters it again

Portending the ghostly world of *Ill Seen Ill Said*, the remaining lines of this poem speculate that this 'faint sound' may well arise from the realm of the dead, and cryptically conclude:

> so the odd time
> out there
> somewhere out there
> like as if
> as if
> something
> not life
> necessarily[8]

It is very much this kind of ghostly revelation, along with the
suggestion that even the dead may be disturbed by visions of
'something there', that Beckett evokes in *Ill Seen Ill Said*. The
peculiarly postmodern quality of this ghostly love story is in turn
best introduced obliquely, by comparison with Beckett's 'Lady
Love', a translation of the Surrealist poet Paul Eluard's poem
'L'amoureuse' (c. 1923). Celebrating the way in which the poet's
lady love moves him to 'laugh cry and laugh', somewhat as
sunshine moves the Proustian hero to 'burst into song', this poem
euphorically confides:

> She is standing on my lids
> And her hair is in my hair
> She has the colour of my eye
> She has the body of my hand
> In my shade she is engulfed
> Like a stone against the sky
>
> She will never close her eyes
> And she does not let me sleep
> And her dreams in the bright day
> Make the suns evaporate
> And me laugh cry and laugh
> Speak when I have nothing to say[9]

Unlike this paean to Eluard's wondrous intimacy with his lady
love, *Ill Seen Ill Said* describes the determination with which its
narrator's eye would 'tear itself away' (59), in order to eliminate all
intimacy with 'she'. For although this dying narrator longs to 'see
her again' (51), he still more fervently desires to die, to be 'shut of it
all' (30), to 'finish with it all at last' (51), to 'Let her vanish' (31), and,
most tellingly of all, to 'say farewell. If only to the face. Of her
tenacious trace' (59). While Eluard's triumphant modernist narrator
proudly counts the ways in which his lids, hair, eyes, hands, shade,
laughter, tears and words are all inseparable from his lady love, the
peculiarly pessimistic and typically Beckettian protagonist of *Ill Seen
Ill Said* despairs of ever severing himself from the 'shade' of his 'she'.

Until its final pages, *Ill Seen Ill Said* reads like a continually
frustrated swan-song, as its narrator incessantly remembers
different aspects of 'she', and regretfully finds that things refuse to
come to an end. Only at the very end of his monologue does 'he'

sense the final 'pip' (59) of his death-rattle. Bubbling and babbling over with *joi de mourir*, he rapturously recounts:

> Then in that perfect dark foreknell darling sound pip for end begun. First last moment. Grant only enough remain to devour all. Moment by glutton moment. Sky earth the whole kit and boodle. Not another crumb of carrion left. Lick chops and basta. No. One moment more. One last. Grace to breathe that void. Know happiness (59).

These lines take one by surprise. Beckett's heroes perpetually aspire to know this 'void', but seldom, if ever, attain its 'perfect dark'. Belacqua, the hero of 'Dream of Fair to Middling Women' (Beckett's first, unpublished novel), fails to make 'his mind a blank' with 'all the candles quenched but one',[10] just as Moran, one of the anti-heroes of *Molloy*, vainly struggles to make his 'memory a blank', while still retaining 'just enough brain to . . . exult'.[11] At best, Moran's imagination cultivates 'a thousand fancies' in order that these may be 'swept . . . away, with a great disgusted sweep', so that he may survey 'the void that they had polluted'.[12]

The narrator of *Ill Seen Ill Said* would similarly reduce 'she' to fancies, or 'pure figment' (20), and sweep them away. But as 'she' discovers, and as the dying 'he' seems predestined to discover, the Beckettian cosmos is devoid of permanent voids, be these real or imaginary. Considered as a whole, rather than in terms of the narrator's dying fantasies, *Ill Seen Ill Said* depicts the process of dying as an interval of painless 'void' sandwiched between periods of unrelieved suffering before and after this 'sense of an ending'.[13] In this respect, the suggestion that the more serene expressions of 'she' are 'Worthy those worn by certain newly dead' (25), alludes quite unambiguously to the way in which sustained serenity is experienced only very fleetingly by the newly dead in Beckett's fiction. Once no longer 'newly dead', 'he', like 'she', seems fated to suffer the torments that the narrator of *Murphy* complacently designates as 'all the usual'.[14]

Of course, the narrator's eventual fate is implicit rather than explicit, and can only be divined, rather than defined, in terms of the disparity between the narrator's assumption that death offers the 'happiness' of 'that void' (59), and the initial suggestion that the dead 'she' suffers from the self-same 'old nausea' (38) and 'ancient horror' (28–9) that the narrator dreads while still alive. Subsequent passages confirm that the dead and the dying in this story suffer identical, or near-identical, afflictions. Like many other of Beckett's recent writings, *Ill Seen Ill Said* imperceptibly intermingles the dilemmas and distress of the living and the dead.

The more that one reads of *Ill Seen Ill Said*, the more one learns about the general human condition, or general inhuman condition, of 'he' and 'she'. Sensitive both the pattern of his own declining days, and to the 'faint comings and goings' (14) of 'she', and looking at and through the material world with the hallucinatory perspicacity of 'an eye having no need of light to see' (7–8), the narrator seems compelled to scrutinise 'she', just as 'she' compulsively contemplates 'a certain spot' (11) in a graveyard near her cabin. While 'she' sits 'Rapt' (14) and 'Riveted' (17) before aspects of her ghostly past, 'he' determines to 'Close-up' (19) and 'enlarge and devour' (23) her image.

Indeed, not content with her image, 'he' would also share her very thoughts as she 'devours', so to speak, other ghostly photographic images in her 'still shadowy album', and yearns to 'be by her when she takes it on her knees', wondering 'what scenes they can possibly be that draw the head down lower still and hold it in thrall' (14). Neither the narrator nor the reader discovers the nature of these 'scenes', for here, as elsewhere in *Ill Seen Ill Said*, details remain infuriatingly elusive. At most, one simply becomes aware of the excruciating pattern of existence as 'he' observes 'she' observing some other ghostly images. To confuse things still further, 'she' is also scrutinised by 'the twelve', a group of ghostly figures whom she all but acknowledges, before suddenly turning away. Introducing this odd process of attraction and repulsion, the narrator explains:

The others are there. All about. The twelve. Afar. Still or receding. She raises her eyes and sees one. Turns away and see another. Again she stops dead. Now the moment or never. But something forbids (15).

Like 'she', the twelve appear to be dead. They are 'her own', and according to the dying narrator, neither 'she' nor the twelve should 'need' one another any more, since, logically speaking, nobody should feel any 'need' any more when dead. Mulling over this argument, 'he' muses:

What is it defends her? Even from her own. Averts the intent gaze
. . . Forbids divining her. What but life ending. Hers. The other's.
But so otherwise. She needs nothing. Nothing utterable. Whereas
the other. How need in the end? But how? How need in the
end? (16).

Impenetrable as they may initially appear, these lines seem to
proffer three main suppositions. Firstly, they hint that however
unlikely it may appear, the dead, like the living, feel compelled
towards others by some sense of 'need'. Secondly, in death as in life,
this sense of attraction seems complemented by an equally forceful
principle of repulsion. 'She' avoids the twelve despite her apparent
wish to greet them, and in his turn, 'he' would 'say farewell' to her
'tenacious trace' (59), despite his obsessive wish to 'see her
again' (51). Finally, these lines also somewhat ambiguously suggest
that death should, in principle, instigate the indifference that
Beckett's Belacqua eloquently defines as 'the neutralisation of
needs'.[15]
Faced by these different possibilities, the dying narrator, like the
reader of *Ill Seen Ill Said*, is highly confused. As his final quizzical
comment hints, he fears that despite all his arguments to the
contrary, the dead may well be plagued by 'need' in the end. In
other words, he weighs the claims of two conflicting modes of
knowledge. Common sense insists that death inaugurates the 'void'
of perfect peace. But the intimations of other, more mysterious,
modes of cognition, such as the visions of the 'eye having no need of
light to see' (8), suggests that the physical demise of the 'filthy eye of
flesh' (30) – or the 'vile jelly' (52) – still leaves the mind exposed to
unspeakable memories and needs in the 'madhouse of the
skull' (20), in that ghostly, ghastly domain 'behind the lids' (39).
As the American poet Robert Lax has suggested, Beckett's recent
writings are most impressive in terms of their sensitivity to this
strange extra-rational realm, where the eye has 'no need of light to
see'. Referring to the opening exchange in Beckett's play *Footfalls*, in
which the ghostly voice (V) tells her daughter, May, 'I heard you in
my deep sleep. . . . There is no sleep so deep I would not hear you
there',[16] Lax comments:

It is down there in deep sleep that Beckett lives, and where all of
us live, but few in our time have been so expert in visiting that
region, in staying there and in bringing back a living report. It isn't

just a matter of visiting – one needs a specially made, specially trimmed vocabulary to bring back true reports. One must understand the rhythms of the realm. One must bring back words and images, its particular music too.[17]

Ill Seen Ill Said and other recent Beckettian texts, such as his play *What Where* and his various poetic 'croaks', seem most interesting of all as precisely this kind of 'living report' from the realm of 'deep sleep'. Beckett defines *What Where* as a 'puppet play', in the sense that its more or less anonymous protagonists, Bam, Bem, Bim and Bom (and the unidentified Bum), are peculiarly impersonal, disembodied figures, and admits that he would like to present an equally anonymous mode of speech, or voice, in his plays, were this possible.[18] In this respect, his most recent writings may all be best understood as attempts to enact or to describe the impersonal, ritualistic actions and intonations of ghostly figures from the depths of 'deep sleep', or the realm that Beckett defines as 'the within'.

According to Beckett, 'expression of the within can only be from the within';[19] that is, ghostly, or visionary experience can only find formulation in the kind of 'specially made, specially trimmed' vocabulary, images and music to which Lax lucidly refers. This unusual kind of vocabulary, image and music finds early formulation in the repetitive refrains of *Waiting for Godot*, when for example, Vladimir and Estragon meditate upon the eerie sounds or utterances of dead leaves, remarking:

> Rather they whisper.
> They rustle.
> They murmur.
> They rustle . . .
> They make a noise like feathers.
> Like leaves.
> Like ashes.
> Like leaves.[20]

Whereas Vladimir and Estragon's exchange offers mimetic analysis of the ghostly conversation between dead leaves, later Beckettian works such as *Footfalls* and *Ill Seen Ill Said* take this process one step further, by offering the mimetic enaction of ghostly voices. Like the disembodied, repetitive voice of May's mother, the narrator of *Ill Seen Ill Said* assumes the rhythms and accents of the Beckettian living dead in such sonorous utterances as: 'Was there once a time she did? Careful. Once once in a way. Till she could no more. No more bring the jaws together' (18). Here 'once' leads to its double echo 'Once once', and 'no more' anticipates 'No more', as the narrator's musings advance in a series of overlapping refrains.

Elsewhere, as in the first lines of *Ill Seen Ill Said*, the rhythms of 'deep sleep' culminate in a kind of muted doggerel, as prose merges into verse, and words such as 'lies' and 'rise' chime together. In a sense, the opening statement, 'From where she lies she sees Venus rise' (7) might just as well be written in verse form, as the couplet:

> From where she lies
> She sees Venus rise.[21]

The haunting 'music' resulting from this kind of repetitive and doggerel writing pervades *Ill Seen Ill Said*. Continually resounding, repeating and repermutating its terms, language itself fades in and out of focus, somewhat as the narrator's memories hover to and fro, in and out of view. In this respect, *Ill Seen Ill Said* records the rhythms and images of *interrupted* 'deep sleep', as the dead 'she' and the dying 'he' tremble and tremor in instants of 'deep awakening' which testify to their continued existence, just as they seem about to enjoy a sense of their long-awaited ending. For all their efforts to nullify intense awareness by reducing reality to soothingly repetitious words and gestures, 'he' and 'she' invariably find themselves brought back to mental life by one or another variant of 'something there'.

On one occasion 'she' appears to sit 'dead still', in the 'still air', observing 'motionless' grass, and evincing what appears to be a 'Voidlike calm' (29). At first sight, then, 'she' seems to enjoy the perfect void that the dying narrator impatiently awaits in his turn. Needless to say, this idyllic stasis gradually disintegrates. The grass 'shivers' with 'faintest shiver from its innermost' (29), and almost imperceptibly, the entire 'old body' of 'she' appears 'ashiver from head to foot' (30).[22]

Eventually the narrator envisages almost everything aquiver, as the sleeves of a suspended greatcoat first impress him with 'the pathos of . . . dangling arms'; next evince the same 'infinitesimal quaver' as all the other objects previously mentioned, or what the narrator terms 'the buttonhook and passim'; and finally lead to the observation: 'She too vacillates. Till in the end the back and forth prevails' (47).

This last sentence is almost identical to the lines in 'something there' which describe the way in which a faint sound animates the eye to such an extent that it opens wide 'till in the end / nothing more / shutters it again'.[23] Like the eye in 'something there', 'he' and 'she' are 'doomed to endure' (9), and to suffer infinitesimal quaver after infinitesimal quaver. Although 'she' is notionally 'already dead' (41), she repeatedly becomes 'alive as she alone knows how' (50). And although 'he' is notionally dying, he repeatedly betrays his susceptibility to mental torment with the expression that he defines as 'the look' (57): a grimace which, like 'that look' in Beckett's *Film*, bears mute witness to the 'anguish of perceivedness'.[24]

Forced 'open wide', like the eye in 'something there', 'he' and 'she' undergo a kind of perceptual rape, as they awaken, time after time, during instants of unwanted mental resurrection. Like most Beckettian heroes, the narrator of *Ill Seen Ill Said* tries to neutralise his anguish by formulating the soothing refrains and anti-narratives which allow deep internal disturbances to be 'ill see ill said. *Outwardly*' (43; my italics).

In the narrator's compressed terminology, deep awakenings, or instants of intense involuntary introspection, activate 'the farrago from eye to mind' (40); that is, the eye's attempt to reduce deep reality to shallow, 'ill seen', outward reality, and the mind's concurrent attempt to conceptualise and verbalise deep reality in equally outward, 'ill said' terminology. As 'he' admits, these 'outward' discourses are 'equal liars both' (40). 'The mind betrays the treacherous eyes and the treacherous word their treacheries' (48).

Ultimately, the 'sad sense' (40) of *Ill Seen Ill Said* derives from three interconnected contradictions. At the level of narrative, there is an obvious disparity between the narrator's deep anguish, and his treacherously superficial, 'ill said' terminology. More generally, *Ill Seen Ill Said* depicts the continual contradiction between its protagonists' desire for a final 'void' and the impossibility of this idyllic sense of an ending. Somewhere in between these contradictions looms the rather more subtle and rather more poignant discrepancy between these progatonists' wish to attain immunity to their 'need' for others, and their compulsive instinct to return, over and over again, to their loved ones.

This third contradiction is not always wholly obvious in *Ill Seen Ill Said*. But on certain occasions 'he' quite patently writes against the grain of his prevailing arguments, somewhat as the speaker of 'PSS', a recent Beckettian 'croak', instructs his hands to both hold him and unclasp themselves, exclaiming:

> head oh hands
> hold me
> unclasp
> hold me[25]

Most of the time, the narrator of *Ill Seen Ill Said* evinces very little wish to hold or be held by anyone; indeed, when addressing the body of 'she', 'he' adopts an almost studiously distant discourse, describing her mouth as 'Unlikely site of olden kisses given and received' (49). Nevertheless, during one particularly elegiac description of the way in which 'she' gently bows her head towards a bowl of 'slop' (35), the narrator's admiration for this graceful movement seems so unusually heartfelt (there is no other word for it), that one suspects that this description offers a veiled projection of the narrator's own desire to be held, clasped and raised with equal grace 'towards her lips'. The narrator observes:

> At last in a twin movement full of grace she slowly raises the bowl towards her lips while at the same time with equal slowness bowing her head to join it. Having set out at the same instant they meet halfway and there come to rest (35).

Whereas Beckett's earlier fiction takes cruel delight in its habitually grotesque descriptions of bodily functions (one thinks, for example, of the passage in *Watt* in which Mary's 'overflowing' mouth is graphically described wtih reference to its shower of 'partially masticated morsels of meat, fruit, bread, vegetables, nuts and pastry'),[26] these beautifully balanced lines offer an image of quite exceptional harmony. Only towards the end of this passage does Beckett's English translation of the original French malevolently transform elegiac plosives into cynical alliteration. Where *Mal vu mal dit* relates that 'une partie retombe dans le bol' (literally: 'a portion falls back into the bowl'),[27] *Ill Seen Ill Said* rather more disparagingly states that part of the 'first spoonful' is 'slobbered . . . into the slop' (35). Here, as elsewhere, Beckett's English testifies to his power 'to claw'.[28]

It is illuminating to compare the contradictions and discrepancies of *Ill Seen Ill Said* with those of Beckett's still more recent *Worstward Ho*, a monologue in which yet another dying narrator similar expresses the desire to 'Know no more. See no more. Say no more', in order to savour 'That little much of void alone.'[29] Like the narrator of *Ill Seen Ill Said*, the narrator of *Worstward Ho* eagerly anticipates his own demise, desiring 'No mind and words', save sufficient faculties 'to joy . . . Just enough still to joy that only they' (29).

Yet for all its studied nihilism, *Worstward Ho* also evinces the same kind of poignant intimacy that *Ill Seen Ill Said* presents in its evocation of 'she' and the bowl that she carefully raises to her carefully descending lips. Describing the harmonious trust uniting an old man and a child as they walk together 'with equal plod', the narrator of *Worstward Ho* relates:

> Hand in hand with equal plod they go. . . . Backs turned both bowed with equal plod they go. The child hand raised to reach the holding hand. Hold the old holding hand. Hold and be held. . . . Joined by held holding hands (13).

One after another, Beckett's 'late' narrators resolve to eradicate their dependency upon company and affection. But eventually, and almost imperceptibly, these same narrators invariably pause before ghostly apparitions of human harmony, and, despite themselves, painfully rekindle the embers of their extinguishable affection for those whom they have cherished and whom they cannot help but continue to cherish, irrespective of their individual or mutual 'ending'. Eventually the dying narrator of *Ill Seen Ill Said* suspects that even the dead may 'need' intimacy and affection, while the narrator of *Worstward Ho* concedes that though notionally 'long . . . lost to longing', his mind may well be 'longing still. Faintly longing still. Faintly vainly longing still' (36).

Employing the same resonant, self-qualifying, and at times, self-negating rhythms as those perfected in *Ill Seen Ill Said*, *Worstward Ho* offers another haunting story of ghostly nostalgia, transporting the Proustian dilemma of 'Time and Space made perceptible to the heart',[30] into the peculiarly Beckettian context of the ill-seen and ill-said time and space of the ill-dying and the ill-dead. 'Always afar' (10), like 'she' and the twelve in *Ill Seen Ill Said*, and 'vasts of void apart' like the protagonists of *Worstward Ho*, the inhabitants of Beckett's 'Shade-ridden void' (*Worstward Ho*, 35, 25) are forever too distant to join one another in 'a twin movement full of grace' (*Ill Seen Ill Said*, 35), and yet never sufficiently distant from one another to enjoy the ideal emotional void, or 'neutralisation of needs',[31] that they associate with the 'joy at journey's end' (*Ill Seen Ill Said*, 56).

Like James Joyce's *Finnegans Wake*, Beckett's later prose reveals the 'savage economy of hieroglyphics';[32] that is, a degree of condensation which requires that texts such as *Ill Seen Ill Said* be read and re-read, until accepted, as it were, on their own terms. Then, as Robert Lax intimates, the reader may gradually become aware of the words, images, rhythms and music of Beckett's incomparable explorations of 'deep sleep', or that realm 'within', between life and death, beyond the habitually 'ill seen' and 'ill said'.

Sometimes, Beckett's archetypally postmodern evocations of perceptual confusion and delusion merely baffle us, and appear little more than 'Confusion amounting to nothing' (20). But on other occasions, they leave 'something there', and appear not so much the negation of the great modernist writers' explorations of inhabitual perception, as an extraordinary extension and elaboration of Proust's and Eluard's meditations upon the mysteries of love. Then, yet again, from 'odd time' to 'odd time', Beckett's haunting images of ghostly, irrepressible devotion leave us 'Riveted' and 'Rapt'.

Notes

1. Samuel Beckett, *Ill Seen Ill Said* (London: John Calder, 1981) pp. 52–3. All quotations are from this edition; page numbers are given in the text.
2. See my 'Beyond Beckett: Reckless Writing and the Concept of the Avant-Garde within Postmodern Literature', *Yearbook of Comparative and General Literature*, 1 (1981) 37–56, for further discussion of the periodisation of modernism and postmodernism.
3. In 'Beckett's Search for Unseeable and Unmakeable: *Company* and *Ill Seen Ill Said*', *Modern Fiction Studies*, 29 (Spring 1983) 111–25, David Read argues that both 'he' and 'she' experience 'the artist's need . . . to be faithful to his true sense of self' (112) and 'progress towards the artist's true goal, inner being' (124).
4. Both David Read (ibid., 113) and Marjorie Perloff, 'Between Verse and Prose: Beckett and the New Poetry', *Critical Inquiry*, 9 (Dec. 1982) 419,

assume that 'she' is still alive. My reading of *Ill Seen Ill Said* postulates, on the contrary, that 'she' is dead.

5. Marcel Proust, *A la recherche du temps perdu*, ed. Pierre Clarac and André Ferré (Paris: Gallimard, 1954) I, 397. My translation.

6. Marcel Proust, *Contre Sainte-Beuve*, ed. Bernard de Fallois (Paris: Gallimard, 1954) p. 83. My translation.

7. *Still*, in Samuel Beckett, *Collected Shorter Prose 1945–1980* (London: John Calder, 1984) pp. 183 and 185.

8. 'something there', in Samuel Beckett, *Collected Poems in English and French* (London: John Calder, 1967) p. 63.

9. *Collected Poems in English and French*, p. 67.

10. Samuel Beckett, 'Dream of Fair to Middling Women', Reading University Library, Beckett Archive MS 1227/7/16/9, p. 76.

11. Samuel Beckett, *Molloy/Malone Dies/The Unnamable* (London: Calder & Boyars, 1966) p. 141. All quotations from Beckett's trilogy of novels are from this edition.

12. *Molloy*, p. 162.

13. Marjorie Perloff, 'Between Verse and Prose', 420, concludes that the dying narrator successfully erases 'the "trace" of the "face" that forever haunts his sleep and his waking'. This 'void', or 'erasure' of the past, seems to me, however, to be only temporary.

14. Samuel Beckett, *Murphy* (London: Calder & Boyars, 1970) p. 124.

15. 'Dream of Fair to Middling Women', p. 38.

16. *Footfalls*, in Samuel Beckett, *Collected Shorter Plays* (London: Faber & Faber, 1984) p. 239.

17. Robert Lax, letter to Nicholas Zurbrugg, 16 September 1984. Lax's own 'reports' appear in his *21 Pages* (Zurich: Pendo, 1984).

18. See *What Where*, in Samuel Beckett, *Collected Shorter Plays*, pp. 307–16. Beckett described *What Where* as a 'puppet play', and discussed his preoccupation with impersonal and disembodied figures and speech, in conversation with Nicholas Zurbrugg, Paris, 28 Jan. 1985.

19. Samuel Beckett, letter to Aidan Higgins, 22 April 1958, in *The Review of Contemporary Fiction*, 3 (Spring 1983) 157. Here Beckett discusses Higgins' story 'Killachter Meadow'.

20. *Waiting for Godot* (London: Faber & Faber, 1965) p. 63.

21. Marjorie Perloff, 'Between Verse and Prose', 416, also makes this point.

22. David Read, op. cit., 118, attributes this quavering perspective to 'the eye's inherent flux', and compares it to the 'tremulous quality' in the paintings of Beckett's friend, Avigdor Arikha (115–16). My own view is that the trembling objects in *Ill Seen Ill Said* are symptomatic of a profound perceptual crisis, rather than testimony to the habitual inadequacy of the eye.

23. *Collected Poems in English and French*, p. 63.

24. *Film*, in Samuel Beckett, *Collected Shorter Plays*, pp. 169, 163.

25. Samuel Beckett, 'PSS', published with a note to Michael Horovitz, dated 17 Sept. 1981, describing this three-poem sequence as 'recent croaks', in *New Departures*, 14 (1982) 64.

26. *Watt* (London: John Calder, 1970) p. 53.

27. *Mal vu mal dit*, (Paris: Editions de Minuit, 1981) p. 44. My literal translation.

28. See Beckett's letter to Alan Schneider of 21 June 1956 in Samuel Beckett, *Disjecta: Miscellaneous Writings and a Dramatic Fragment*, ed. Ruby Cohn (London: John Calder, 1983) p. 107.

29. *Worstward Ho* (London: John Calder, 1983) p. 18. All quotations are from this edition; page numbers are given in the text.

30. Samuel Beckett, 'Proust' (1931), in *Proust/Three Dialogues with Georges Duthuit* (London: Calder & Boyars, 1965) p. 58.

31. 'Dream of Fair to Middling Women', p. 38.

32. Samuel Beckett, 'Dante . . . Bruno. Vico . . Joyce' (1929), in *Disjecta*, p. 28. In 'The Poem within the Play in Beckett's *Embers*', *Language and Style*, 17 (Summer 1984) 193–205, Wanda Avila offers a very comprehensive analysis of the 'savage economy' of Beckett's emergent poetic prose, paying particular attention to its 'obtrusive irregularity' and 'intrusive regularity', its 'syntactic parallelism' and its 'syntactic fragementation', as well as its various rhymes and repetitions.

11

Voyelles, Cromlechs and the Special (W)rites of *Worstward Ho*

Enoch Brater

I

Who is the reader for Beckett's late fictional prose? Stories of the '[m]eremost minimum' presented in 'syntaxes upended in opposite corners' are unlikely to command for long the attention of any popular audience.[1] A narrative technique that looks so much like a grammar for being elsewhere[2] requires that the reader who stays with it be something more than the 'gentle skimmer' whose competence and fidelity Beckett summons to help out in *Murphy*.[3] Joyce's ideal reader suffering from an ideal insomnia will be required to do one more turn when he picks up the likes of *Worstward Ho* or *Ill Seen Ill Said*. Of course, if the reader has made this author's acquaintance before, and few but the initiated would dare to venture into such dangerous territory, some of these verbal adagios will not sound entirely unfamiliar. Yet a story that depends for its life on another story, and another one before that, and both by the same hand, is likely to demand a comprehensive knowledge of Beckett that only a few diehards have the time and inclination to possess. The more of Beckett one reads, however, the more of Beckett one understands. But the same is true of any author. What, then, makes Beckett's case so special?

Let us look for a moment at *All Strange Away*, a not so very late piece of fiction Beckett wrote in English in 1963–64 but did not release for publication until 1976–78.[4] Although this enterprise shares with *Imagination Dead Imagine* its first line as well as its preoccupation with the angles of a diagram, the fiction is also full of connections to other Beckett works – works past and works still to come. *Godot* is here ('Stool'), *Not I* ('Sitting, standing, walking,

160

kneeling, crawling, lying, creeping'), *A Piece of Monologue* ('Light out, long dark, candle and matches, imagine them, strike one to light, light on, blow out, light out, strike another, light on, so on'), *Ill Seen Ill Said* ('aha'), *Still* ('deasil'), *The Unnamable* ('rotunda'), *Molloy* ('beehive'), *Krapp's Last Tape* ('rubber ball'), as well as the 'something there' of Beckett's poem of the same name. A system of self-referentiality like this, an intertextuality that borders not only on the obsessive, but on the downright narcissistic, is sure to be available only to a coterie. For the rest of humanity the network will remain closed, or at the very best a kind of 'caviar to the general', the cult of elitism Hamlet shares with his beloved players. Yet Beckett's text suffers from an inaccessibility even more basic than this. To put it bluntly, at first glance the unsuspecting reader has no idea just what in the world is going on here – and, to make matters worse, the tactic seems to have been deliberate on the author's part. Language as a vehicle of communication appears to have broken down completely.

That which seems so difficult and mysterious, even frustrating, is far less so, however, on subsequent readings. How comforting the statement and restatement of things we cannot hope to understand becomes with every repetition, a re-experiencing of the text based on familiarity of rhythm rather than content (accent on the first syllable) or our initial reaction of vain discontent. Suddenly new mysteries intrude, ones we had hardly thought possible on 'first aperçu'.[5] Before long we find ourselves reading the formerly unreadable, imagining the unimaginable, naming, and with considerable accuracy, the unnamable. Our phenomenology of perception, challenged, shortcircuited, and perhaps redirected, is once more discovered to be mercifully intact. We have survived one more rite of passage, the *passage* of this text, and we are ready once more to resume the struggle, 'worstward ho'.

All Strange Away serves to remind us that every act of reading is a secret ceremony we must all undergo. As if to bring the point home, this text, moreover, buries within itself the 'traces blurs signs'[6] of some other poetic rituals as well: 'A noir, E blanc, I rouge, U vert, O bleu: voyelles . . .'. The line is from Rimbaud[7] and Beckett colonises it as 'Fancy dead, to which now add for old mind's sake sorrow vented in simple sighing sound black vowel a . . .' (128). Rimbaud's 'black vowel a' is in fact the only vowel sound we hear in the title *All Strange Away*, which features two cases of assonance, the first syllable of 'away' echoing 'all', the second echoing 'strange'.

The sound of 'ay' in 'away' emphasises this 'black vowel' even further: that is how the letter itself is pronounced. Sound and sense are in a new relationship, for together they formulate the possible meanings of a text. Rimbaud's 'Voyelles' pairs vowels with certain colours: A, E, I, U and O engender certain images, which correspond to the colour and the shape and sound of each vowel. Language is reduced to a matter of fundamental sounds ('no joke intended', to quote Beckett himself on this point).[8] Rimbaud's sequence reverses the normal progression of U and O in order to highlight alpha and 'O l'Oméga' with their tempting Biblical overtones ('I am the alpha and omega, the beginning and the end'). Beckett will play with this idea too. Emma (M–A) and Emmo (M–O) accomplish a number of things. Giving alpha and omega a back seat, they not only serialise Beckett's other M-heroes, but also bring to mind another important work of nineteenth-century French literature, *Madame Bovary*. Emma Bovary, too, might have been delineated in the following way (though certainly not by Flaubert): 'First face alone, lovely beyond words leave it that, then deasil breasts alone, then thighs and cunt alone, then arse and hole alone, all lovely beyond words' (119). Such metonymic description is characteristic of Rimbaud's poem too, where the 'lèvres belles' stand in for the whole woman.

In *All Strange Away* Beckett keeps his eye on all that is black, denaturing Rimbaud's chorus of colours. Within the cube and later the rotunda black (or its opposite, white) predominates. In this piece we read about 'white lava mud', 'peeling plaster' (125) and 'bleached dirt' (121). The cube is appointed as follows: 'Sheets of black paper, stick them to the wall with cobweb and spittle' (117). Once the rotunda comes into full view, other items begin to disappear: 'long black hair gone, long black lashes on white cheekbone gone' (124). The figure placed there sits in a '[b]lack shroud . . . till it all perishes and rots off of him and hangs off of him in black flitters' (118). The last image recalls the text for the vowel A in Rimbaud's poem, where we read 'noir corset velu des mouches éclatantes/Qui bombinent auteur des puanteurs cruelles'. Both lines include items of clothing which 'fly', an image evoked by 'flitters'. The 'puanteurs' corresponds to 'rotting'. Beckett's text will also speak of flies, as in the 'dying common house or dying window fly' (120). The cube, furthermore, contains an image of 'ivory white', with 'ceiling flaking plaster or suchlike, floor like bleached dirt, aha, something there' (121). A simile dependent on 'like', however, can make things equivocal. The black coverings cannot endure, can never be as pure and eternal as the whiteness of a white rotunda.

Dark and light make sense as emblems for death and imagination in the opening line of this piece, 'Imagination dead imagine', next described as an 'A place' (117). Black prefigures death, but images require light to be seen. 'Fancy', used as a synonym for imagination here, supports this correspondence. Its root is 'phaos', light. The entire phrase, moreover, is circular in that it begins and ends with imagination, thus corresponding to the letter 'O', which brings closure to Rimbaud's 'Voyelles' with 'Ses Yeux'. Although imagination, white, and the circle dominate Beckett's scene, death dances in the privileged centre, as witnessed by the placement of the letter A in the diagram (should the reader himself fancy to work all of this out). 'O' continues to pervade the atmosphere of Beckett's text in the guise of cycles, as of light to dark to light, but 'A' asserts itself at the end with a clear allusion to Rimbaud's 'black vowel a'. But this, too, is ironic. Fancy does not die at the end of this text: it is, instead, still there, still there as herald to its own beginning in the reader's imagination, one more strange Beckett piece 'for to end yet again'.[9]

II

Beckett's reliance on Rimbaud points out just how various the rituals are that language has at its disposal, should the writer care to take advantage of them. Even the elementary sounds of 'voyelles' can be coloured with meanings, some of which Beckett explores in his own diagrammatic way in *All Strange Away*. In *Ill Seen Ill Said* Beckett will make use of rituals of a very different sort. Although we do not normally associate his fiction with Celtic or Druidic monuments, the cromlechs dotting the Irish landscape of Beckett's childhood, *Ill Seen Ill Said* makes unusual use of them.

Cromlechs (the most famous of which is probably Stonehenge in England) were of course used by the Druids for plotting astronomical events. The circles of monoliths were also the sites for mysterious ceremonies involving animal and human sacrifice. The language of *Ill Seen Ill Said* makes many references to stars, the moon, the sun and other celestial bodies. 'From where she lies she sees Venus rise', the opening line of this story, is soon followed by 'she watches for the radiant one' and 'she savours its star's revenge'.[10]

The use of colour is similarly derivative. When preparing for battle or sacred rites, the ancient Celts would cover their bodies with 'woad', a plant substance that would make them look vaguely blue. Ward Rutherford notes that the Druids also had an 'odd custom of treating their hair with lime wash which not only bleached it, but made it stand back from their heads'.[11] In light of this material, let us now read a few choice selections from *Ill Seen Ill Said*: 'Save for the white of her hair and faintly bluish white of face and hands all is black' (7); 'her long white hair stares . . . as if shocked still by some ancient horror. Or by its continuance' (28–9).

Wherever it is that the figure is sitting in *Ill Seen Ill Said*, the surrounding environment comes curiously close to describing a cromlech. At Stonehenge, for example, there are fifty-six holes with chalk stones to mark the cycles of the moon. In a cromlech celestial events are viewed from an altar stone through spaces between the surrounding stones referred to as windows. Beckett renders his scene this way: 'Chalkstones of striking effect in the light of the moon. Let it be in opposition when the skies are clear. . . . quick to the other window to see the other marvel rise. . . . How whiter and whiter as it climbs it whitens more and more the stones' (9). At Stonehenge, furthermore, the diameter is frequently given as somewhere between 610 and 630 feet. Beckett measures his fictional space as follows: 'The two zones form roughly a circular whole . . . Diameter. Careful. Say one furlong' (9). Now a furlong is 660 feet. Beckett also states that 'her' passage is as though from 'one tier of a circus to the next' (27), the term 'circus' frequently being used to denote the different levels of stone circles comprising a cromlech.

Is all of this mere coincidence? Probably not, for the ancient rituals of *Ill Seen Ill Said* are only just beginning. Into this 'zone of stones' (13) enter human figures, 'come what may. Twelve' (10). Thirteen celebrants seem to have been involved in the Druidic rites, and Beckett's lone ghost-woman is perhaps the thirteenth. The buttonhook, mentioned far too often in this text to be ignored, is a real teaser. Is this the cult object of some mysterious religion, 'silver pisciform' (18) and engraved with scales? Rutherford even mentions it as a distinct possibility. The Druids indulged their tastes in personal adornment, their cloaks, for example, being secured by an intricately wrought pin, brooch or buttonhook of gold or silver. Even the cryptic date in Beckett's text ('Tu or Th 17') (38), together with the '[o]ne April afternoon' (57) points to a Druidic event not to be missed. For although the main Feast of Beltain is on 1 May, the actual festival starts much earlier.

Beckett, of course, has not gone anthropological on us. The pervasive use of ancient ritual in *Ill Seen Ill Said*, like its verbal counterpart in *All Strange Away*, is really there to point our way to something else, something that has to do with accessibility and communication after all. Ancient patterns and literary precedents are not so easily forgotten and, even if these fail us, we can always count on habit to be 'a great deadener'.[12] A seemingly obscure allusion in Beckett can sometimes perform marvels of invention, opening up a text for us that first seemed dreadfully esoteric. Nevertheless, a note of caution remains, on which we take from no less a source than *Watt*: 'Obscure keys may open simple locks, but simple keys obscure locks never.'[13] After all, the 'critic' may have got it 'ahll wrahng', Beckett's own sigh of resignation about so much interpretation of his work.[14] In any case, my point is simply this: in this upended fictional universe there are still things to latch onto, cromlechs and voyelles, that provide a tradition and a context for all that follows. It is Beckett's 'raid on the inarticulate',[15] a new way to make things strange that helps, finally, to make 'all' that seems so 'strange' in this late work go 'away'.

III

Worstward Ho provides us with the curious rite of a text far more accessible as a whole than in any of its parts. The work leaves an indelible impression, lines running rhythmically through the head, even though the reader, like Watt staring out at the picture hanging on the wall in Erskine's room, is at a loss to tell how the effect is achieved.[16]

First the body. No. First the place. No. First both. Now either. Now the other. Sick of the either try the other. Sick of it back sick of the either. So on. Somehow on. Till sick of both. Throw up and go. Where neither. Till sick of there. Throw up and back. The body again. Where none. The place again. Where none. Try again. Fail again. Better again. Or better worse. Fail worse again. Still worse again. Till sick for good. Throw up for good. Go for good. Where neither for good. Good and all.[17]

Beckett's dedicated reader, that 'gentle skimmer' so tenderly appealed to in *Murphy*,[18] will soon recognise the themes that keep this very particular piece of fiction going somehow 'nohow on' (7 *et passim*). For the more of Beckett one reads, the more Beckett one reads quantitatively per work. As one grows in familiarity with the seeming incongruities, the more readily they seem less incongruous. A narrative which, like Beckett's *The Unnamable*, 'can't go on',[19] yet doggedly refuses to stop until it gets itself 'said said said missaid' (36), is by now the expected, almost welcome company on this writer's unnamable road to nowhere and back again, something we are tempted to call, for want of a better word, the void. Equally recognisable is that overly fastidious voice which cannot help commenting on itself as it goes compulsively along, the subject/ object relations that are at once precise and indeterminate, and the general ambiance of no 'I', no 'have', and, it almost goes without saying, no 'being'.[20] Absence is, once again, a featured presence; so much, as the narrator of 'Enough' puts it, for the 'art and craft'.[21] Word processing unexplainably continues, but with a noticeable difference: all the good words have already been used, sometimes by this same author, and only the worst ones seem to remain, 'springes', as Polonius says, 'to catch woodcocks'. Language is 'sick': the ether, pun on 'the either', makes us '[t]hrow up for good' (8).

Given such an unenviable position, beyond *Lessness*, beyond *Fizzles*, beyond *Ill Seen Ill Said*, the writer can do no more than put his best foot forward, this despite the fact that he is, quite literally this time, putting his foot right into 'it':

> It, say it, not knowing what. Perhaps I simply assented at last to an old thing. But I did nothing. I seem to speak, it is not I, about me, it is not about me. These few general remarks to begin with. What am I to do, what shall I do, what should I do, in my situation, how proceed? By aporia pure and simple? Or by affirmations and negations invalidated as uttered, or sooner or later? Generally speaking. There must be other shifts. Otherwise it would be quite hopeless. But it is quite hopeless.[22]

Hopelessness, however, has never been a special obstacle in Beckett's world. His heroes seem to derive special nourishment, if not downright inspiration, from it. Buried up to the waist in mother earth, potted in urns, riding bicycles bent out of shape, queuing up inside flattened cylinders 'fifty metres round and sixteen high for the sake of harmony',[23] or dragging their feet, like Watt, in a series of 'funambulistic' staggers, they are forever going on, especially in words: 'call that going, call that on'.[24] Such calculated athleticism provides a tempting analogy for the vocation of writing, just as a body wracked with pain offers us a convenient metaphor for what generations of writers, in the struggle to tell their stories, have done to the fragile little body of language itself. The story Beckett's heroes are determined to tell is always the story of getting itself written, finished before the body gives up, the company is gone, or, as in the case of *Malone Dies*, the pencil (a Venus) simply runs out. Success or failure, not life or death, is the fabulist's ultimate conflict. The setting is officially the '[m]eremost minimum' (9), often no more than a thought, and the style, as always, is more a question of vision than technique.[25] The antagonist is language; the protagonist is the word and, as in the present case, not necessarily the best one at that.

Language has always been at the centre of Beckett's fictional universe and in *Worstward Ho* even the title seems to proclaim the '[u]nworsenable worse' (33) of 'that near true ring' (23). Words drive the reader on, 'worstward ho'. And what strange words they are. Ever since 'Whoroscope' (1930) Beckett has been partial to the neologism.[26] 'Worstward ho', significantly without the exclamation point (what is there to exclaim about?), is an immediately obtainable pun, one which, moreover, adds some flesh to the sanctity of the word. The phrase intertextualises a Renaissance play, Webster and Dekker's *Westward Hoe* (1607), and also a Victorian novel set in Elizabethan times, Charles Kingsley's *Westward Ho!* (1855). Beckett not only makes capital of the dark overtones of riding westward, made famous by another seventeenth-century writer, John Donne, but also prepares us for his own use of the kind of poetic energy T. S. Eliot so much admired in the dramatic language of the Tudor and Stuart playwrights.[27] The 'pox', 'ooze', and 'gnawing' of *Worstward Ho* are a modernist's attempts to make new an archaic but still muscular Jacobean vocabulary. And every Beckett reader will find satisfaction in the recognition that in *Worstward Ho*, where the word has become the ultimate hero, it too has a name that falls in which the long line of M's and W's marching triumphantly through the repertory, a weak and private but nonetheless pervasive joke that may in part explain the 'ho' – what Arsene in *Watt* calls 'the *risus purus*, the laugh laughing at the laugh, the beholding, the saluting of the highest joke, in a word the laugh that laughs – silence please – at that which is unhappy'.[28]

The title, then, which seems at first so straightforward, indeed almost a self-parody, is not really so straightforward after all. For 'worstward' is neither backward nor forward but somewhere in between. Although some of its overtones are strictly on the level of a crossword puzzle, other implications of this 'word go'[29] are more serious. Like so much else in this work, the title begins by making us uncertain and ends by making us insecure. The structure of *Worstward Ho* will follow a similarly unsettling pattern. Set up typographically on the page as a sequence of paragraphs, the piece presents a series of starts, some of which prove to be false:

> Where then but there see – (12)
> Where then but see there now – (12)
> The void. How try say? How try fail?
> No try no fail. Say only – (17)
>   Next try fail better two. The twain.
> Bad as it is as it is. Bad the no – (22)
> Next – (23)
> The eyes. Time to – (26)

Such abandoned work may prove all but unreadable, but it is certainly not unspeakable. Like the lines from *The Unnamable* quoted earlier in this essay, and like the Director's command to his female assistant in *Catastrophe*, Beckett's language in *Worstward Ho* demands of us that we say it. The piece is in fact written as a recitation, a self-performing artifact, something that needs to be heard, not read silently in a study. In this work it is the saying, to paraphrase a key line in *Molloy*, that constitutes the inventing.[30]

Worstward Ho thus offers us a language reduced to its most human and tender form, words meant to be spoken and words meant to be heard, preferably in the dark. You cannot *write* words like 'unworsenable worse', something far worse than *the worst*, but you can certainly say them, and with impunity, even when the result is the kind of language Beckett admired in Joyce's 'Work in Progress' (later *Finnegans Wake*).[31] A work limited to 'more', 'less', and 'worse' is simply not enough. 'I use the words you taught me', Clov laments in *Endgame*. 'If they don't mean anything any more, teach me others. Or let me be silent.'[32] But the silence, like the sex on Hamm's dog, goes on at the end. Until that time, and that time will come, prefixes and suffixes must be put energetically to work. The spoken language of *Worstward Ho* needs 'unworsenable' (33), 'unmoreable' (43), 'unlessenable' (33), and the great tongue-twister 'unmoreable unlessable unworsenable evermost almost void' (43). The paragraph structure, constantly backtracking on itself and echoing its own ineptitude, is stanzaic, a set of strophes and antistrophes featuring refrains which are choral and aural:

On. Say on. Be said on. Somehow on. Till nowhow on. Said nohow on (17).

It stands. See in the dim void how at last it stands. In the dim light source unknown. Before the downcast eyes. Clenched eyes. Staring eyes. Clenched staring eyes (10–11).

Less. Less seen. Less seeing. Less seen and seeing when with words than when not. When somehow than when nohow. Stare by words dimmed. Shades dimmed. Voice dimmed. Dim dimmed. All there as when no words. As when nohow. Only all dimmed. Till blank again. No words again. Nohow again. Then all undimmed. Stare undimmed. That words had dimmed (39).

Like May in *Footfalls*, we 'must hear [these] feet', these sounds and rhythms 'however faint they fall'.[33] The sound in these stanzas *is* the sense.

In *Worstward Ho* the sound/sense relations are extended to antonyms of a most unusual kind. The mind/body dichotomy is framed in a language which is not only 'lying' (11), but 'stands' (8), '[t]wo too' (26). Polarities are not polarities and yet are polarities, simultaneously so-say, un-say, and mis-say: 'Far and wide the same. High and low. Unchanging' (16). Things are not bad, they are the worst; things are not small, they are '[m]eremost minimum' (9); things are not far, but '[f]ar far' (20); things are, finally, not said, but 'said said said' (36), only one vowel away from sad. Lacking the articles *a*, *an*, and *the*, we are not sure which description is confined to which limitation. And on those rare occasions when an article introduces a little variety into the emerging composition, such determination provides only a very distorted close focus: 'a child and yet a child', '[a] man and yet a man', the latter '[o]ld yet old' (44–5). Double negatives are supposed to yield something positive, but not in this work: 'Whence no farther. Best worse no farther.

Nohow less. Nohow worse. Nohow naught. Nohow on' (47).

Spoken language, even when delivered in the 'arsy-versy'[34] syntax of *Worstward Ho*, normally presupposes a speaker, but in this fiction Beckett makes us hear the rhythms of speech without the intrusion of an identifiable speech act. Unlike Beckett's drama, where the source of language is carefully controlled (Mouth in *Not I*, the Reader in *Ohio Impromptu*, or the Speaker so aptly named in *A Piece of Monologue*), this prose work confronts us with no such mediating presence. Words are, instead, decentred, offering us no local habitation and certainly no name. The absence of an identifiable speaker creates the greatest mystery here, but at the same time it allows us to study language in a pure sense. Psychological factors like motivation, the rich subtext of intrigue and self-interest any speaker inevitably brings with him, can now be held at bay. Language is finite, experience is not. How then can language be a diagram of experience? Not only are words limited, they are tainted with imprecision and cluttered with the multitude of meanings they embody. Before an action or an image can be captured in words, it is over. Replacing the speaker with the speech itself liberates language from one of its principal restraints. Language can now have a being for-itself and a being by-itself, moving on with a vigour and a seeming autonomy of its own. In *Worstward Ho* Beckett asks us to question the words themselves, where the words are going to, not where the words are coming from.

In making the language the story, and not the vehicle for a story, *Worstward Ho* represents a considerable advance over an earlier work like *Company*. Yet in Beckett a step forward is always a step backward, a further reduction of what is already a reduction. Consider what happens in *Company*. Although this work shares with *Worstward Ho* a language which 'lies' flat 'on [its] back in the dark',[35] such concentration on the essence of words is often in conflict with passages of intense lyricism:

A strand. Evening. Light dying. Soon none left to die. No. No such thing then as no light. Died on to dawn and never died. You stand with your back to the wash. No sound but its. Ever fainter as it slowly ebbs. Till it slowly flows again. You lean on a long staff. Your hands rest on the knob and on them your head. Were your eyes to open they would first see far below in the last rays the skirt of your greatcoat and the uppers of your boots emerging from the sand. Then and it alone till it vanishes the shadow of the staff on the sand. Vanishes from your sight. Moonless starless night. Were your eyes to open dark would lighten.[36]

Clearly, such a passage focuses our attention not on the words themselves, but on the images, on what the words can be made to say. Indeed, the whole effort here seems to capture in language a fleeting memory torn from the past. *Worstward Ho* attempts to scuttle such literary adventurism as romanticism of the worst sort, a 'Wordsworthy'[37] opportunism that makes language the slave of sloppy sentimentality. 'But to hell with all this fucking scenery', Malone reminds himself when he, too, begins to wax similarly eloquent.[38] In *Worstward Ho* language is bent on defending itself against the ravages of such figurative enticement:

> The words too whosesoever. What room for worse! How almost true they sometimes ring! How wanting in inanity! Say the night is young alas and take heart. Or better worse say still a watch of night alas to come. A rest of last watch to come. And take heart (21).
> Next the so-said seat and germ of all. Those hands! That head! That near true ring! Away. Full face from now. No hands. No face. Skull and stare alone. Scene and seer of all (23).

One of the great ironies of Beckett's attempt to 'desophisticate'[39] language in *Worstward Ho* is the uncanny way his words have of resurrecting themselves. Despite Beckett's most earnest endeavours to denature words, their properties of being keep trailing clouds of glory (there is Wordsworth popping up again) behind them. What Barthes called language's 'secondary memory' will not let language lie still.[40] Images, no matter how cryptically rendered, keep insinuating their immediacy into this supposedly empty text: 'Clenched eyes. Staring eyes. Clenched staring eyes' (11). As if to make matters worse, the image goes so far as to allow us to watch how it gets itself made, from 'clenched eyes' to 'staring eyes' to the inevitability of 'clenched staring eyes', '[t]hree pins', as Beckett declares in the penultimate stanza, for '[o]ne pinhole' (46). The writer's hands are 'crippled' (22). The attempt to make language forget its secondary memory is a myth, like the belief in *The Lost Ones* that there exists a way out. But, and here is the *but* that keeps the fiction going on, 'No try. No fail' (17). The process of reducing language until it can go no farther makes the outline of the void more precise, even though the void itself (of which, as in *Godot*, there is no 'lack'),[41] can never be fully defined. Here language, a finite mechanism, reveals its endless variety and its boundless potential, approaching that infinity that is experience itself.

But in *Worstward Ho* Beckett is not content to leave us with just another demonstration of how language fails once again to say nothing, 'a little yes, a little no, enough to exterminate a regiment of dragoons'.[42] Into this work Beckett builds a man, a woman and a child, and it is from this primary family, rather than from the flea in *Endgame*, that 'humanity might start from there all over again'.[43] Even though they may '[t]ry again', only to '[f]ail better' (7), it is their frail endurance, walking 'hand in hand' (13), that keeps the life of language – and life itself – going on. For 'preying', a word used so often in this text, is also, inescapably, a homonym for 'praying'. The '[d]int of long longing' is finally 'lost to longing' (36) itself. The resolution of the conflict comes with the acceptance of the conflict, just as the text comes to rest in silence.

Language lies, then, in *Worstward Ho* as something more than one of the several 'loopings of the loop' we find in Beckett's repertory.[44] That quality of being less has now degenerated into that quality of being worse. And yet there is still no occasion to despair. Quite the contrary: the language is almost heroic in its mad determination to go on. The void cannot be conquered, but it can still be described, especially when part of the description is the writer's inability to describe it. In this enterprise the writer shares with us the challenge his words must face. By doing so, by risking so much, the potentially abstract and inhuman reaches out to us in what is, for Beckett at least, a new kind of humanity. For though this work lacks a speaker, it by no means lacks a voice. The voice, is, unmistakably, Beckett's. *Worstward Ho* is a communion in words, what writing, for better or worse, has always been all about. Words, even the worst ones, exist in time and space. Only silence is their great extinguisher, but even in that 'dim void' (12) words ask us to remember them:

> Footfalls echo in the memory
> Down the passage which we did not take
> Towards the door we never opened
> Into the rose-garden. My words echo
> Thus, in your mind.[45]

In *Worstward Ho* Beckett's words are there to assure not only the reader, but also Beckett himself, that language never really lies: even in the dark silence that threatens to overwhelm us all – reader, writer, listener – this language defiantly 'stands', a marvel of invention and a monument, finally, to something more than itself, as a text, in the very best sense of the word, for company: ' – Hypocrite lecteur, – mon semblable, – mon frère!'[46]

Notes

1. *Worstward Ho* (London: John Calder, 1983) p. 9, and *All Strange Away*, in Samuel Beckett, *Collected Shorter Prose 1945–1980* (London: John Calder, 1984) p. 118. All quotations from *Worstward Ho* and *All Strange Away* are from these editions; page numbers are given in the text.
2. See H. Porter Abbott, 'A Grammar for Being Elsewhere', *Journal of Modern Literature*, 6 (Feb. 1977) 39–46.
3. Samuel Beckett, *Murphy* (London: John Calder, 1970) p. 60.
4. See James Knowlson and John Pilling, *Frescoes of the Skull: the Later Prose and Drama of Samuel Beckett* (London: John Calder, 1979) p. 136.
5. *The Lost Ones*, in Samuel Beckett, *Collected Shorter Prose 1945–1980*, p. 161.
6. *Ping*, in Samuel Beckett, *Collected Shorter Prose 1945–1980*, p. 149.
7. Arthur Rimbaud, 'Voyelles', in *Oeuvres complètes* (Paris: Gallimard, 1972) p. 53.
8. Quoted by John Fletcher in *The Novels of Samuel Beckett* (London: Chatto & Windus, 1970) p. 227.
9. *Collected Shorter Prose 1945–1980*, p. 179.
10. Samuel Beckett, *Ill Seen Ill Said* (London: John Calder, 1982) p. 7. All quotations from *Ill Seen Ill Said* are from this edition; page numbers are given in the text.
11. My information about the Druids and ancient Celts, as well as Stonehenge, is from Ward Rutherford, *The Druids* (Wellingsborough: Aquarian Press, 1983), and J. A. Macculloch, *The Religion of the Ancient Celts* (Edinburgh: T. & T. Clarke, 1911).
12. Samuel Beckett, *Waiting for Godot* (London: Faber & Faber, 1965) p. 91.
13. Samuel Beckett, *Watt* (London: Calder & Boyars, 1970) p. 122.
14. See Alan Schneider, 'Waiting for Beckett', in *Beckett at Sixty* (London: Calder & Boyars, 1967) p. 39.
15. 'East Coker', in T. S. Eliot, *Four Quartets* (London: Faber & Faber, 1963) p. 31.
16. See Samuel Beckett, *Watt* (London: John Calder, 1970) pp. 126–7.
17. *Worstward Ho* (London: John Calder, 1983) p. 8. All quotations are from this edition; page numbers are given in the text.
18. Samuel Beckett, *Murphy* (London: John Calder, 1970) p. 60.
19. Samuel Beckett, *Molloy/Malone Dies/The Unnamable* (London: Calder &

Boyars, 1973) p. 418. All quotations from Beckett's trilogy of novels are from this edition.

20. See Israel Shenker, 'An Interview with Beckett (1956)' in *Samuel Beckett: the Critical Heritage*, eds Lawrence Graver and Raymond Federman (London: Routledge & Kegan Paul, 1979) p. 146.
21. 'Enough', in Samuel Beckett, *Collected Shorter Prose 1945–1980*, p. 139.
22. *The Unnamable*, p. 293.
23. *The Lost Ones*, in Samuel Beckett, *Collected Shorter Prose 1945–1980*, p. 159.
24. *Watt*, p. 29; *The Unnamable*, p. 293.
25. See Beckett's famous statement on this point in his 1931 essay on Proust (in *Proust/Three Dialogues with Georges Duthuit* (London: John Calder, 1965) pp. 87–8): 'For Proust, as for the painter, style is more a question of vision than of technique.'
26. 'Whoroscope', in Samuel Beckett, *Collected Poems in English and French* (London: John Calder, 1977) p. 1.
27. See John Donne, 'Good Friday, 1613. Riding Westward' in *The Metaphysical Poets*, ed. Helen Gardner (Harmondsworth: Penguin, 1966) p. 86. See also T. S. Eliot, *Selected Essays* (London: Faber & Faber, 1951).
28. *Watt*, p. 47.
29. *A Piece of Monologue*, in Samuel Beckett, *Collected Shorter Plays* (London: Faber & Faber, 1984) p. 269.
30. See *Molloy*, p. 32.
31. See 'Dante . . . Bruno . Vico . . Joyce' (1929), in Samuel Beckett, *Disjecta: Miscellaneous Writings and a Dramatic Fragment*, ed. Ruby Cohn (London: John Calder, 1983) pp. 19–33.
32. Samuel Beckett, *Endgame* (London: Faber & Faber, 1958) p. 31.
33. *Footfalls*, in Samuel Beckett, *Collected Shorter Plays*, p. 241.
34. *All That Fall*, in Samuel Beckett, *Collected Shorter Plays*, p. 31.
35. Samuel Beckett, *Company* (London: John Calder, 1980) p. 7.
36. Ibid., p. 7.
37. *Murphy*, p. 74.
38. *Malone Dies*, p. 279.
39. 'Dante . . . Bruno . Vico . . Joyce', p. 28.
40. See Roland Barthes, *Le degré zéro de l'écriture* (Paris: Seuil, 1953).
41. Samuel Beckett, *Waiting for Godot* (London: Faber & Faber, 1965) p. 66.
42. *The Unnamable*, p. 305.
43. *Endgame*, p. 27.
44. *Malone Dies*, p. 269.
45. 'Burnt Norton', in T. S. Eliot, *Four Quartets*, p. 13.
46. Charles Baudelaire, 'Au lecteur', in *Baudelaire: Selected Verse* (Harmondsworth: Penguin, 1967) p. 156.

12

Beckett's New *Godot*

Colin Duckworth

The *Godot* phenomenon has gone through several stages, which have been recorded and analysed in detail.[1] Inevitably, Beckett's first major intervention in the production of the English version (he directed it in German at the Schiller Theater, Berlin, in 1975) has occasioned several further changes. The overall significance of these changes, and of his directions to the actors involved in the 1984 production, is that we can now have a clear insight into his own view of his most famous play a third of a century after he wrote it.

The production in question was that of the San Quentin Drama Workshop, founded by ex-convict Rick Cluchey, which was scheduled to come as a main attraction to the Adelaide Festival, then do seasons in Melbourne and Sydney, and an extended tour of Europe and the USA. Beckett's own involvement with the production was short but very intensive. When I met him in Paris a couple of weeks before he was due to start rehearsals in London, he said, shaking his head sadly, 'What can I do in ten days?' He was, at that stage, very pessimistic about what he could achieve in such a short time with actors whom he had not worked with before *in those roles* (even though he had worked with them on other plays). The cast had already been working for several weeks in Chicago under the direction of Walter Asmus, who had been his associate director for the Berlin production of *Godot*; between them, they thought they knew fairly clearly what Beckett wanted, and envisaged the London rehearsals as a fine tuning process. They were very wrong. At the time Beckett was speaking to me in January, he was already preparing some major changes that would cause Asmus and the actors to look at the text and their roles afresh and, at times, aghast.

Unfortunately, I was unable to remain in London to sit in on the rehearsals, as they were delayed slightly.[2] However, through the good offices of Rick Cluchey and of James Knowlson, I was able to obtain a copy of Cluchey's Faber edition, annotated by Beckett for this production; I attended several performances and made careful notes of textual and directorial interest, and used these as the basis of a long and detailed recorded interview with Rick Cluchey (Pozzo), Bud Thorpe (Vladimir) and Larry Held (Estragon) in Melbourne.

Beckett scholars owe them a considerable debt for the light they throw on the reasons and motivation for some of the changes made in this new version.[3] The discussion was not, I think, without its historical importance. One might compare it with, say, a discussion with the cast of the Globe Theatre about the Bard's own production of *Hamlet*, with regard to what he actually did for and to the actors on stage. For the actors had the experience not only of having been directed by Beckett in the play that in so many respects changed the face and direction of European theatre in the 1950s, but also of being in on the creative process, the evolutionary dynamic process, of arriving at what Beckett must reasonably expect to be his final *Godot*. Where, I wondered, did the motivation for this production come from, how was it all arranged? Cluchey replied that it was the result of nearly ten years' persistence; little by little Beckett had agreed to undertake the production of *Godot*, *Endgame* and *Krapp's Last Tape*, within the limits of his energy and schedule.

The organisation and arrangement of rehearsals created many tensions, frustrations and conflicts; five weeks under Asmus in Chicago, then ten days with Beckett at the Riverside studios in London, did not constitute the ideal schedule. Was the relationship between actor and writer–director at all strained during this process, I wondered. Cluchey replied that it had not been at the time, but after fifty or more performances the actor finds the need to experiment:

> In rehearsal, Beckett was the task-master, and although you are obviously thrilled at doing the work at that time, you find that all you can do is maintain concentration, because he is giving you very little time to assimilate his direction. The tendency is to want to stop and ask him what he meant by such and such a direction.

Would Cluchey recommend having to transfer from one director to another?

> I would certainly do it again, under those circumstances. I cannot speak for the others – I know it was particularly painful for Walter Asmus. It was no secret to any of us that he suffered deeply at the

rearrangement of the human furniture in the play, of the choreography, when the various elaborate moments set up by Beckett in the Berlin production came crashing down. The thrill of having a writer of Beckett's talents redirect and change – beyond just cutting, but also adding – had a great impact on everyone.

For Bud Thorpe, what was gained in this production was in human qualities ('the characters now definitely have souls'), whereas their previous production had been highly stylised and, as Rick Cluchey put it, 'balletic'. From working with Beckett, said Thorpe, one gained an insight into 'the inside terror, the inside hurt of giving these characters souls. They now have an incredible depth, they're no longer caricature of human beings.'

It is presumably from the comparison between the current production by Beckett, and Cluchey's previous production, that Donna Foote found the characters in the new *Godot* 'more sympathetic', and the production as a whole 'more human, more accessible – and ultimately more beautiful than its precursors'.[4] One wonders what productions she had previously seen: certainly not the Royal Court production in 1965, with Nicol Williamson's moving Vladimir and Jack McGowran's anguished Lucky, or Peter O'Toole's production at the Nottingham Playhouse with Frank Middlemass's Lucky, which he managed to make both hilarious and immensely touching. Even my own humble production at the Maidment Theatre, Auckland, sent people away with lumps in their throats and tears in their eyes.

There is nothing new, then, in a *Godot* whose characters are not 'caricatures of human beings'. Bud Thorpe did, in fact, respond to my reservations, by qualifying the statement thus: '*Our* evolution was a transition from caricatures to more of a human quality.'

Larry Held had some very revealing comments to make regarding the effect Beckett's direction had on his interpretation of the role of Estragon. Were there, I asked, vast, sudden changes of characterisation?

No – the basic character was there and remained; but the levels on which that basic character worked were expanded considerably. There were moments that I felt very happy with, moments that were very amusing, that had been developed in Chicago, but suddenly they had the life taken right out of them. And that, initially, was a problem for me; but that is always an actor's problem – having to accommodate the director's wishes. And in this case, the director also happens to be the writer. It became very obvious to me that Beckett's work is always in a state of flux and evolution, and that this was how he felt at this particular time, how he saw the play at this time, hence this is how he was going to direct it.

The possibility of a *definitive* production of the play, analogous to the definitive version of a text that every scholarly editor wants to bring out, seems vitiated by two factors: first, the frame of mind of the writer–director during any given set of rehearsals; and secondly, the fact that Beckett was having to work with and through the temperaments of actors whom he had not hand-picked (as he had in the case of the Schiller Theater production). Nevertheless, the point was strongly made, in our discussion, that this most recent version was important because it was what Beckett wanted to say in 1984; after a minimal rehearsal period it might well be, and it is true that given another ten or twenty days he would no doubt have made further crucial changes – but this is the latest version Beckett has given us to date. Is it the best? Is it an improvement? Let the discussion speak for itself:

> CD: The contrast between the characters of Vladimir and Estragon does come out very strongly in this production, on account of the harshness, edge and bitterness that Estragon has, compared with the extreme gentleness and mildness of Vladimir. Was this part of Beckett's vision of the characters?
> BT: When Walter Asmus was building and preparing us for the roles and the meeting with Beckett, with the soul-searching for the human qualities, our own temperaments became accessible. You can search and search for a genuine performance, but you also have to accept the fact of what that actor's temperament is. I don't think Walter or Beckett could have fought that fact; it was accepted that we were two human beings trying their best in a very difficult portrayal.
> LH: What you're saying is that you are gentle and kind, and I'm a grouch.
> BT: Definitely. That's what I'm trying to say. [*Much laughter*].
> RC: Beckett, now approaching his eightieth year, would like to clear up, if possible, any misconceptions about what he intended

by the play; and in the latter half of the twentieth century, to improve what he himself agrees was a quickly-done translation into English, given that the standing text was not overly admired by himself, the creator. Beckett is here saying 'Let us be observant, let us take our cues from this production of the English.' But if he had had ten more days, I'm sure he would have cut, added, cut, added, orchestrated, rearranged, in an endless process, because the play is full and rich.

CD: What do you think about the wisdom of letting authors loose on their own work thirty years later? It isn't guaranteed to be an improvement, is it?

LH: With Beckett, it is an evolutionary process. Sure, in some people's eyes it is going to be far worse now, perhaps, but it is still very important because that is what he is doing and saying *now*, not thirty years ago.

CD: If one looks at what he has done to this text in terms of his own development as a dramatist since *Godot* was first written – which has been a gradual paring away, a whittling down, a more and more dense and poetic approach to what language can do, inevitably if he were to start from scratch on *Waiting for Godot* now, he would write a totally different play – it would be a concentration, judging by intervening works such as *Breath*, *Footfalls*, *Not I*, *Catastrophe*, *Rockaby*. They are all sonnets as compared with epics.

RC: What we are dealing with here is Beckett's view of the human condition as evidenced by these rites of passage to the later part of this century. He's focused on the changes around him, as a dramatist, as a poet, and what he has said is, 'Let my poetry be one thing, but let my understanding of the human condition be another.' And this otherness is what we are directed towards. Our understanding of his understanding of it is very complicated. For example, in the midst of this whole process, he comes up to Larry and says, 'Do it this way'; Larry has the right to turn around and say, 'But what do you mean?' Yet we all know there isn't time for a whole lot of explanation, and the more Beckett tries to explain the more tenuous it can become.

CD: So you all had to take a lot of short cuts.

RC: From our bridge of five weeks' work into Beckett's vision of it, I would say so.

BT: It comes down to incredible trust: trust in Beckett's judgement and in there being a reason for it. If there was time later in the day, we could ask, 'What do you mean by that, Sam?' In the meantime, let's just keep on going; we've got a lot to do.

LH: We all had the problem of finding what he wanted some other time, some other place – perhaps it came during another performance, perhaps you'd suddenly think, 'Ah, now I know how to do that, now I know what the truth of that is.' It always fell back on us.

Cluchey had a comment to make about Beckett's approach to *Godot* in 1984:

Beckett is saying: 'this was superfluous, that was too poetic, too much of a stage gimmick, I don't need these weeds coming up to choke the garden. I want to cut out the weeds, to get right back to the human plank, to reduce my philosophical content – not to make it obscure, but to give it a silence, to give it deeper silences, to disallow the puppetry of the characters, the vaudevillian aspect of the play, the clown and Chaplin routines, and to grow into the focus of the human condition in 1984.' Less grand, if you will, none the less poetic, however, with as much economy and minimalism in the form, to allow us to look at the content. It is evocative of Beckett's genius that he can come to us thirty years after [the first productions of the play] and remove obstacles to our understanding from the text, or rather, obstacles to our *hearing* of the play. He has orchestrated the way we hear and see it so that it is precisely what he wants. He has finally got us to listen.

CD: He is still, of course, working through the filter of your own individual talents and interpretation, and within ten days there is really very little he could do as far as the fine tuning is concerned.

BT: That's a good point; he was just beginning to warm up and become comfortable with the script that he threw down too many times during the first three days of our getting together in London. As the days progressed, you could see his energy and excitement building, and he knew that time was just going to end it, when he had to go back to Paris and we had to move on to the Adelaide Festival. Near the beginning of rehearsals I remember seeing him knock himself on the head with his knuckles, saying, 'I can't do anything because I don't know the script.' We had spent so much time with it, and he had come in new to it; but at the end of those ten days, he was ready to continue. I too wonder what kind of performance we would have ended up with in ten more days. I think it would have been quite remarkably beyond, beyond.

CD: So it isn't quite the definitive production that it could have been, according to some commentators?

LH: I don't think one could ever reach a definitive production. After ten days we would have reached a certain point, then another ten days . . .

BT: We also have to bear in mind that we are *a group* – the only group Beckett will work with as a group. We have to go back to the Schiller Theater production to find the actors he chose – Wigger and Bollman and Raddatz, and Klaus Herm. They, their physical types, were his choice. But he has accepted a group, with us, and has worked well within those talents. But we have worked with him many times, unlike an actor pulled out of the ranks to work with a master.

CD: The comments that you have made about the warmth and humanity and soul coming through in the characterisation in this production would seem to indicate that the playing under Beckett's direction is much more on a human and perhaps more realistic level. The very first words of the play, Estragon's 'Nothing to be done' (9), were accompanied by a large gesture (which was presumably Beckett's direction), which seemed to me anything but a naturalistic one; it was a heightened, rhetorical, gesture. So the play started off on that level – slightly stagey.

LH: Initially, when I first sat down and did that, it felt awful, but I knew it was something Walter [Asmus] had carried to Chicago from Beckett's Berlin production, and I thought I'd work on it myself, and I've come to enjoy it. Yes; it is a *large* gesture.

CD: Conversely, Vladimir loses quite a lot of the anger the original text calls on him to express. For example, there is no longer any anger when you say, 'Nothing is certain when you're about' (14), as is directed in the text. There is very little anger when you come back on stage, after going off for the first time to pee. This is all part of the 'mildification' of Vladimir. On the other hand, both of you are quite sadistic towards Lucky, to an extent that I've not seen before, in the way that you tease him – particularly Estragon. So there are surprises for me in these two characters – which is a great enrichment. But I wonder, did they just grow, or are they things Beckett said something about?

RC: I think his comment holds true here, that Estragon is 'of the earth', therefore he's the one to kick the bags, and to approach Lucky about the bones, and to be concerned about the rope around his neck, whereas Vladimir, being more orientated away from the earth, has the other concerns, which can be quite sarcastic and vicious. But on the other hand, I remember Beckett saying of Pozzo, 'I don't want any more of this overbearing landowner, all this barking.'

BT: I know we talked about the beating up of Lucky, which no longer happens in this production [when they remove his hat after his monologue (45)]. Sam just waived it off, and said, 'It never did work anyhow.' The loss of violence here seems to show more of a human element instead of always the physical.

CD: The reference to Estragon's being beaten up during the night is still there. It is still a fact that as soon as he goes back into society he becomes a victim. In view of that, what is he doing at the side of the stage at the beginning of Act II, in full view of the public? Why isn't the stage empty, as it says in the text?

LH: Yes, he's visible; it's just something that happened. In Chicago I used to stand upstage facing out, which is what Beckett did in Berlin. But then he didn't like that in London, so he wanted me to be *there*, visible but in the shadows. So I suppose I was never not there, except for the brief moments when we ran off.

CD: That increases the extent to which you are tied to that spot, as far as the audience is concerned; because if you're coming in from nowhere on to the stage, you have gone anywhere; but they do not now get the sense that you have gone away and come back.

RC: But this now reinforces the similes in the play; Beckett wants the circularity, he wants these mirror images and echoes, one built upon the other. So the beginning of Act II is the echo of what Didi did in the first act. In effect, it's a case of 'You were there, and now I'm there.'[5]

Bud Thorpe, at this point, stressed the inadequacies of the Universal Theatre stage and its unsuitability for this production, which was blocked for a proscenium stage with much greater depth. Discussion then centred on what I consider to be one of the most extraordinary, repeated, and yet simple changes to the text; namely, the exchange:

– Let's go.
– We can't.

– Why not?
– We're waiting for Godot.
– Ah! (14 *et passim*)

which has now become 'Ah, yes!'. That 'Ah' has always been open
to multiple interpretations from actors playing Estragon, from anger
to despair to 'Ah?', and so on. It would seem, I suggested, that the
interpretation has now been narrowed down, because there is less
the actor can do with 'Ah, yes!'. How did the change come about?

LH: I believe it first came about in Berlin, when it became 'Ach,
ja'.
RC: Yes, it was inspired by Bollman, who played Estragon.
Beckett loved the way that phrase sounds and turns. For example,
when we were rehearsing *Krapp's Last Tape* in Berlin, Beckett told
me, 'I nearly called the play *Ah, Well*.' The poet comes out eternally
in Beckett, you see.
CD: That would indicate that the 'Ah, yes' is rather wistful?
LH: The full story is that when Walter [Asmus] came to Chicago,
it was 'Ah, yes'; then for a while in London it was somewhere
between 'Ah' and 'Ah, yes', and it finally came down on the side
of 'Ah, yes!'. But I can still remember the way Sam was doing it: 'A
. . . agh . . .', but with a 'yes' on the end, suggesting 'Still the
same old thing, still the same old thing'.
BT: I remember that Larry was sometimes saying 'Ah', and
sometimes 'Ah, yes', and Sam said, 'Well, which is it going to be,
because we have to have uniformity.' After some whispered
discussion it was decided it would be 'Ah, yes'.
LH: But it certainly started with the German: 'Ach, ja' is better
than 'Ach'.

I then queried the change from 'Eleven' (28) to 'Ageless', which
causes the loss of a laugh-line. Previously Estragon's irreverent
answer was either a put-down implying 'Don't bother me with silly
questions', or a dig at Vladimir for his 'infantile', overexcited
protests about Pozzo's treatment of Lucky. I suggested that this has
now become a much more portentous and unfunny response.

LH: You say it was the loss of a laugh, but Beckett didn't think it
was funny. In fact, he finds a lot of the play very unfunny. And
when he finds something unfunny, he can make it unfunnier still.

So he shook his head and said 'That's a terrible line, I never liked that', and he looked down, scratched his head for a bit, then said 'Ageless'. We said, 'OK'.

[Perhaps the French and German Estragons' reply was preferable to this: 'Ask *him*' (Vladimir)].

We then moved on to the major cuts that have been made in this latest version of *Godot*, and the reasons Beckett had for making them. The suppression of the suggested names for Lucky's dance ('The Scapegoat's Agony' and 'The Hard Stool') came about simply because he thought 'it wasn't progressing fast enough'. It must be borne in mind that despite this and the many other (sometimes considerable) cuts, Beckett has lengthened the playing time enormously: it is now almost three hours, and previous productions that have left quite adequate time for full value to be given to the pauses and silences that form an essential part of the Beckettian score have lasted as little as two hours.

Pozzo's vaporiser routine has gone. Was Rick Cluchey just told to cut it, or were there reasons given?

RC: In the general process of tightening up the play, Beckett is disallowing these rather useless items of furniture and delaying tactics; he has also disallowed the pipe. I feel that Beckett definitely made the correct choice here; it slows the action.
CD: That's true for the vaporiser, too, is it? That always struck me as a good routine.
RC: Yes, but it's a prop; he's already got their attention, that was Beckett's comment. He wants to keep the focus.
CD: So this is part of the process that has also been applied to *Krapp's Last Tape*, for example, cutting the bananas and the drawer and the keys and so on . . .?
RC: Yes, he's cut the banal from them.

I wondered if Beckett had said anything about the deletion of Vladimir's comment to Estragon, 'I'll carry you. (*Pause.*) If necessary' (32). Bud Thorpe recalled that 'this was one of the cuts that came on our first day of rehearsal in Chicago, 7 December 1983. Walter [Asmus] sat down and said, "Before we do anything, we're going to go through the script and make cuts." That was never discussed. It had already been cut in the German production.' [But it remains in the published German text (Suhrkamp, 86)].

CD: It's a nice little touch to Vladimir's character, though, isn't it? The immediate generosity, then the caution.

Cluchey came in at this point with a comment about the status of these changes: 'Beckett will not impose any of these cuts on the published editions of this play. "The text is the text", quote, Beckett. But in the production, directed by Beckett, depending on who the actors are, he makes these abrogations of text, for the sake of that given production.'

CD: So anyone directing this in future needn't feel that he's got to stick with these changes?
RC: Correct.

[The fact remains, however, that Beckett was carrying over a number of changes from the Berlin production, which had had a very different cast].

There is at one point a line with a very menacing tone about it, Pozzo's reply to Estragon's question about whether Lucky ever refused to dance: 'He refused once. (*Silence*.)' (40). That has been cut. Cluchey saw this as part of Beckett's acute ear for the extraneous, now that he has directed it several times. He finds the unnecessary painful.

CD: That is a good indication of how subjective the idea of what is necessary or unnecessary in the text is. I would personally regard that a very important line as far as Pozzo's character is concerned. But he's lost some of his viciousness and sadism anyway: there's been a kind of 'nicification' of Pozzo's character in this production, and this is part of it, maybe?
RC: Correct. Again, it's Beckett's attempt to make him more human, and to make the event on stage more accessible to the theatregoer.

When Pozzo loses his watch, he decides that he must have 'left it at the manor' (46). The new version adds: 'On my Steinway.' Cluchey remembered that Beckett commented, 'Well, if he's got a manor, he must have something in it. Why not a Steinway?' Everybody laughed, and he said, 'OK, it's in.' I commented that this rather grand piece of bourgeois furniture seemed at variance with the new run-down Pozzo: he wears no socks, he has holed knees in his trousers, he is much closer to Didi and Gogo that I have ever seen before. Cluchey recalled that even in the Berlin production he was less shabby; but since then, the world has changed, and so has Beckett's image of Pozzo:

> RC: I think Beckett is focusing here on the disintegration that has gone on in an accelerated fashion in this part of the century. What were the trappings of the bourgeois landowner have now disintegrated into decay and dependence and vulnerability, as we see the shape of the world changing as well.
> CD: So there is now a faded gentility about him.
> LH: But who's to say that Pozzo *has* got a Steinway?

There is a rather extraordinary addition to the Faber edition, indicated in square brackets, below:

> ESTRAGON: I'm in hell!
> VLADIMIR: Where were you? (74)
> [ESTRAGON: To the foot of the rise.
> VLADIMIR: No doubt we are on a plateau. Served up on a plateau.
> ESTRAGON: They're coming there too!
> VLADIMIR: We're surrounded!]

That reference to the plateau dates back to the original French edition of the play; Beckett has omitted it from all English editions, but included it in the German version, both for the Schiller Theater and for the Suhrkamp edition. It became part of the English version in Chicago. The actors had varied reactions to it:

> BT: In my philosophy, if there is no way out, you are on a plateau, there is no place to go save where you are.
> RC: The plateau here is the stage. These are actors being served up. It is a poetic metaphor for their situation.
> CD: And it adds to the image of Didi and Gogo as passive victims of some force outside themselves, doesn't it?
> RC: Well, if the play is based on waiting, and everybody paid to come in and wait with us, then yes. It is rather diabolical.

Another addition occurring in the new version is partly to be found in the original French edition, and partly stems from the

Schiller Theater version: in Act II (Faber edition, 88), Pozzo and Lucky are about to leave; Vladmir creates a lovely moment in the new version when he relates to the blind Pozzo what his carrier is doing:

POZZO: As you please. Let me go! Up!
VLADIMIR: He's getting up.
POZZO: He'd better.
VLADIMIR: He's picking up his bags. Now he's all set.
POZZO: Whip!
VLADIMIR: Where do you go from here?
POZZO: No concern of mine.
VLADIMIR: How changed you are.
POZZO: Whip!

Here, then, Beckett has reintroduced into Pozzo's lines some of the menace he removed with the line 'He refused once.' And in Cluchey's opinion, he has emphasised the reversed circularity of the play's structure. In response to my comment that he delivered the line 'No concern of mine' rather jocularly, as if relieved of the responsibility, Cluchey replied: 'Pozzo is now in the reverse position, he's in Lucky's position in the first act; they've changed places. Beckett uses one dimension of his characters' humanness to point up the opposite in the other character. Or, if they are a human tandem, they are linked together by more than the rope. In Act II, Lucky is the motivator.'

Another addition (in square brackets below) comes to us in this new version from the French, via the German:

VLADIMIR: I wonder is he really blind.
ESTRAGON: Blind? Who? (90).
[VLADIMIR: Would one truly blind say he had no sense of time?]

This incorporation of 'Un vrai aveugle dirait-il qu'il n'a pas la notion du temps?' (84) leads one to marvel at its omission earlier. Bud Thorpe was presented with it for the first time in Chicago: 'It is a beautiful addition; and it's an echo from when Pozzo says earlier, "The blind have no notion of time. The things of time are hidden from them too", and Vladimir replies, "Well just fancy that! I could have sworn it was just the opposite"' (86).

In the new version Godot has grown another possibility for the colour of his beard: Vladimir asks the boy, 'Has he a beard, Mr. Godot? . . . Fair, or . . . (*he hesitates*) black (92) . . . [or red?]. According to Thorpe, this is a direct echo of the story of the man who went to the brothel (half-told by Estragon (16)). This is taken from the Schiller Theater version. As Ruby Cohn has pointed out, this is a remarkable addition that pointedly relates Godot to a smutty story – 'the physical and metaphysical, the vulgar and ethereal'.[6] So, Beckett has now added a scatalogical level to Vladimir's curiosity about Mr Godot's appearance (for those who are wide awake enough to make the connection), a level which automatically detracts from the awed seriousness of the question as it had previously read, a level which would justify, now, a jocular reading by Didi, perhaps even with accompanying 'Haw, haw!' and affecting his next line (in response to the Boy's suggestion that it is a white beard): 'Christ have mercy on us!' (92).

In his original published translation of *Godot*, Beckett made no attempt to find an English alternative to the Macon country and its vulgar rhyme (61). The new version has an American equivalent, 'Napa . . . Krappa', a Beckettian in-joke, but more accessible to American and Australian audiences who are perhaps less likely to be acquainted with French wine-growing regions. According to Bud Thorpe, the suggestion came from Marty Fehsenfeld (in the audience during rehearsals for Walter Asmus's own production in New York), when the cast was looking for a local equivalent. They had also tried to find an Australian equivalent, but without success, rejecting the Hunter Valley, as it invited too vulgar a rhyme.

The new version of *Godot* in performance has a strange atmosphere in each act, when the moon comes up and the dying fall starts; a kind of dreaminess descends, as is normal at this point in the play, but also having a lunatic effect on Estragon's voice, which takes on a trancelike drawl. Larry Held recalled that 'in Chicago the end of each act was much more in keeping with the rest of the play, but when Beckett got hold of it, he said that when the moon rises, neither character has anything left, they're both exhausted, they're at the end. It really was a problem, trying to achieve this. The way we had been doing it had a certain dynamic which was now lacking; we had to adapt to what was not thrust upon us. Then Beckett came up with the direction that we should "speak with the tone of moonlight in our voices"'. Bud Thorpe commented: 'For any director to say that, one would say "What *is* it to talk like moonlight?", but we understood what he meant: the draining process, the fatigue in our soul, the heat of the dusk has now turned into the paleness of moonlight. A steel-blue moonlight tone, the softening of the voices, the lack of energy; let the moon take the energy from the voices – that will give you the feeling that it is now night. That's what Beckett seemed to be saying.'

The final textual point discussed brought in the wider question of the extent to which Didi and Gogo are self-consciously performing for the audience and aware of the audience's presence. Under Beckett's direction, Larry Held spoke Gogo's line, 'Where are all these corpses from?' (64), and his line, 'There's no lack of void' (66), straight out to the audience. Was this Beckett's idea, to make a deliberate appeal to the audience's presence?

> *BT*: I think Beckett does purposely want to smash that fourth wall, and to demonstrate that people are sitting in chairs as easily as if lying in a box. The reaction, if there is going to be one, could be almost that of a corpse, watching and waiting. I don't give any heavy philosophical meaning to it.
>
> *CD*: It does cut away at the authenticity of the characters on stage, though, doesn't it? It turns them into actors.
>
> *BT*: It does. It is a fine line we have to tread, working so hard to give the character a human quality, and yet move the left foot on the tightrope and you realise you are an actor delivering poetic prose in play form.

There are several other excisions and additions that future critical editions will have to incorporate. A few of them, which there was no time to discuss with the cast, but which affect either characterisation or the overall quality of the play, deserve our attention here.

Pozzo undergoes a considerable transformation. Excised from Act I are 'I'm not in the habit of smoking two pipes one on top of the other', the whole of the second pipe routine, his proud assertion, 'I am perhaps not particularly human, but who cares?', and the ensuing pipe relighting (28–9). The aim – and result – is to tighten and avoid drag, but the cuts also reveal Beckett's determination to humanise Pozzo, as does the excision of Pozzo's worn-out whip routine (37). It was sensible of Beckett to cut Estragon's repeated invitation to Pozzo to sit down (the first is on p. 36), and the whip-cracking routine was never really convincing, but its omission does reduce the accumulated evidence that Pozzo's powers are waning and his world dwindling.

One strange piece of heaviness is introduced in Act I, where Vladimir asks if Lucky will be able to walk, and Pozzo (in the existent English version) replies ruthlessly, 'Walk or crawl!' (45). The new *Godot* lines revert to the French text. Where the French text reads:

VLADIMIR: Mais va-t-il pouvoir s'orienter?
POZZO: C'est moi qui l'orienterai (39)[,]

the new *Godot* has:

VLADIMIR: Will he be able to orientate himself?
POZZO: I will orientate him.

This seems somewhat stilted and Gallic; even a translation of the German sounds more natural:

VLADIMIR: Will he be able to find his way?
POZZO: I shall show him the way.[7]

Once again Beckett has reduced Pozzo's harshness; no longer does he drive Lucky on relentlessly, but he acts as his guide, thus making his loss of sight in Act II worthy of our pity. This difference always existed between the French and English Pozzos; but it is significant that Beckett has now opted for the softer and more sympathetic Pozzo.

Finally, Beckett has instructed some remarkable cuts towards the end of Act II. All the exchanges from Pozzo's question '. . . but are you friends?' down to Estragon's 'Expand! Expand!' have gone, and all the references to 'the Board' from 'I'm going' to 'Some diversion!' (86–7).

It is difficult to explain this textual vandalism, perpetrated on some of the most magical moments of the play: the confusion about the sunrise and the sunset, and Vladimir's beautiful speech about night drawing nigh, with Estragon cutting right through the sentiment with his down-to-earth 'How much longer must we cart him around?' No; these pages cannot go.

The changes ordered by Beckett in 1984, thirty-five years after *Godot* was written, open up some fundamental questions about the definitive text (as distinct from definitive performance). This is generally taken to be the last text authorised during the author's lifetime. In the technical sense, this is the one performed by the San

Quentin company – that is to say, future critical editions should relegate excised passages to mere variants. This is a very gloomy prospect. It makes one wonder whether authors should be let loose on their plays thirty-odd years later. We now have a different play, a 'new' *Godot*, which can be regarded in some important respects as an impoverishment of the original. It would be good to be able to forget it, but it exists, on paper, in the Reading University Library. As a performance piece, as live theatre, I must regard it as an aberration for the most part; but for Beckettian scholars it is invaluable. This is the vision Beckett now has of a greyer world, glimpsed through the filter of his later works. It is an incomparable barometer of the evolution of the Beckettian world view over thirty years.

Notes

1. Textual variants, evident from comparing the manuscript and the Editions de Minuit version of the French text with the Faber and Grove Press English texts, are to be found in my critical edition of *En attendant Godot* (London: Harrap, 1966). Differences betwen English versions are studied by Hersh Zeifman in 'The Alterable Whey of Words: the Texts of *Waiting for Godot*', *Educational Theatre Journal*, 29 (Mar. 1977) 77–84. Zeifman accepts the Faber (London, 1965) version as definitive; it corrects the bowdlerisms imposed by the Lord Chamberlain in the original Faber edition. Some variants have no explanation other than Beckett's own wishes at the time of preparing his English translations for the successive Grove Press (New York, 1954) and Faber (1956 and 1965) editions. The same applies to the new performance text referred to in this essay as the 'new' *Godot*. Beckett's further textual and directorial instructions are analysed by Ruby Cohn in *Just Play: Beckett's Theater* (Princeton University Press, 1980), pp. 256–66, and in 'Beckett's German *Godot*', *Journal of Beckett Studies*, 1 (Winter 1976) 41–9. Page references in this essay are to the Faber edition (1965) of *Waiting for Godot*, and to the Harrap edition of *En attendant Godot*. The German edition of *Warten auf Godot* was published by Suhrkamp (Frankfurt, 1953), and reprinted with parallel French and English (Faber, 1965) texts in 1975. References to the German version are to the latter edition.
2. For an account of the rehearsals see Bryan Appleyard's 'Noises off, murmurs on', *The Times* (London), 25 Feb. 1984, 8. Other accounts appear in Peter Smark's 'Rehearsing with Beckett', *The Age* (Melbourne), 10 Mar. 1984 (Saturday Extra), 3; and in Donna Foote's 'Beckett's Return', *Newsweek*, 19 Mar. 1984, 16.
3. The impact of *Godot* at San Quentin Penitentiary (California) and the subsequent establishment of the San Quentin Drama Workshop have

been chronicled by Martin Esslin in *The Theatre of the Absurd* (Harmondsworth: Penguin, 1968) pp. 19–20. Cluchey was its founder and artistic director, and performed many Beckett plays before being invited by Beckett to work as an assistant on the Schiller Theater production of *Godot* in 1975. In the current productions he was playing Pozzo, Hamm and Krapp. Bud Thorpe joined the SQDW in 1976, and was playing Vladimir and Clov; Larry Held, the only Australian in the cast, joined the SQDW in 1973, and first worked with Beckett in a production of *Endgame* in Berlin.

4. Donna Foote, 'Beckett's Return', *Newsweek*, 19 Mar. 1984, 16.
5. Beckett's own diagram for the beginning of Act II, reproduced below, confirms that Estragon's presence from the start of the act was a deliberate decision, intended to be symmetrical with what he calls 'E's and V's inspections' on pp. 13–15 of the Faber edition. This diagram appears opposite p. 57 of Cluchey's copy of the 1965 Faber edition:

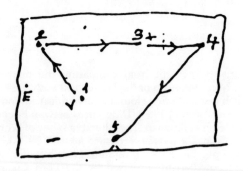

1. Back to audience, head raised, listening .
2. Inspection off.
3.   "   tree
4.   "   off
5.   "   boots + song

cf E's - V's inspections *Act II* pp. 13-15

6. Ruby Cohn, 'Beckett's German *Godot*', 42.
7. Cf. Suhrkamp edition, p. 116.

13

Company for Company: Androgyny and Theatricality in Samuel Beckett's Prose

S. E. Gontarski

The voice has been *dramatic* since its appearance in *Molloy*, and the possibilities of staging it were enhanced in 1965 when Beckett assisted two friends in such an enterprise: Jack MacGowran with his anthology, *Beginning to End*, and Shivaun O'Casey on her production of *From an Abandoned Work*. Since the composition of *Krapp's Last Tape* (1958) the line dividing Beckett's prose monologues from his stage monologues has grown less distinct, as Beckett has explored the theatrical possibilities of the monologue as thoroughly as he explored its fictive variations in his postwar trilogy of novels, *Molloy*, *Malone Dies* and *The Unnamable*. Hints of that generic androgyny were implicit early in Beckett's dramatic efforts. Colin Duckworth and a number of other critics have remarked on the degree to which *Waiting for Godot* (1949), for instance, had been developed from Beckett's first extended piece of French prose fiction, *Mercier et Camier* (1946), left unfinished and published as such in 1970 in French and 1974 in English. *Krapp's Last Tape* was similarly developed from an abandoned but subsequently published prose text, *From an Abandoned Work*. And the genetic decision about a text like *Not I* came late in the work's composition – it could as easily have become a work of prose fiction.[1]

It is not surprising, then, that as Beckett's own position on keeping 'genres more or less distinct'[2] has softened, as he has become less resistant to what Ruby Cohn calls 'jumping . . . genres',[3] numerous forays into the prose have been made. E. T. Kirby and his Projection Theater, for instance, adapted *Molloy* to the stage in 1969. Joseph Dunn and Irja Koijonen of the American

Contemporary Theater adapted *The Unnamable* in 1972. Mabou Mines staged a variety of texts, beginning with *The Lost Ones* in 1972, *Mercier and Camier* in 1979,[4] *Company* in 1983, and most recently, *Imagination Dead Imagine* in 1984, a work the group originally planned to adapt in 1972. Joe Chaikin and Steve Kent combined portions of *Texts for Nothing* and *How It Is* in 1981 as *Texts*. And Gerald Thomas did two versions of *All Strange Away* both in New York in 1984, one at La Mama and another at the Samuel Beckett Theater. Thomas has also worked with actor Ryan Cutrona on a radio version of *Fizzles*, but the stage version of three of the tales, with the same actor, was directed by Liz Diamond in 1984.

My own entry into what has become an increasingly crowded field is an adaptation of *Company* which opened at the Los Angeles Actors' Theater's Half-stage in February of 1985 with Alan Mandell as the Figure. This *Company* was the English language version of *Compagnie* directed by Pierre Chabert at the Théâtre du rond-point (Paris), which opened on 15 November 1984, and has the distinction of being the only adaptation of his prose work with which Beckett has directly involved himself.

Certainly one of the attractions to staging *Company* is that it is among the most textually androgynous of Beckett's works. It was written at a time when Beckett seemed to be consciously exploring the common ground of fiction and theatre, immediately after *A Piece of Monologue*, the most narrative of Beckett's dramas. Indeed, *Company* offers a striking complement to *A Piece of Monologue*: it may be the most dramatic of Beckett's prose narratives, one which works equally well on stage and page.

The most fundamental question about staging *Company* was determining the stage image. Beckett, Pierre Chabert and I agreed that one fundamental flaw of adaptations needed to be avoided. The staging should not attempt to illustrate the text literally. We would make no attempt to dramatise the stories of the second-person voice, nor illustrate the image of the third-person as described – that is, the speaker would not be lying on his back. And even if the speaking voice goes through a process of hypothesising similar to the process a writer like Beckett might go through in creating his imaginative figments, the stage image should not overtly suggest that Figure is a writer: no notebook, no desk, no bookshelves. The image we settled on, then, was something between an illustration of the episodes and a reading of the text: a sole figure sitting in a chair. This would keep the emphasis on the words and avoid the pitfalls of other adaptations, which, in order to render concretely the illusive imagery of the fiction, resorted to a variety of highly technical images which often became ends in themselves. The central figure in *Company*, the figure we see on stage, is imaginative, a figment, and ought to remain so in production. The vignettes of the second-person are, despite their obviously autobiographical roots, likewise imaginative renderings, and trying to dramatise them would alter their thematic function. Language is central to *Company*, and Figure's phrasing, the often baroque, inverted, elliptical, poetic phrasing of both voices, is as much a source of company as the actual hypothesising. Language itself is as much a theme in this work as are creativity and human isolation. We wanted to retain as much linguistic emphasis as possible and still stage a drama. In short, we were limiting the range of theatrical sign systems working with language to transmit the theatrical message, and such reduction of what some theatrical semioticians would call 'transmitters' (that is, body, voice, costume, props, lights, etc.) is a fundamental characteristic of Beckett's own direction.

Once that central icon was determined, it was then possible to develop an approach to staging. Pierre Chabert's initial conception was to minimise the speaker's corporeality by staging a floating head. He decided to mask the source of light and so created a black box large enough to accommodate the lighting and the figure sitting on a black chair. Shrouded in a black cassock, the actor's body would be invisible save the head, lit by sourceless light. In addition, the huge wooden box was mounted on rubber wheels, and could move so slowly and silently across the stage that movement was not consciously perceptible. At some point in the performance the spectator simply realised that the speaking figure was no longer in his initial position. When Beckett attended his first rehearsal on 8 November (a week before opening), however, he made some fundamental alterations in staging. He rejected the movement for one, and was not altogether happy with the floating head image (perhaps because it evoked *That Time* too directly). He suggested that the third-person figure be more fully lit and dressed in grey pyjamas and a grey robe. He further cautioned the distinguished French actor Pierre Dux not to anticipate the voice, which, although it was spoken live by the actor, was projected via a remote microphone through three speakers. The figure must, Beckett insisted, be surprised by the voice and with his failing eyes search out its source. For the actor this meant that he must start to speak while his head was still bowed against his chest and maintain the same voice quality as he lifted his head to search out the source of the voice.

What was clear from the earliest rehearsals was that even as a prose work *Company* already contained a fundamental dramatic structure, a dichotomy between second- and third-person voices, and Beckett's characterisation of the two voices reflected the contrapuntal relationship not only between each section but within them as well. The third-person voice, he noted, was 'erecting a series of hypotheses, each of which is false'. The second-person voice was 'trying to create a history, a past for the third-person', each episode of which the third-person rejects, insisting, in effect, 'that was not I'. The adaptation was designed to develop as much of those contrapuntal elements as possible. The first change I made for the English language production was that instead of having Figure speak both voices as Pierre Dux did, I taped the second-person segments. This immediately solved a number of production problems and opened up additional staging possibilities. For one, Figure could now truly be a listener, and I was freed from trying to mask his moving lips, a lighting problem which plagued the French production and was never adequately solved. More important, I could more easily establish two separate modes of stage action, a speaking or hypothesising mode and a listening or searching mode, and play the one against the other, both visually and aurally.

In the hypothesising mode Figure could move and speak normally in his chair. Here he existed in real time. The listening mode, however, would be highly stylised. As listener, Figure would move in slow, balletic motion searching out the source of the voice, one source at each of the two far corners of the theatre and one directly above his head. The voice could be slow, deliberate, almost flat, and the effect generally would be to suggest that time too had slowed. Further, taping the second-person voice also allowed me to manipulate the sense of theatre space. I was working in a very small, intimate theatre to begin with, and the initial effect created was claustrophobic. By varying the amount of echo and reverberation on each taped segment, I could open up theatre space, create the illusion in the dark that the voice was coming not only from a variety of sources but from varying distances, some from very far off, others whispers in his ear. I divided the second-person segments among the three speakers so that figure's head moved slowly, almost painfully, to search out the source of the voice; the pattern of complex light changes (almost 100 light cues in 65 minutes, and most of those during the listening mode) enhanced that balletic motion by creating a series of silent facial sculptures.

Taping the second-person voice allowed for an additional series of counterpoints. Normal time could be played against slowed time, normal motion against slowed motion, hypothesising voice against the flat voice of memory and/or imagination, the full light of the speaking head against the varying chiaroscuro of the listening head, rejection of the voice against acceptance of the voice: in short, light against dark, movement against stasis, sound against silence. As Beckett suggested, the lighting in *Company* should have 'musical possibilities'. That is, it should not only illuminate and as such reinforce the metaphor of imagination, but the light should also control the rhythm and pace of the drama, punctuating each paragraph into discreet segments and enhancing the fugal nature of the performance.

I also wanted the production to reflect two fundamental themes of the work: first, the strength and potential solace of the imagination as company; and second, the weakness and failure of the imagination as company, that is, its failure finally to alleviate man's most fundamental condition, loneliness. Unlike Chabert's production, which was staged on a proscenium stage in a 250-seat theatre, my Los Angeles *Company* was intimate in character. The Half-stage was converted into a black box, so that there was, in effect, no stage at all. The audience shared Figure's space. The theatre's sixty seats were reduced to thirty, arranged in an irregular pattern so that each spectator would have clear sight lines, but would not have the comfort of sitting next to anyone. As a precaution against spectators moving their chairs, the seats were bolted to the floor and covered in black floorlength crepe. 'Most funereal things', Krapp might have said.[5]

As the audience entered the dimly-lit black box with the strange looking chairs, they had little hint of what the visual theatrical image might look like. The dim lights faded to dark and the spectators heard, 'A voice comes to one in the dark. Imagine' (7).[6] At that point the lights faded up on a dishevelled figure in grey bathrobe and pyjamas sitting in a black chair, a reflection of the black chairs on which the audience sits. Figure appeared noiselessly, on a chair beautifully conceived by designer Timian Alsaker, as if the audience's imagination had brought it into being. For some sixty-five minutes Figure hypothesised and listened amid the audience, on intimate terms with it. Then, as the voice asserted that despite the solace of imagination, the pleasures of mathematical calculations, the contemplation of formal symmetries, and the companionship of hypothesising, Figure is – as he always was (fade to black – lights up) – 'Alone' (89). Lights fade to black and Figure silently disappears. Dim house lights return, and the audience is, as it always was, alone. A curtain call would only dispel that moment of intimacy and bewilderment. And audiences were puzzled at play's end. They generally did not know whether the play was over, whether to applaud (most did not), whether to leave the theatre. Even after the exit door was opened, spectators sat still, unsure what to do.[7]

Once the basic contrapuntal, fugal relationship between modes was established, between second- and third-person voices, the next step was to establish the relationship of Figure to voice. Almost all of the incidents that voice iterates are painful to Figure. They suggest a loveless childhood where the boy was rebuked or derided by his parents for his comment on the perception of the sun (12–13), or for his report of being able to see the mountains of Wales from his 'nook in the gorse' (33) in the Wicklow Hills. There is the lovelessness of parents 'stooping over cradle' (66); the lack of parental concern for a child who, in desperate need of attention, throws himself from 'the top of a great fir' (28); or the embarrassment of the child's being on exhibition, standing naked at 'the tip of a high board' before the 'many eyes' of his father's cronies as he is urged to 'Be a brave boy' (23).[8] The child in the memories seems never to have been the boy or the man his parents wanted. He was busy, even in those days, developing the light of his imagination, one of the work's dominant metaphors.

Voice also recounts some embarrassing and naive incidents: the boy who believes he can play God by intervening in the life of an ill hedgehog, the child who can look out the summer house window to see that 'all without is rosy' (54), or the young adult who believes that his path (literal and metaphorical) is straight, 'a beeline' (48), and looks back one morning to see the counterclockwise pattern in the fresh snow: 'Withershins' (52). The incident is wryly comic even as it also suggests the plight of man living the pattern of the sinistral spiral of Dante's hell. Even the sensual moments are painful. The erotic episode of his feeling the 'fringe of her long black hair' (66) on his face is intimately connected to the story of the loved one's pregnancy, with its puns about her being late. The episode's concluding line hints at the disastrous end to the love affair, 'All dead still' (58).

Figure resists that voice for numerous reasons. The memories are, of course, painful; but he also resists the simplified notion that a sum of memories (or stories) will add up to a history, a life. And even if the voice recounts incidents from his past more or less accurately, memories are not historical but fictive – selected, reordered, re-emphasised versions of past incidents. Philosophically, the separation of voice and Figure allows for the dramatisation of a phenomenological theme. In order to be perceived, voice needs to be objectified, separated from the perceiver, and so voice must always be something other than the subject, the self; it cannot be accepted as part of the I. In fact, both figments Figure creates, the figure of one lying on his back in the dark and the voice he hears, have been objectified and thereby separated from the perceiving self. That is, they are not I; 'I am not what I am conscious of', Figure implies to us throughout the play. That dichotomy, moreover, also destabilises the perceiver since, according to Sartre in *Being and Nothingness*, only the known can *be*; the perceiver, the knower, the Figure is a *nothing*. The perceiver is the opposite of what is perceived, what is known, the *en soi*, being, and so the perceiver is a nothing to the perceived's being. What Figure recoils from at the mention of the 'I' when he says 'quick leave him' (followed each time in production by a blackout) is the confrontation not only with the nothingness of his self *per se*, but with the self's objectification once it has been perceived and the infinite regress of nothingness that a self-reflexive consciousness entails. Figure resists accepting the voice as part of himself as soon as he hears it, as soon as it is objectified and 'known', which process simultaneously nullifies the knower. The play dramatises once again the difficulties and paradoxes entailed in being and consciousness. Consciousness, or the *pour soi*, Sartre tells us 'is always something other than what can be *said* of it'.[9]

And yet voice is appealing. Despite the pain and embarrassment evoked by it, 'little by little as he lies [in both senses] the craving for company revives. . . . The need to hear that voice again' (55). The craving not only suggests that voice helps him pass the time, is a companion through the long *nuits blanches*, but that it is also the fountainhead of creativity, the source of the art we witness on stage. And so the fugal quality of *Company* suggests an aesthetics. Art is a counterpoint, a dialectic between the formalist hypothesising and the subconscious voice from the past. *Company*, drama and prose text, is precisely that sort of fugue. In production the formalist aesthetics implicit in the text was made explicit by recapitulating at the conclusion all the lighting patterns, visual imagery and sound variations used throughout the play.

The theatre piece *Company*, then, is in many respects a development of, a conception beyond, translation of the prose text into the language (or sign system, if you will) of theatre. The prose text posited a duality between a 'he' voice and a 'you' voice, while the narrator, the nexus of those two voices, was barely suggested. In this translation of *Company* the narrator is our principal – albeit illusive or ghostly – icon, mediating the two pronouns, sharing characteristics of both, but refusing to identify with either. That is, to the character sitting in his room, neither the creature he creates lying on his back, an extension of his imagination, nor the voices that he hears in the night, another extension of his imagination, are essentially part of the 'I' sitting in the chair, because both figments and voices have been objectified and thereby separated from consciousness, or the perceiving self. And yet he is connected to both through the act of perception.

In the play we picture a narrator sitting in a room listening to voices very like his own memories and creating a figure of one lying on his back in darkness. But consciousness can also perceive itself sitting in a chair perceiving memories. The hypothesiser himself is not a stable, core reality, not a transcendental creator, ego or signifier. He keeps an eye not only on his creature, but over his shoulder as well, wondering not only about his created figment but whether he too is only figment, created creature, imaginative construct, *en soi* to another *pour soi*, *en soi* to his own *pour soi*. And so, finally, he is, for he is not an actual hypothesiser, Beckett continually reminds us, but an actor, a representation in an art work created by a particular set of cultural forces that for convenience we call Samuel Beckett. But this Samuel Beckett too is glancing over his shoulder, wondering if he too has been written. One characteristic of consciousness, Sartre notes, is that it is capable of being conscious of itself being conscious. In contrast, however, to Sartre, who rejects the possibility of an infinite regress, positing a transcendental ego, Beckett explores the fictive possibilities of such an infinite regress by suggesting an infinite series of devisers: 'Devised deviser devising it all for company' (64). A transcendental unity is finally always arbitrary, for one can always ask, 'Who asks in the end, Who asks? . . . And adds long after to himself, Unless another still' (32).

From its opening theatrical image, then, *Company* emphasises a point Beckett has been exploring at least in the late plays, that one source of dramatic action and conflict is a tension created by playing narrative against visual imagery, ear against eye, the story we hear against what we think we see. The play opens with precisely such displacement – a figure in a chair recounting the story of a figure on his back; a figure hearing voices and hence negating his own being; the spectator perceiving the figure hearing the voices, negating himself. *Company* as drama is not merely a set of visual images in concord with the text, with dialogue, but is at the same time a set of disharmonies. The iconography of stage image and the syntax of language – in short, what we see and what we hear – are as often in conflict with one another as in concord, and the drama more often than not resides precisely in such tension, that displacement of one by the other (to adapt a psychoanalytic metaphor). Much of Beckett's drama, certainly the late drama, resides in such displacement. As a drama *Company* shares characteristics with Beckett's early plays: the figure in *Company* is passing the time as Didi and Gogo are in *Waiting for Godot*, or as Winnie is in *Happy Days*. And much of the imagery evoked by the voice, the 'you' portion of the text, suggests travel, but like the action in *Godot* and in *Mercier and Camier*, the movement is heading '[n]owhere in particular' (*Company*, 30).

But *Company* is more strikingly of a piece with Beckett's late, ghostly plays, plays during which we question our own perception, the existence of the images we see before us on stage: hence Chabert's interest in the moving box and my interest in altering the sense of theatre space by manipulating sound. *Company* is certainly part of Beckett's late Theatre of Immobility. Figure himself, the icon we see before us on stage, is the confluence of memory and imagination, and exists in fact as the tension between those forces, as does the figure lying on his back in the dark, as does the work we witness before us on the stage. In many respects the text acquires resonances through its translation into stage language. When Figure wonders whether or not there may be another with him in the dark, he is invoking the ritual we call theatre, fictions for *Company*, where there is always someone with you in the dark – even if his chair is not beside yours.

Notes

1. See especially Chapters four and nine of my *The Intent of Undoing in Samuel Beckett's Dramatic Texts* (Bloomington: Indiana University Press, 1985).
2. Samuel Beckett, quoted by Ruby Cohn in *Just Play: Beckett's Theater* (Princeton University Press, 1980) p. 207.
3. Chapter 11 of *Just Play* is entitled 'Jumping Beckett's Genres'.
4. Cohn, pp. 224–9, p. 287n.
5. *Krapp's Last Tape*, in Samuel Beckett, *Collected Shorter Plays* (London: Faber & Faber, 1984) p. 59. The adaptation mine resembles most in this respect is the Mabou Mines version of *The Lost Ones*, which was at first intended only as a reading and demonstration. Once the notion of reading was abandoned, designer Thom Cathcart conceived the idea of seating the audience within a black, foam rubber-lined cylinder. (See Cohn, p. 225).
6. Samuel Beckett, *Company* (London: John Calder, 1980). All quotations are from this edition; page numbers are given in the text.
7. For a theatre festival in Madrid, 'Muestra sobre la vida y la obra de Samuel Beckett', which ran from 28 April to 5 May 1985, *Company* was performed four times in a 200-seat theatre on a proscenium stage. We could not, of course, duplicate the Los Angeles production in the Madrid space, but we tried to achieve some of the original intimacy by building a ramp into the audience.
8. The autobiographical nature of these vignettes is evident from Deirdre Bair's *Samuel Beckett: a Biography* (London: Jonathan Cape, 1978). The biography was published some two years before the appearance of *Company* (1980).
9. Jean-Paul Sartre, *Being and Nothingness*, tr. Hazel E. Barnes (New York: Philosophical Library, 1956) p. 439.

Index

203

DATE DUE

GAYLORD   PRINTED IN U.S.A.